NIGHT JASMINE TREE

DEBU MAJUMDAR

BO-TREE HOUSE

Published by
Bo-Tree House, LLC
1536 Lowell Ave., Bellingham, Washington, WA 98229 USA
www.Botreehouse.com.

First U.S. print edition 2021
Identifiers: LCCN 2021913528

Publisher's Cataloging-In-Publication Data
(Prepared by The Donohue Group, Inc.)

Names: Majumdar, D. (Debu), author.
Title: Night jasmine tree : bittersweet stories of an Indian youth / Debu Majumdar.
Description: [First U.S. edition]. | Bellingham, Washington : Bo-Tree House, 2021.

Identifiers: ISBN 9780996851657 (paperback) | ISBN 9780996851671 (hardcover) | ISBN 9780996851664 (ebook)
Subjects: LCSH: East Indian Americans--Family relationships--Fiction. | Retired teachers--United States--Fiction. | Families--India--Fiction. | Caste-based discrimination--India--Fiction. | Hindus--India--Fiction.
Classification: LCC PS3613.A35364 N54 2021 (print) | LCC PS3613.A35364 (ebook) |DDC 813/.6--dc23

Cover watercolor painting by Patricia Loughlin, Lummi Island, WA and Mountain View, California.

CONTENTS

To Catherine
For her unconditional love

Also by Debu Majumdar

From the Ganges to the Snake River (Creative nonfiction)
Sacred River: A Himalayan Journey (Fiction)
Viku and the Elephant (Children's story)
Viku to the Rescue (Children's story)
Viku and the Ivory Thieves (Children's story)
Viku Goes to School (Children's story)

By deeds alone one is an outcaste,
By deeds alone one is a Brahmin
            — *Gautama Buddha (Sutta-nipâta, 142)*

BELLPORT, NEW YORK

OCTOBER 2005

Chapter One

The Snake and the Frog

Shankar stared through the window at the October rain pounding on the roof of the Volvo in the driveway. He enjoyed looking at the rain and loved hearing its drumming sound—*the same in India or in the U.S.*

"You want more tea?" his son, Samir asked.

Shankar turned from the window. Everyone was home on this rainy Sunday. He, Samir, and Julie had stayed at the table after breakfast, sipping tea and lazily reading the newspaper. Durga had taken the grandchildren to the living room.

"Yes, a little more." Shankar pushed his cup forward and looked at his son's face. When Samir was relaxed, like this morning, he resembled a typical round-faced Bengali with sleepy eyes. Durga had chosen the name for their son; it meant a breeze, an early morning fragrance, a companion. Early in her pregnancy, she had told Shankar, "If we have a boy, I want to name him Samir. I feel so happy." They both liked the name so much they could not imagine any other, not even a nickname for their boy.

Gingerly, Shankar cradled his teacup, sniffing the familiar aroma. "What a rainy day! Just like rainy season in Calcutta. You know, we lived with rain pouring down for several days at a time."

"Yes, and fortunately, I'm not on call," Samir said. He was a cardiologist.

Julie, their daughter-in-law, looked across the table at Shankar with a radiant smile. "I also remember the rainy season in India. It was quite

3

something! But this rain will stop tomorrow." She brushed a strand of dark brown hair away from her face and opened the Styles section of the *New York Times*.

Julie and Samir had met when they were both students at Columbia, and they had immediately found a similarity in their outlooks on life. Julie, born in Connecticut, was of mixed Irish-Dutch descent and had been raised in a Unitarian family. She always had an optimistic outlook, like saying with confidence that the rain would stop tomorrow. Samir's parents had not taken him to any church or temples but raised him with the Vedic ideals of Hinduism, teaching him many Hindu and Buddhist stories from India. This had given him his core spiritual center.

Shankar put down the paper and took his cup to the living room, stopping near a window that faced the large eastern white pine tree in front of the house. The hard, metallic sound of rain on the car became softer in this room.

The grandchildren left what they were doing and flanked him. Ten-year-old DeeDee drew a face on the steamy window with her finger. Her younger brother, Raja, stood glum, hands in his pockets, his legs pressed against the radiator.

"Tell us a story, Grandpa," DeeDee pleaded. "I'm sick of this rain." Her two braids, tied with little magenta ribbons, swung as she turned to him. "When you were little, did you play house on rainy days?"

"Oh, no! We huddled in bed and read books." He looked at her closely. Her complexion was like Julie's, but not quite. She clearly had Indian blood in her, making her skin glow like creamy tea. Normally so lively, today she was sullen. Perhaps she needed something to keep her occupied.

"When the rain stopped," Shankar said, turning to Raja with a twinkle in his eyes, "sometimes we went outside and played soccer. The field had patches of water, but we played anyway." His heart lifted at the memory. "It was lots of fun, slipping and sliding on the muddy ground. We came home covered with mud and totally drenched."

"That sounds messy, but I guess you had fun." DeeDee moved to the French doors on the north end of the long living room and stared out through the screened porch.

Shankar thought of the small field behind his childhood home in Dum Dum. There, he and his friends had dug out many bushes to make a soccer field. Many little creatures would come out of the ground under the bushes and overturned rocks—lizards, frogs, snakes, and colonies of ants and spiders. He remembered children didn't get an allowance then and they could barely pull together a rupee and some coins to buy a rubber ball. They also did not have goalposts, and they used old bricks to mark the goals.

"Can I go out and play, Grandpa?" eight-year-old Raja asked. He could not stay still and fidgeted; his large ears prominently framing his gloomy face.

Shankar shook his head and eased onto his favorite blue armchair. "You'll get sick if you play in this weather. India is a warm country. Still, my mother was always mad when we played in the rain." Thoughts of the monsoon brought memories of his two sisters huddled together with him in bed—eating, chatting, and laughing while rain beat on the closed shutters.

He looked around the living room, brightly lit with tall lamps, the yellow Oriental carpet brightening it further. Flower, their golden retriever, slept curled up on the carpet. Durga sat in the corner near the bookshelf, reading. Lamplight shone on her, illuminating her mocha complexion. Shankar liked her heart-shaped face the first time he had seen her. Her countenance still emanated a lively vigor. Her long salt and pepper hair fell loosely to the middle of her back. She did not want to color her hair, saying more than once, "I want to age naturally."

A profound happiness came over Shankar, and a serene smile spread across his face. This was all he had wished for when he left India—to build a happy family without any burdens of the past hovering over them. He had not become a famous physicist, but he had succeeded in his wish. Then, out of nowhere, his father's face came to him—inflamed, swollen, and tight with emotion, eyes narrowed, body bent forward and forefinger shaking reproachfully at him. Shankar closed his eyes. After so long, why couldn't his first twenty-three years fade into oblivion?

"I bet Grandpa had lots of adventures in the rainy season when he was a little boy," Samir said to his children, as he came into the living room. He parked himself on a chair and pulled Raja onto his lap.

Shankar turned toward them, pleased to see his son. Samir was right. "Yes, I did," Shankar said, relieved to be called away from thoughts of his father. DeeDee was now in front of the east window looking blankly at the rain falling on the hemlocks. The sight troubled Shankar. She was certainly bored. He was rarely that low-spirited during the rainy season in Calcutta. He wanted to teach the children how to make the paper boats they would construct on rainy days and float them in the drain channels along the street when the rain stopped. But no—that required participants with cheery spirits.

"I'll tell you what happened in one rainy season," he said, addressing DeeDee.

She turned and eagerly came closer. "Tell us, Grandpa."

"There are five seasons where I grew up," Shankar began, "and each season brings something new." Shankar pulled DeeDee close to him on the arm of his chair. "The two-month rainy season brought frogs. They were everywhere—in fields, in puddles, in drains, and under rocks. The big ones croaked day and night. I went to bed with their noisy symphony and, when I got up, they were still croaking."

***

One-Eyed Frog

One day, I was returning from school and saw a green thing moving in the water of an open drain. I stopped and looked at it carefully. It was a snake. It had a frog in its mouth but couldn't swallow it, as the frog was too big for the snake. Both were struggling—the frog fighting hard to get out and the snake laboring to swallow it.

The frog wiggled its dark-green-black body, desperate to get away from the predator. It fought for its life, squirming in the death grip of the snake but was unable to free itself. I felt sorry for the frog. I got a big stick and hit the snake. But the snake wouldn't let go of the frog; so, I beat the snake hard near its head. That did it. The snake promptly let go of the frog and escaped. The frog lay there half dead. It did not have the strength to move, and it looked absolutely helpless. I nudged it with the stick and was surprised to find it alive. One side of its head was damaged, but its body was throbbing with each beat of its little heart. I wondered what to do when another boy stopped to look; I told him what had happened. The boy was bold and picked up the frog. 'Ah! The snake has destroyed the left eye. This frog is too weak to survive.' He put it down and left.

If the frog stayed on the road, a dog or cat or even a crow would surely kill it, and if I pushed it into the drain, the strong flow of water would drown it in no time. I couldn't leave the pulsating frog to die there so I took it home.

As I entered the house, my younger sister Parvati, who followed me everywhere, saw me. I avoided her gaze and went into my room, closing the door behind me.

Now I didn't know what to do with the frog. I knew my mother wouldn't like it in the house. So, I quickly hid it inside an empty *kunjo*, a clay pot used to store drinking water. Kunjos are large at the bottom and have long, narrow necks. I didn't have any other place to keep the frog hidden, and I didn't tell anyone about it.

The frog lay there as if it were dead.

That night, I put a little fish curry and rice from my dinner into the pot, not knowing whether a frog would eat that. I thought it might like a piece of toast, but that would draw attention from my mother because we only had toast in the morning.

Frogs eat live insects, worms, and other tiny animals. This, I knew. I had no net or gadget to collect those, but I didn't want it to die. So, I kept on giving it fish and rice.

I heard no noise for three days. *Had it died?* I used a flashlight and saw it was there and, miraculously, alive. I continued giving it food from my plate.

A few days later, I heard a little noise from inside the kunjo; it seemed like the frog was moving. That made me happy. Relieved.

Then, one day, the sun came out and I planned to take the kunjo outside to turn the frog loose. But when I came home from school, I found my mother waiting for me instead.

"What have you done in your room?" She began. "It smells terrible." The red *sindur* mark on her forehead glowed in the sunlight. I stared at the bright blue border of her white cotton sari. I was nervous, but before I could say anything, she said, "I found the smell came from the kunjo. It reeked of rotten fish. I took it out and had to clean your room."

What the frog hadn't eaten must have rotted, but I was so engrossed with the frog I didn't notice the smell. I was horrified that she had found out my secret and looked at her blankly. But my mother was not annoyed with me. She put her hand on my shoulder. "Be sure to tell me next time if your room smells bad."

"Where is the kunjo?" I asked her anxiously.

"Oh, the kunjo? There was a frog inside it. It was too big to come out through the neck. It must have gotten in when it was small and got bigger." She looked at me, but I remained silent. "The kunjo broke while I tried to get the frog out. We lost a good kunjo because of that stupid creature."

She hadn't figured out what I had done!

"What happened to the frog?" I inquired nervously, trying not to arouse suspicion.

"That frog was peculiar," my mother said instead of scolding me. "As soon as it came out, it jumped to the right—sideways back to your room. Any other frog would have jumped forward, but no, not this one. I had to chase it around because it would always move to the right. It finally got out through the window."

"It went to the field outside?" I asked her, quite agitated.

"Yes. Change your clothes and come for a snack." She looked toward my room. "I don't know how you could sleep with that awful smell!"

I didn't answer her and rushed inside to look through the window. Perhaps the frog was sitting just outside. My mother called me to come to the kitchen, but I ran out to the field. Puddles were everywhere and hundreds of frogs jumped away in all directions as I looked for a frog with one eye. I stayed there for a long time, but it was impossible to find the frog that jumped only to the right.

***

"I'm glad you saved the frog," Raja declared.

Shankar's facial muscles tightened. Those memories of his early childhood were sweet; but thinking of all that followed made him wince. He felt the hair on the back of his neck rise.

He simply stared at Raja's face for a few seconds. "I never liked snakes."

"Me neither," DeeDee said.

"I wish I could catch big frogs here," Raja said wistfully and came to stand in front of Shankar.

"Someday I'll take you to the place where I grew up." Shankar leaned toward Raja. "And we'll collect frogs together."

"Take me too, Grandpa," DeeDee pleaded.

"Of course, you will come."

Shankar shifted his view to the hemlock hedges and wondered whether the field where he played in his childhood was still there, or if the land had now been filled with houses; there might not be puddles for frogs and boys to play in anymore. Then he thought of his mother; perhaps hiding the frog was the first time he hadn't told his mother the truth.

She would not have allowed the frog inside. So why tell? It came to him that this was probably not the first time, as he realized how deftly he had avoided the frog's discovery. Even at that tender age, he understood their family boundaries and had slowly stopped being open with her.

Sixty years had passed by since that incident. His mother was dead now. Her face came vividly to his mind, stirring a dish on the coal-fired mud cook-stove in the kitchen where she spent most of her time. Shankar's regrets grew as he remembered something, she had asked him to do— being their only son—but he had not done it. How could he? No one could imagine how events would develop the way they did. Even a Delphic oracle could not have envisioned it.

Chapter Two

The Letter

A utumn was almost over, and today was the second Halloween for Shankar and Durga in Bellport. Shankar sat in the living room in his favorite blue armchair, admiring the few red and yellow leaves still left on the trees lining the street when DeeDee, with Flower at her heels, came running, quite excited. "Grandpa, Grandpa, you have a letter from India." She gave him the blue aerogram. Her face glowed. From her expression Shankar could see she thought he must be extremely pleased to get the letter. "Open it, open it." She stood in front of him, bouncing from one foot to the other.

Shankar examined the envelope addressed to Shankar Lahiri 411 42nd Street, Philadelphia 19104, his very first apartment in the U.S. Such an old address! The letter had been redirected to the Department of Physics at Penn, then Michigan State University in Ypsilanti, and finally to Bellport. It was from his younger sister. He could barely read her handwriting: Parvati Bhattacharya, Bhatpara, West Bengal, India. The worn-out letter had gone through many hands from that tiny village in West Bengal to Bellport, New York. This was her second letter to Shankar. He had received the first one in 1959 in Philadelphia, but he hadn't opened it. The moment he touched that first letter, anger quite unlike he had ever felt burst like a bomb within him. He tore it to pieces and threw them into different waste baskets in the physics building for good measure.

Now he stared at this new letter. He squinted at the aerogram as the muscles in his face tightened into a hard expression and his breathing became rapid and shallow. Why had she written to him again after so many years? 'Pajee meye! Sweet-faced, spineless girl.' She was someone he had counted on to understand and support him when he needed it the most. But she had bluntly refused, hurting him deeply in a way that would last a lifetime. He had tried hard for years to forget her twisted facial expression during their last meeting, but it floated back to him in this moment. That reaction was so unexpected from his beloved sister! Since then, he didn't want to know anything about her or any of his family in India. They didn't exist as far as he was concerned. He felt an urge to tear up this letter too and throw it away.

Then he saw DeeDee's inquisitive face and put the letter in his pocket. "I'll read it later." He pulled her closer. "It's from my younger sister Parvati. So ... how was school today?"

DeeDee didn't want to talk about school. "You never told us much about your sister. Did you play with her?"

Parvati's girlish face came to Shankar; what dreamy eyes she had. "She is four years younger than me. I also have another sister, three years older, but I played with Parvati more often. When she was little, she would follow me everywhere. You know, we didn't have many toys, but we had each other, and we played together all the time."

It pained Shankar to bring these thoughts and memories up from the depths of his past, but his granddaughter was not someone he could often refuse.

"How nice you had a sister to play with!" Her face brightened with the thought. "What kind of games did you play?"

"Ordinary games like hide and seek. When I was young like you, we went around the neighborhood and explored the fields. We often found live lizards, frogs, and other little creatures in the bushes. Mother didn't like it when Parvati brought dead birds or nests home." Shankar chuckled, to his own surprise. "Once Parvati brought a stray puppy into the house. It was a cute but smelly little dog. Father was so enraged. He thought dogs were inauspicious and brought bad luck. He threw it out the door and rebuked Parvati severely. She locked herself in the bedroom and cried and cried. She wouldn't come out to eat or even open the door. Mother and my older sister had to entice her with sweets before she came out."

"I think I would like her, Grandpa."

Shankar studied DeeDee for a few seconds and saw how happy she was hearing about his sisters. "Parvati was a sensitive girl. One time, she didn't like what Mother told her and she left the house after announcing she would never come back. After a few hours, when she didn't return, we looked for her. She hadn't gone to any neighbor's house and no one had seen her. My mother was very distressed. I found Parvati sleeping under a bush." The memories flowed from Shankar's lips as though they were uncontrollable, having been unlocked after years of determined avoidance.

"You looked out for her." DeeDee's face beamed.

"You know brothers and sisters do that for each other." Parvati's young face glowed in his mind. Even at that age she had a mind of her own. "Once I had done something that we both knew mother wouldn't like," Shankar began, "but Parvati didn't tell her."

DeeDee's eyes widened. Her hand went to her chest. "Grandpa, what did you do?"

"Oh ... I shouldn't have told you that."

"But please grandpa, tell me."

***

Climbing a Date Tree

One early autumn Sunday I was studying in my room when my friends called me from outside. Very few people had telephones in those days; friends simply dropped by. I peeked through the window and asked, "What's up?"

"We have found a date tree with orange-red dates, just ripe to eat," Bikash told me.

"So, why didn't you pick them?"

"We cannot get them by throwing stones," Debjit replied.

"None of you can climb the tree?" I asked in a haughty tone.

"No," they said together. "That's why we have come to you."

Pride immediately burned within me. They came to me because they couldn't climb a date tree! I had never climbed a date tree either. But I thought for sure I could do it. I'd show them what a good climber I was. "It's no big deal. I can do it."

My mother overheard our conversation and called to me as I crossed the courtyard toward the front door. "Shankar," she said sternly from the veranda around our courtyard, "don't try to show off when you don't know how."

"I know how to climb trees, Ma." I resented her interfering with my imminent demonstration of tree-climbing prowess.

"Date trees look simple but are treacherous. Think why the other boys aren't climbing the tree."

"Don't worry, Ma. I know what I'm doing."

"I don't want you to climb date trees." Her face was tense, forehead furrowed tightly, and eyes boring into me.

"All right, Ma. If I find it difficult, I won't climb the tree." I rushed out the front door.

I didn't notice my sister Parvati behind me; she had followed me out. "I want to see you climb a date tree." She looked at me, eyes pleading.

"No. You can't come with me right now. I'll bring some dates for you."

"I'll tell Ma if you don't take me." She glared.

I didn't want to take her, but I was in a hurry to go out for the adventure, so I caved. "You must remain quiet."

"You are awesome," Ranjit told me when I came out, as he gave me a brotherly punch.

When they arrived below my window, my friends had been a little gloomy, but now they perked up. They didn't want other boys to get those dates before us. We increased our pace. My friends led me toward the tree, a little distance away. We usually didn't go to that place, but I had passed by once or twice before. There was a curved pond with a small island in the middle. That was a novelty, and I admired the scene. I even wanted to go to the island, but I was afraid snakes lived there. Older boys were playing soccer in the field next to the pond. Soumen showed me the date tree on the far side of the field and pointed to the two large bunches of delicious-looking dates hanging near the top. They were of a smaller variety, not like the large kind you buy in the market. Only a thin layer of flesh covered a long seed, but they have a superb, delicate flavor.

"Can you climb it?" Soumen asked me, pointing to the straight trunk.

I gave him an indignant look. Why was I there if I couldn't climb the tree?

"It must be easy for you," Bikash told me quickly. "You are such a good climber."

The tree wasn't very tall, and I thought it would be easy to climb. The dates looked ripe—bunches of little red-orange fruits shining in the sunlight. It didn't occur to me why the others, especially the older boys, hadn't already picked them. I took off my shoes. I wanted to show my friends how *able* I was; I started to climb immediately.

A date tree grows straight up like a coconut palm. You need special skills to climb a coconut tree because its trunk is smooth. I had always admired the men who climbed tall coconut trees. They put a small hoop of rope between their feet and hop up, holding the smooth trunk with their hands. They climb fast, like monkeys. They have no fear. But the trunk of a date tree is rough because the stems of its old fronds stay stuck to the trunk. I decided to climb the tree by holding on to these old stubs. I moved up ten feet quite easily. But as I went a little farther, I found the stubs were not strong. Something had caused them to rot.

I kept on going because I was determined, and too high up now to admit defeat. I stood on the lower stubs and held on to the upper stubs for balance. But the higher I went, the looser the stubs became. That was bad. Then I discovered little red ants.

Their bites hurt a little and itch a lot. They were there for the sweet dates—hundreds of ants running up and down in lines, everywhere. This made me nervous. I searched for stable stubs to hold on to. One came off in my hand and I threw it down to the ground. The situation quickly became precarious, but I couldn't think of giving up. I kept on climbing, sweat poured over my brow as I inched upward.

When I neared the top, closer to the dates, several ants walked on my hands. One bit me. When they bite, they curl up as if putting all their strength in the bite. I rubbed my hand against a stub and crushed the aggressive creature. I noticed a few more on my hands and I tried to blow them away, but I couldn't; they were too many. I began to panic. Standing there with no strong stub to hold on to became difficult and many ants were crawling over my arms. Several were on my neck, where one bit me. The spot started to itch badly. I put my foot one step up and placed my hand on a higher stub, but as I pulled the stub to lift myself, it came loose, and many ants crawled out from under the stub. The ants had a colony there and thousands scrambled all over the tree trunk and all over me. I tried to hold on to another stub, but it also came off.

I must have fainted because I don't remember falling. I only recall my friends lifting me up. They carried me to the pond, put water on my face, and massaged my back, which hurt terribly. My sister dutifully removed ants from my arms and legs.

When I finally sat up, the island was before me and I saw it had similar date trees with bunches of dates hanging on several shoots. They were redder and even more plentiful than those on the tree I had just fallen from. I kept on gazing at them because the trees looked beautiful with large, green leaves and red-orange dates; then I understood why the older boys had left them untouched. They were smart.

My friends brought me home. Parvati had run ahead of us. She stood at the gate and whispered to me, "Ma is in the kitchen."

I went in quietly and lay down on my bed. I saw a tall brass vase on the table with tuberoses. The sweet fragrance of its milk-white flowers filled the room. I thought how my mother loved those flowers and if they were there, she must be in a happy mood.

Soon I heard her voice from outside my door. "How come you are back so early?"

"The dates were not worth the trouble, Ma," I told her. I wanted to, but I couldn't tell her how foolish I was. My pride held me back.

***

Your sister helped you, but you were naughty, Grandpa," DeeDee said, snuggling up to Shankar. "You should have told your mother. "I can't wait to tell Mommy when she comes home." DeeDee skipped upstairs with Flower bounding after her, wagging her tail.

Shankar hoped the story had distracted her from the letter; the impending rush to get ready for Trick or Treat would let her forget it completely. The house felt silent after the sounds of her steps faded. Shankar stared at the beige wall, sitting still. The memory of chasing toddler Parvati around a night jasmine tree came to him. The tree, about twenty feet tall, was on the empty lot next to their house. Night jasmine trees bloom in late autumn; the tiny white *shiuli* flowers with orange-red stems fall in the wee hours of dawn and fill the air with sweet fragrance. Shankar loved it when the ground beneath the night jasmine tree was covered with flowers, a very pretty sight. They couldn't play there for fear of stepping on the flowers. Instead, he collected them, and Parvati made garlands for the deities in the *thakur ghar*, their worship room. He remembered the day when workers came to build a house on the lot and the tree was chopped down. Parvati was a little older, but she was still upset. She gazed silently at the woodcutters from the window with tears streaming down her burning cheeks.

Shankar slumped in the armchair. He couldn't conjure the fury that had led him to shred her first letter. Parvati had been a sweet child, but how quickly she had changed. He remembered how she had turned in disgust and rushed away from him when he went to her College to gain her support for Durga as his prospective wife. She couldn't provide him the support he desperately needed, if not in outright solidarity, at least in sympathy. He couldn't accept the harsh reality of her rejection. He had become increasingly repulsed by her response over the years.

He developed a hollow feeling in his chest. He took the letter out from his pocket and vacillated for a few moments; memories of young Parvati kept him from throwing it away. Instead, he hastily opened the envelope; his breath halted in his lungs. As he read the words before him, his facial expression changed from stiff enmity to profound sadness. "Oh, my God ..." he whispered to himself. He read the letter again from the beginning and held it in his hand, staring at the words.

How she had suffered! Because of his bitterness, Shankar had refused to inquire about his own family and did not care, banishing them into oblivion. He had no knowledge of what happened to Parvati. This was a tragedy of the worst kind. He stood up and paced the living room. His outrage against his father reignited with greater force than before. It was a tsunami, and he felt justified in abandoning him.

"Cruel, insensitive man!" He must consult with Durga immediately.

Parvarti's life flashed through his mind from her birth to teenage years. She was such a passionate and good-hearted girl, caring even for the stray dogs and cats in the neighborhood. She would sneak out food from her plate and feed the dogs outside, taking milk in a small saucer for cats. She had to bear many scoldings from mother and had fights with father for bringing home stray dogs and cats, ending up crying alone in her room. "The little dog was shivering in cold," she confessed to Shankar later. "I brought the dog just for the night."

She cared not for herself or the punishments that would surely come from caring for these helpless animals. How could Shankar forget the real Parvati for so many years over one moment of callousness? Though it was pivotal in his own life, it was but a rare occurrence in his little sister's life.

Her young face on another night came to him. It was the night when he was too scared to sleep alone. That evening, he heard a frightening story of a man with a green coconut who called boys through the window at night to capture them and take them away forever. Shankar was afraid such a man might come to his window and call his name. Parvati stayed with him that night.

He never understood how she could behave so harshly during their last meeting. That was not the Parvati he knew, but it burned in in his mind's eye for decades, overriding the time they had shared as children. He had loved and cared for her, but she threw that love away, and the result had been tragic for them both. Now he was more than certain that was not the real Parvati. Sadly, he had not realized this before. His throat choked and tears came to his eyes.

Until this moment he had blamed his father for all that happened to him, and now he saw how their father had ruined not only his but also Parvati's life, destroying the entire family. His resentment against his father grew intense. The Parvati he had encountered outside her college for the last time, was not the real Parvati he knew. It was his father talking through her. As a result, he had turned his mind away from her and abandoned his responsibility as an elder brother. What should he do now?

He must talk with his wife.

Where was Durga? He had called, but she was nowhere. Then, his older sister's weeping face came to him—crying when she was leaving home after her marriage. So many years back, but that was the last time he had seen her. Shankar put his hands on two sides of his head and exclaimed, "My God!"

Chapter Three

Older Sister

Shankar's sister, Uma, was three years older than he. When she got married, Shankar was about to graduate from high school. She had looked after him so affectionately since he was a toddler. He remembered her fondly.

Abruptly he stood up and his hand banged the small table next to his armchair. The book, *'Particle Physics and Inflationary Cosmology,'* he had planned to start reading fell from the table. He hurried toward the porch without picking it up; then instead of going to the garden, he returned and paced the living room. Uma's young face hovered in his mind with many memories of her. How they had secretly tended an egg together to hatch a koel bird in their house. She had often invited him to join when she played house with her friend. The two girls pretended to cook and serve dinner to him. They used various wild fruits as fish, meat, and vegetables and cooked them in a make-believe oven of bricks; they used little, round, silky leaves as *rooti* or sometimes as *luchi*. They served dinner using big leaves as plates. His part was to sit on the ground or on a brick and pretend to eat. Sometimes his older sister sent him to the field—their market—and he brought various leaves and wild fruits to cook.

Shankar remembered his older sister when she was a teenager—two long braids hanging by her ears. How soft and affectionate her dark eyes were. Then she was married off and gone to a place far away from Calcutta. He had not seen her or had any communication with her since then. He stood near the porch window and blankly looked out toward the sky. Her thirteenth birthday came to him vividly, as if he had gone back in time.

***

Blue-eyed Doll

The birthday party was to be held in the evening. That morning, while they were having breakfast, their uncle, his father's younger brother, told my older sister, "I have a special present for your birthday. I hope you'll play with it even after you become an adult and get married." He gave her a box. "You can open it now."

Her face glowed when she opened the box and saw the doll. She picked it up and held it close to her. Its eyes were blue, and it had long eyelashes. She uttered a happy cry and ran to show the doll to our mother.

Many brought gifts for her later, but compared to the doll, they were ordinary. I had not seen so grand a doll before. My sister fell in love with the it immediately. Who would not? Even I wanted to play with it, but she would not let me touch it. "You can play with it after all the gifts are opened," she promised. Her braids swung by her ears as she left me.

In the afternoon, I saw the doll on a table while she was busy with mother. I lifted the doll. Its body was light and translucent. I wanted to look at it more carefully and took it over to a window. As I was examining it to satisfy my curiosity, she saw me from the veranda and shouted, "Don't touch my doll."

"I'm not." I quickly put it back on the table.

My sister was never selfish. She shared her toys with others, but that doll was so special, she wanted to be the first one to play with it. Mama had told us so. I knew that, but why couldn't I look at it for a few minutes? But I dared not and left the room.

I hoped our cousins would arrive soon. I roamed the house for a while. The rooms had already been decorated and they looked nice. I had gone out early in the morning to collect fresh flowers from several local fields. The flowers I had picked were there in vases along with gardenias and tuberoses from the market. The fragrance of these flowers made the rooms elegant and announced the special occasion.

Finally, the cousins started to arrive. Chinta came in late afternoon. I immediately recognized her high-pitched voice and went to her. She was always jolly, and I followed her as she moved around the house. She was from the city; she was not afraid of anything. She was a little bossy, but I liked playing with her. "Where are the presents?" she asked me, "I want to see what she got."

I took her to the room where the presents were assembled on a large table my mother had covered with a beautiful, lacy tablecloth. Mother had also hung colored paper chains at the windows, so the room looked rather festive.

Chinta went around the table and looked at the presents for a while, but she was not impressed until she discovered the doll at the center. "Huh, that's a fine doll."

"Uncle brought it from New Market in Calcutta," I bragged.

"Really?" she expressed a little surprise and picked it up. "Look," she showed me, "the doll's eyes close when I lay her down." Indeed, it was the finest doll I had ever seen.

I told her to leave the doll where it was and she did, but she kept on eyeing it until we left the room.

More relatives and cousins came in the evening. Candles were lit, and more gifts piled up on the table. Bright lights and the fragrance of tuberoses continued transforming the room into a place worthy of a celebration. When new guests came, my older sister escorted them to the room so they could place their gift on the table. I also came along with her. My mother's oldest brother came last. Then, as soon as he and my sister left the room, Chinta said, "I'm bored." She picked up the doll. "Let's play a little in the other room," she whispered. "She's too busy to notice."

Chinta left the room with the doll before I could say anything. I simply followed her to the next bedroom.

This room was not decorated; its only light came from one hurricane lamp that glowed dimly because its glass was sooty. She asked me to bring a candle. By the time I had searched the house and found a large candle, she had pulled a table close to the bed. He put the candle on the table, but it was not steady, so she put some books around it. She laid the doll on the table and started to play. "She needs a pillow," she said, talking to herself. "Hmm. What could be her chair?" She looked around and found the sewing basket. She took things out of the basket and arranged them on the table. "That's better."

"You like how I made her bed?" she asked me.

Then I heard my sister's voice, "I don't see the doll on the table."

We heard footsteps around the house and soon several children and my sister came to the room. "There's my doll!" my sister shouted from the doorway. Her voice startled Chinta. She was caught! She wanted to hide the doll and instinctively stretched her hand over the table, but she bumped the book holding the candle and it fell. She tried to lift the candle but, in her hurry, she tipped the sewing basket over, and cotton balls rolled out. Before she could do anything, the cotton and papers surrounding the doll caught fire and smoke curled toward the ceiling; fire from cotton and papers surrounded the doll.

"Fire, fire!" all children shouted.

I did not remember exactly what happened next because it happened so quickly. My sister rushed to the table and recovered the doll. Someone threw a bucket of water on the table. When it was all over and more lights were brought to the room, Chinta had disappeared. I saw my sister standing near the table and looking at the doll. Dark soot covered her beautiful present; one cheek was pressed halfway in and the beautiful pink glow of the doll was gone. Tears welled up in my sister's eyes and she started to sob. How hard she cried, holding the doll in her hands. She would not let Mother take it from her. Mother had to carry her out of the room with the birthday girl's arms wrapped around the doll. She lay on her bed with the burnt doll and cried. She would not come out. All heard her sobs, but no one could go to her room and console her. How could we? That was the only magical thing she had ever received in her life. And no one had any spirit to sing "Happy Birthday" to her.

Uncle promised to buy her a new doll, but that never happened.

***

For a long time, Shankar did not know what had happened to the burnt doll. Everyone avoided talking about it. He had a feeling she had not discarded the doll. How could she? Even in its half-burned, melted state, it remained the most precious possession his sister could own. But as time passed, everyone else forgot the incident.

When his sister was getting married and their mother was cleaning the house, she discovered the doll, wrapped in Uma's old clothes, hidden in a drawer. Only the feet stuck out. She stared at the package silently for several seconds. "I don't want her to be reminded of that sad event now," she said with sigh. "Shankar, throw it away quietly in as far a place as possible."

I took the doll to a trash bin near the train lines. I opened the package and saw the damaged doll. Under all the soot, I could still see a little blue color in one eye. Like my mother, I stared at the once-beautiful doll. Tears came to my eyes thinking of my sister's sadness. One only dreamed of getting such a gift. I could not look at it anymore. I threw it in the bin and turned away.

***

Everyone loved Uma's happy demeanor. But Shankar remembered, as the time of her marriage had drawn closer, she became quieter and sad.

One day, he had gone to the roof and found his older sister sitting alone. It was dusk, the sun's light almost gone from the sky. "What're you doing here alone?" he asked her.

"Thinking." She got up and stepped near him. "Thinking that once I go away to Allahabad, will I ever be back again?"

"Don't they come to Calcutta often?"

19

"Rarely, I heard." She looked at the trees in the distance for a second. "You'll not forget me. Will you, Shankar?"

"No. I will never forget you."

"Please write to me," she pleaded, putting her hands on his shoulders. "And tell me all that happens here."

And Shankar had promised. "Sure, I will."

"You know, if you don't write to me, no one else will. I'm afraid I'll be forgotten."

"No. No. We won't let that happen."

A happy smile crossed her pensive face. "Let's go down."

Shankar now felt she had a premonition that those were her last days in the house.

How hard his older sister had cried when it was time for her to leave for her husband's home. This was a true farewell, not simply going to live in another house; it was a farewell to her life in her birth family. All Bengali girls shed tears at this time. But for her, it was like banishment – her husband's house was not in the next block or town – it was all the way across India. She clung to her mother, begging not to be sent away. Tears poured down her cheeks, streaming in torrents. His mother also cried. Shankar remembered tears had come to his eyes too. When he tried to say something soothing his voice choked and nothing audible came out of his mouth. His sister had to be pulled away by three other women. She held on to one corner of her mother's sari, and it came unwrapped.

"Be happy in your husband's house." His mother could not say any more and covered her face with the end of her sari.

Shankar went to college soon after. He remembered he had written her a cursory letter once; he had felt shy and uncomfortable as he had never written to her or any other relative before. Just a young college student, barely out of high school, what would he write to his older, married sister? So, for one reason or another, he had not written again. They had no telephone service in those days, and their mother wrote to her once each year after the annual Durga puja, as custom required, but she could not write intimate letters. The letters were simple inquiries about her and her husband's well-being, ending with a blessing. Family letters were read by all, so there could be no private questions or notes. Shankar's mother's lack of education also held her back, a situation common to many mothers in India in that era. What was there to write but simple queries. Travel was impossible. His mother had no other alternatives—a sad situation when daughters go far away after marriage. As time passed, his older sister occupied less and less of his family's and Shankar's thoughts and dwindled into memory, recalled once a year as duty required.

Shankar stared, unseeing, into the middle distance for some time. Thoughts of his older sister pricked his conscience. She had loved him and taken care of him as older sisters do. But he had conveniently forgotten her. Then a disquieting thought flew into his mind. Did he forsake any trace of responsibility to his older sister? Had he behaved like his rigid father?

Shankar strolled slowly to the far end of the yard where the tall walnut trees were. A stab of regret hit him. He had been completely focused on his own interests and his own misery and had not cared for his two sisters. How could he open his heart and share his woeful situation? He must talk with Durga immediately; she was the only one who would understand him.

He returned to the living room, stood at the window, and gazed outside, brooding. How his life had gone! It had become a mess—more so because he had knowingly shielded his son from his life in Calcutta and deprived him of his heredity. And this secrecy and his indignation against his father had made him an unhappy and a pathetic person.

How did it all come to this stage? He agonized while waiting for his evening walk with Durga.

INDIA

SHANKAR'S YOUTH

Chapter Four

Sacred Thread Ceremony

S hankar grew up in the sleepy suburb of Dum Dum, on the northern outskirts of Calcutta, known for almost a century for a nearby ammunition factory and military cantonment. Originally, many settled here to work at the factory, but other types of people followed and made it a thriving community. His family lived in the interior, about half a mile from the train station. One and two-story brick and cement houses occupied the neighborhood, with many empty lots occupying spaces between homes.

During his early youth, roads in the neighborhood were not paved and no streetlights were put in for several years. Small farm plots and large trees added a humble village atmosphere to the area. Boys gathered fruits by throwing stones or by climbing the mango and other fruit trees when no one watched. One of his pastimes was exploring the skimpy forest patches that dotted the vicinity. When he grew a little older, he and his friends ran, played hide and seek, and swam in the nearby pond used by farmers. Life was simple and idyllic for any child who lived there.

Sweet innocence and freedom to play both in and out of the house marked his early years. No one asked Shankar to study hard or participate in religious ceremonies and being the only son, he received extra care from his mother. His happy childhood started to change, however, as the time for his sacred thread ceremony approached.

Shankar's family belonged to the brahmin caste, the highest caste in the Hindu religion. Brahmins were the educated class in ancient times, responsible for teaching, maintaining spiritual knowledge and performing religious ceremonies as priests. The sacred thread event was to initiate Shankar into the age-old traditions of the family—to learn the sacred texts and perform priestly services as needed in the community. After this initiation at the age of ten, his actions and behavior were expected to take on the religious aspects of a proper brahmin adult. Weeks before, it had been impressed upon him that this would be one of the most important events in his life. This would bring a new birth for him, a new life where he would become a full-fledged brahmin.

A white cloth embroidered with flowers on the edges hung over the central courtyard of their house. This 10-foot by 10-foot canopy was held up by strings attached to hooks on the walls. A large, decorated mat covered the floor making the courtyard festive. His father had brought deities from the Thakur Ghar—a special room in the house for religious activities. Uma and Parvati had enthusiastically made colorful paper chains and draped them around the courtyard. Shankar knew his sisters were treating this event with more joy and reverence than the festive *pujas* their family performed each year. He sat in the lotus position under the canopy on an embroidered cushion. His head had been shaved for the ceremony, but a small tuft of hair, a *tiki*, was left at the back of his head. Many don't keep this little tuft in this ceremony anymore, but his father insisted on it.

"This is an ancient tradition." He said sternly. "It reflects our status as true brahmins. We do this because we are the keepers of the religion."

Shankar had fasted for this auspicious occasion—his initiation to the sacred thread. Earlier in the morning, he had taken a bath and his father had taken him to the local Shiva temple to pray to the great Lord Shiva. His father had draped a small new *dhuti* around his waist. He had a loose cotton shawl on his upper body. Sitting there, he looked to be an obedient little boy.

A solemn atmosphere pervaded the courtyard. Earthen oil lamps burned on decorative stands; smoke rose from the incense burners; and fresh flowers and many dishes of sweets and cut fruits lay near the deities as offerings. Shankar's father and a priest recited Sanskrit mantras, and relatives and guests sat or stood around to watch the ceremony.

The priest rang a small bell several times. It was supposed to be a joyous festival, but Shankar felt more overwhelmed than joyous. His father, along with the priest, performed ancestor worship where Shankar offered rice balls and water to their deceased souls.

"Always remember, son," his father told him, "ask for blessings from ancestors before any important activity."

Shankar was in a daze. He simply followed what he was told to do. A fire was built during the formal ceremony. Ghee was fed to the fire along with other offerings and the priest and his father uttered mantras in Sanskrit to

Agni, the fire god. As instructed, he also offered flowers with sandalwood paste, *durva* grass, leaves from the *bel* tree, and grains of unhusked rice to the fire. This went on for more than an hour. Shankar's initial enthusiasm quickly subsided; he felt bored and blankly watched his father's and the priest's activities. Occasionally he glanced at his sisters and cousins quietly chatting and laughing and wondered when the ceremony would end.

Then the priest put *panchagavya* on his tongue and asked him to swallow it. It was a mixture of milk, curd, ghee, with a few drops of cow dung and cow urine. Shankar felt uneasy and disgusted but followed what the priest and his father told him to do. He took it in quickly. The priest sounded the bell vigorously. The ceremony reached a crescendo, the priest took a loop of sacred thread he had made from three cotton strands and put it over Shankar's head and across his chest. It hung from his left shoulder down to the right side of his waist. The priest told him to wear the sacred thread all his life. His father whispered in his ears the Gayatri Mantra from the Rig Veda, the most sacred mantra in the Hindu religion. They repeated the mantra, along with the priest, three times. The ceremony ended and his father pronounced, "Now you are twice born, the same as your ancestors."

Shankar was the center of attention. Many people came for the occasion. Relatives had arrived several days earlier, and brahmin family friends were also invited. The guests gave him presents—new clothes, books, a watch, money—and all congratulated him. Delicious food had been cooked. The ceremony ended with a scrumptious feast.

The next day, his father started to teach him about religious practices and worship services. He taught Shankar how to perform *ahnik*, the daily ceremony of the Hindu religion, with hands folded in prayer, reciting ancient religious texts, and meditation. His father did ahnik every morning and would not take any food or drink until he had performed this ritual. He would repeat the ritual again after sunset before taking any food or drink. He instructed Shankar to do this every day.

When Shankar went back to school, his classmates teased him about his shaved head and his tiki. The shaved head was not a problem, as many had done that for various reasons, but the tiki caused him anguish. One boy pulled his tiki, saying, "See, your head comes along with it!" He ran away, laughing. "Just checking."

One boy asked from a little distance, "How did the cow's urine taste?"

Other boys snickered behind him. Shankar ignored them but started to wonder about the ritual. Sure, cows are important, but did he have to eat their dung and urine? And this tuft of hair on his head? That was more embarrassing than anything in the world. Other brahmin boys didn't have a tiki for their sacred thread ceremonies. But his father had said, "We are the true followers; they have deviated from the path."

"I do not want to have the tiki," he told his father after returning from school.

"You must have it. Removal of the tiki would be a disgrace to our family tradition." His father loomed over him, his expression one of thunderous fury.

"I cannot go to school with this on my head," Shankar cried and fled to his room.

After a few days he cut off the tiki with scissors from his mother's sewing basket, causing a big commotion with his father. Shankar stayed in his room.

His father paced around the courtyard in a fury but had to consent in the end. After all, the tiki was gone, and he knew how students would mercilessly tease someone with a tiki. But he insisted that Shankar devote his time primarily to mastering the sacred texts and learn to perform religious services, the main activities of their family.

Shankar started to change after the 'tiki incident.' He became a little reserved in his dealings with his father. Although still very young, Shankar found it hard to love him. He obeyed his father, but remained wary. In later years he thought the episode was a harbinger of strained relations to come.

Chapter Five

A Growing Divide

S hankar! Come home right now!"
He heard the loud call, and his heart sank. He was the next batsman, waiting for his turn. Their team needed eight more runs to win. He pathetically looked back toward his house. "I have to go!" He glanced wretchedly at Soumen. "My father will be angry if I'm late," he sighed, dragging his feet away from the cricket field.

"You're almost eleven now," his father scolded him, as he entered the courtyard, somewhat dimmed by the setting sun. "One year has passed since your sacred thread initiation! Still your mind is scattered." His father stood near the thakur ghar. "Wash your hands, feet, and face. Change your clothes and come to the altar."

Washing was the routine when returning from outside, a normal practice in all families. What was not common was that his father would sprinkle a few drops of Ganges water on his hands and feet to cleanse him from inauspicious places he might have passed through.

His father sat in front of the altar and instructed Shankar. "Take a little Ganges water in your right hand and sip it three times, saying 'Om Vishnu, Om Vishnu, Om Vishnu.' Then follow your practice of the evening ahnik prayer ceremony."

After an hour, when they emerged, night was upon them. The electric light was on in the courtyard.

"You know, we are the custodians of our religion," his father told him. "We originated from Brahma's mouth and must uphold the ancient

29

traditions. It is our sacred duty." He watched his older daughter going to rooms around the courtyard with an earthen lamp in her hand, welcoming the gods and goddesses. "You cannot while away your time playing cricket. You have too much to learn. Eat something and go to your regular studies."

He obeyed but walked away with only the desire to know: did they win or lose the cricket game?

Chapter Six

Lower Caste Rice

S hankar started reading Bengali detective stories in sixth grade. The name of his favorite detective was Kiriti Roy—the Bengali Sherlock Holmes. He read many Kiriti Roy books. The boys in his class exchanged those books with each other and talked about how Kiriti Roy could predict many things about a man after only one look at his clothes or his manners. Each time someone brought a new Kiriti Roy book, the rest would vie to borrow it first, even if the book was second-hand with worn-out pages.

Since he got along well with his classmates, they often gave him the first chance to borrow their books. There was another reason for treating him differently: he was the top student in the class and his classmates knew he studied the ancient scriptures with his father, which they had heard of but never read. Many were a bit in awe of him because of that. They didn't know his life at home was a life of strictures and limits.

One day, Mintu told him he had finished a new Kiriti Roy book. It was about a black diamond ring stolen from a prince's estate. Mintu could loan it to Shankar for two days, but the book was in his house.

Black diamond? Shankar was immediately intrigued. He was not sure what it was, but a black diamond ring must be unbelievably valuable. Who could steal it from a prince's estate with so many sentries guarding it? His mind could not stay still. When the teacher went to the blackboard to explain the properties of an isosceles triangle, he gestured to Mintu that he wanted the book and would return it in two days. Mintu agreed and nodded.

Shankar accompanied Mintu home as soon as school was over. They came to a huge rice field hemmed in by irrigation ditches. "This is our farm." Mintu pointed out the rice plants. "My family grows rice. Sometimes I work in the field too." The plants were only a few feet tall and yellowish green; Mintu's house was next to the rice field. In the courtyard of their house, Shankar saw, for the first time, a *dhenki*, used to dehull rice. It was like a mortar and pestle but built horizontally and operated by foot. Mintu said they used it only to make rice for their own consumption, the rest went to a mill. He brought the book from inside the house.

While they were talking, Mintu's mother brought two bowls from inside the house. "Here is some puffed rice and *guhr* for you two. An after-school snack." She looked at Shankar's face and her plain facial expression changed to delight. She gave an approving nod to her son and left.

"Guhr from date syrup," Mintu told Shankar, "Very tasty. Try it. We make it in our house."

Shankar didn't know what to do. He wanted to tell him he couldn't eat in their house. His family belonged to the highest caste. They would not eat food cooked by a non-brahmin and would not enter a non-brahmin's home except for religious purposes.

Shankar knew most of his friends at school were non-brahmins. He didn't know any prince or warrior caste students, the kshatriyas. His friends belonged to either the vaishya caste of the merchants and farmers or the shudra caste of laborers and service providers. There were many sub castes among these two major castes, but that didn't matter. There were no untouchables in his school, those who performed the lowest, the most menial of all jobs—cleaning toilets and dealing with dead bodies of men and animals. He mixed with all his classmates and played with them, but taking food in a non-brahmin's house? No one in his family did that.

Shankar knew he must not eat the snack Mintu's mother had so lovingly offered. However, the words would not come out of his mouth and he froze. He struggled and finally took his bowl to Mintu, saying, "I'll eat only a little as I must go home now." He poured most of the puffed rice into his classmate's bowl keeping a tiny amount for himself.

Shankar walked home in slow hesitant steps. He felt shame, and, when he reached home, he could not tell his family he had eaten in a non-brahmin house. His mind churned silently, questioning their traditions and why they followed such strict rules that no one else had to follow.

Chapter Seven

Curiosities and Contradictions

S hankar's best friend, Soumen, asked him to come along to a distant part of Calcutta to meet a friend of his father's who was close to his family. Soumen admired him and was so fond of him that he called him 'uncle.'

"He is unusual," Soumen said. "He joined the military after college and has travelled all over India. You'll like him."

Shankar was intrigued and went with him to South Calcutta. He was a jolly man and entertained them with stories of his life. He had climbed mountains in Nepal with Sherpas, dived deep in the ocean near the Maldives to explore the coral and spent dark nights with the army in wild forests. The two young boys were mesmerized by this man and wished they were with him on those adventures. The man took them to a posh restaurant for a treat. Shankar had never entered such an elegant restaurant, or any restaurant at all for that matter. His family never ate out. How hesitantly he had examined the surroundings! The uncle ordered omelets for everyone; Shankar hadn't eaten an omelet before. He was curious and kept quiet. But when the dish arrived, his immediate reaction was, "I cannot eat that."

The man laughed. "These are made of duck eggs, not chicken. I eat this often." Then looking at Shankar's hesitant face, he said, "Look, I'm a brahmin too. Try it. It's okay." Shankar took a bite. It was not bad! Salty, spicy and a little hot because of the chopped green chilies. And it had an odd, overpowering flavor he had never tasted before. Then he saw the onion bits; he felt like throwing up. His family didn't eat onions; his mother said, they increased 'passion.'

On his way home, he felt a little excitement, as though he had done something daring and gotten away with it. And nothing happened to him. He didn't feel increased passion or any reduction of his alertness as his mother had confidently predicted. However, as he neared home, fear and remorse grew in him. After some hesitation, he blurted out to his mother, "I tasted egg today. Another brahmin gave it to me." Shankar did not mention the onions.

She gave him a strong rebuke. "We raised you in our culture. How could you do this?" However, after some time she gently said, "Never do this again. If your father comes to know of it, he will force you to purify your body by eating cow dung."

Shankar remained fearful for many days, but nothing happened. His mother must have kept it quiet for his sake.

One evening, Shankar's father came home from school with a stranger. He rarely invited anyone to their house. The man looked different from a Bengali. He was tall and muscular with a sharp nose, bright eyes, and dark, curly hair. He had an aura of command. While his father wore a white dhuti, a long shirt, and sandals, this man wore western clothes: pants, shirt, jacket, and black leather shoes.

"This is Saurabh Ranjan, a teacher from Bihar," his father told him. "He has come from Patna to learn our teaching methods. Ask your mother to make tea for us." His father took his guest to the outside room.

Shankar's father taught high school Sanskrit; teaching Sanskrit, the ancient language of the Hindu religion, was hard. The teachers in the school appreciated his father's knowledge of religious texts and his style of teaching. What impressed Shankar was that although his father was strict, the students were obedient and followed his instructions well. He wondered what special reason his father had for inviting Mr. Ranjan home.

As soon as the stranger entered their house, Shankar's mother pulled her sari to cover her face and retreated to the kitchen. She and Shankar's sisters did not appear before the visitor. His mother gave Shankar a tray with tea in the best cups they had along with a plate of Bengali sweets—round white syrupy *rasogollas* and triangular salty *nimki* crackers—to take to them.

After the man left, Shankar's father went to the kitchen and asked his wife to throw away the plate and the cup used by Mr. Ranjan. She was startled and looked at her husband questioningly.

"Ranjan could be a brahmin last name," his father said, "but in Bihar, people take such last names as Ranjan, Gaurav, Prakash to hide their caste. I do not know what his caste is. We cannot use these again."

Shankar's mother lowered her eyes and threw away the dishes. They crashed against the floor near the cemented drain.

They had few fine things—certainly, very few items like this cup and the saucer. Shankar understood his father's rational but felt sad. Couldn't they wash these well enough to be used again, at least for other guests?

He was intrigued and found out that Saurabh Ranjan's real last name was Chaudhary; he was a brahmin. Changing last names so no one can figure out one's caste was a movement started in the Indian state of Bihar in the 1940s to stop caste-based socio-economic violence. A change of surname does not change one's caste. Last names such as Singh, Sinha, Mishra, and others, belong to many castes. It was even fashionable for movie stars to take Kumar or 'Prince' as their surname; Dilip Kumar was born a Muslim and Ashok Kumar, a Hindu brahmin. This way their popularity was not hampered by caste biases.

At school, Shankar mixed with all students, brahmin and non-brahmin, and they treated him equally. He was slightly lighter in complexion, but no one appeared to be that different from him by looks or by their behavior. He continuously thought about his father's pervasive idea of their superiority and didn't agree, but his father was firm in his belief. Shankar read more of the sacred texts compared to other boys, but he could not feel superior to them. He felt confusion and shame. However, he could not open up to talk about this with any of his friends, and kept these thoughts inside.

His father had set the rules in their family and those were based in his proud brahmin identity and his belief that they were the religious guardians of an ancient culture. His father had told him more than once that they were the upholders of the Hindu religion. No one in his family asked questions or even examined how they lived. His sisters followed the traditions and listened to what their parents told them. They seemed to be happy that way. But questions percolated in Shankar's mind. He wondered if he was different and not suitable for following the traditions of his family and their brahmin caste. He had no one to ask, as raising a question or expressing a doubt was considered disrespectful of his father and their tradition.

He remained in quiet rumination for much of his youth, wondering from time to time if what his family followed was truly the religion, or just his father's prejudices. There was no acceptance there of the changing world.

CALCUTTA, PRESIDENCY COLLEGE, 1951 - 1955

Chapter Eight

College Admission

I t was a Monday late in May … or perhaps it was early June—Shankar couldn't remember exactly when. He had gone to Presidency College to see the admissions list. He knew he did well in the high school final exam and would surely get admission, but he wanted to verify that his name was on the official list and see when classes would begin. Only a few students were in the wide corridor with heavy columns and arched walls next to the driveway. He found the list on the wall posted inside a glass-covered announcement box. His name was on the first page. He saw a girl coming along the corridor; she had a heart-shaped face, large eyes, long black hair, and a spritely gait. She was not fair, so did not qualify as pretty in the customary Bengali definition, but she was comely and graceful and had a vibrant demeanor.

She stopped at the board near him and nervously scanned the list. After a few tense moments, her face relaxed, pleased. "Did you find your name?" she asked him shyly.

He nodded and looked at her, astonished that she spoke to him.

Their eyes met, and she quickly looked down. "Good. We're both in."

"Will you study Arts or Science?" he asked, his tone a little hesitant.

"Arts." She glanced around.

Shankar understood her apparent anxiety. There were no other girls. Only a few boys loitered in the driveway some distance away. He himself had never spoken alone to an unknown girl. He wondered whether to go away or say something more. He looked at her and, for some reason, felt at ease. He ventured, "Which school are you from?"

"Shalkia Girls High School." She pulled her cotton sari tightly around her shoulders.

"I'm from Hindu School," Shankar announced with some pride. "Many students will be here from my school."

Shalkia Girls High was not known for its ranking – not like his own, which was one of the top high schools in Calcutta. *She must be exceptionally good to gain admission into Presidency College,* thought Shankar.

"I'll be the only girl from my school." She looked at his face. "And the first to get admission in Presidency College." She said coyly. "Everyone here will be new to me."

"There will be many from different schools," Shankar assured her quickly. He took a step back from the notice board. "I want to see the classrooms upstairs. Do you want to come?"

She nodded and followed. It was bold of him to ask, and yet, adrenaline swirled with the comfort she seemed to stir in him. They climbed the wide, long stairs quietly.

Many first-year students were visiting the classrooms and chatting, all eager to start college.

The classrooms lined a colonnaded corridor, which surrounded and opened onto an interior courtyard. Pigeons flew in and out among the rafters, boldly announcing their presence with sounds of rustled feathers and soft but excitable coos. The classrooms were all similar— benches for the students, a table and a chair for the professor, and a long blackboard on the wall behind the desk. Open windows brought in lots of light. In one room, the blackboard was covered with equations and diagrams. No one had erased the board after the last lecture.

"You will study science, right?" She glanced at the board.

"Yes. Physics."

"We'll have different classes."

Shankar studied her without speaking. Her eyebrows were pretty. He didn't want to stare, but he enjoyed looking at her. "You'll have a very long commute every day!" He acknowledged.

"Yes, but I have to. Education is the most important thing in our family."

A little taken aback, Shankar saw the determination on her face. He liked her openness.

There was nothing left to see upstairs. They started down the stairway. Classes would not begin for another week.

With nothing else to reasonably do in the building or say, she began to leave. "I'll go home now." She turned slightly to walk away.

He didn't know what prompted him, but he asked, "What's your name?"

"Durga, Durga Datta." Her eyes flickered to his face for a moment, then lowered, and she left.

Shankar knew Datta was not a brahmin name, but that didn't matter, as most of his classmates were non-brahmins. He softly repeated her name, 'Durga, the Mother Goddess.' Indians name children after gods and goddesses—either for the family's main deity or for some god-like characteristics they hope their child will emulate. Goddess Durga is the feminine power that fights against evil to safeguard her people, and to bestow upon them a prosperous life.

Shankar realized he forgot to tell her his name.

Before Shankar fell asleep that night, he thought of Durga—her smooth skin and slim, graceful body. Bengali society prefers light skinned girls, but to Shankar she was beautiful, an embodiment of her inner strength and lively spirit.

Chapter Nine

Romeo and Juliet

S hankar studied science, but English and Bengali literature were compulsory for the first two years for all students. He was not very enthusiastic about English, but on the first day he went early to English class. After the bell, before the class started, all the girls came together and occupied the first two rows of benches. When the professor called the roll, he heard Durga's name and looked up. Their eyes met and she acknowledged him with a slight nod. He didn't know why, but after seeing her in the class he found the English literature class fascinating and started to pay attention. The girls left together at the end of the class, and there was no chance of saying anything to her. He didn't think of connecting with her anyway, as that would be quite unusual, but he liked the fact that she was in the class with him.

They didn't have a chance to talk with each other for several weeks. There was a taboo against meeting and talking with girls back then. And what would he tell her? But he knew she was aware of his presence in class and that gave him a wonderful feeling.

Then, one day, he saw her in the library. Their eyes met, so he walked over to her, but then he hesitated and stood there awkwardly, wondering how to appear casual.

"Hi," she said with a shy smile.

That made it easier. "How is everything going with you?" he asked, trying to appear nonchalant. But inside, his heart beat fast.

"Fine."

"Your commute from Shalkia?"

Her eyes widened in delight that he remembered this detail about her. "I'm used to it now."

"This section of the library is a nice quiet place to study. I do my physics homework here." He looked around; there was no one he knew. "That day we met, I forgot to tell you my name," he told her shyly.

"I know your name."

"How?"

"All the girls know your name," she said with a sparkle in her eye. "The boy who's always in the library."

"Really!" Then he saw that she was trying to hide a smile.

She quickly changed the subject. "I came to look for *Romeo and Juliet*. I want to write my report tonight, but all copies are checked out."

"You can borrow mine." He tried to sound confident and reassuring.

"Are you sure?"

He took the book from his bag and handed it to her.

"Thank you. I'll return it soon."

"No. No. There's no rush." He forced himself to appear at ease but inside he was shaking. He finally relaxed under her kind gaze.

"Thank you again." She went out of the library.

Shankar watched her slender figure move away with a gentle, self-assured pace. He kept looking at the exit for some time. On his way home that evening, he bought a used copy of Romeo and Juliet from a sidewalk bookstall on College Street.

Chapter Ten

University Canteen

When Shankar came down the stairs to go to his class in Baker Laboratory, Durga was standing in the corridor. Boys and girls rushed by her to their classes.

She came forward when she saw him. "Could you meet me in the library today around 12:30, near the bulletin board?" There was nothing extraordinary in her manner or appearance. She wore a light blue cotton sari, practically no facial makeup beyond perhaps a little powder, and her hair was in a thick braid down her back. A light blue cloth bag, printed with little magenta elephants, hung from her shoulder. She expressed no overt emotion, but there seemed to be pleading in her eyes.

"Sure." He nodded.

She quickly walked away to her class.

Shankar couldn't keep his focus on physics. He stared at the board and heard little of what was said as the professor drew magnetic force lines from a rectangular magnet. Was Durga in some kind of trouble? He fidgeted on the bench and, as soon as the bell rang, he left class without talking to his classmates. He swiftly walked to the library. It was only a few minutes after noon. He pretended to read the notices on the board and prayed his friends would not find him there.

Finally, Durga came, walking hurriedly. She stopped short when she saw him. "I wanted to return your book." She paused for a moment and said bashfully, "And I brought something for you to taste."

"For me to eat?" His mouth fell open.

42

Her face glowed and she moved a little closer. "My mother makes the best *pati-shapta* in the world—you know, rice flour crepes with *kheer* and coconut paste inside. I brought some for you to thank you for letting me borrow the book." Seeing his surprise and discomfort, her demeanor changed from reserved to a playful smile.

"How nice of you!" Shankar was stunned but pleased. And relieved she wasn't facing some trouble. But he felt a little awkward and looked toward the library. "We can't eat in the library. We could go to the cricket field, but …" he stared helplessly at her. Being seen in the company of a girl would start all kinds of gossip. Suddenly he got an idea. "Let's go to the university canteen. Very few students from our college go there."

She followed him across the street next to Baker Laboratory and onto the university campus. Shankar led her through several corridors to the canteen. Neither of them said a word. He had a pleasant feeling being with her, but he was also a little nervous, as he had never taken a girl to a place for a rendezvous. He had chatted with some of the girls in classes but never met one alone—certainly not clandestinely. His parents would have a fit if they knew.

The canteen was noisy and bustling, mostly with older university students. They found an empty table in the corner and took it.

"Do you come here during Tiffin?" she asked after taking her seat.

"Sometimes." The calm expression on her face helped him relax. The nervous feelings caused by this surreptitious meeting quieted. "The vegetable *chop* is excellent here. Do you want to try it?"

"Maybe. First you have to try my mother's patishapta." She pulled out an aluminum box from her bag and gave him two. Shankar took a bite.

"Fantastic," he said, as he savored the sweet coconut filling. "I wanted to know how you were doing, but I never had a chance to ask you."

"I wondered about you too."

He reached out for the second patishapta. "How are your classes going?"

"Good. I might fail in math, but everything else is fine." She chuckled.

"I'll fail in English. Math and physics are fine."

They both found this humorous. Gradually, Shankar felt at ease with them being alone together.

Time passed by quickly in small talk; it appeared to Shankar she was as happy as he with their surreptitious tiffin meeting.

"Now you can get me a vegetable chop," she reminded him after some time.

On the way back, when they came to the street in front of Baker Laboratory, Shankar suggested, "You go through the college. I will go by College Street. I don't want—"

"I understand. But if you want to discuss English sometime, let me know."

"That would be great. Next Thursday at the canteen? Same time?"

She nodded and entered the college. He watched as she slipped away and noticed how beautifully her braid swung against her slim back.

It was too late to go to his math class, so he walked cheerfully toward the library.

***

When Shankar got home, the sun was still up. His father was in his room hunched over a dinner plate, removing small pebbles from rice. People believed the rice mills added stones to increase the weight of rice, but no one had found a way to stop them. The pebbles had to be removed before cooking to make the rice edible. His father called him in.

"Are you practicing your prayers and mantras every day?" His father raised his head and caught him in his icy gaze.

"I do it when I get up and also before falling asleep."

"Good. How about reading the Bhagavad Gita? Have you memorized the *slokas*?"

"I try, but Baba, it's not easy to remember them." Shankar's face stiffened. He removed the bag from his shoulder and avoided his father's eyes. "Besides, I have so much to study for my classes."

"Listen. Studies are fine, but you cannot deviate from learning the Vedas, the Upanishads, and the Gita. That is why we are here. You must."

"Baba, I have to balance this with my own goal in life." Shankar surprised himself as he had never dared speak so directly to his father before.

"What goal?"

"I want to do research in physics."

"Fine, but you cannot neglect studying the scriptures. This is our family's tradition. Not physics."

Shankar stared at his father for a moment. His confusion turned into resentment. He had so much homework in math and physics. Not to mention writing up lab experiment results. Where was the time to read scriptures? There was no way he could get his father to understand the goal he had set for himself. His father only thought of his own goal for his son—to be an esteemed scholar of scriptures and perhaps a priest! Shankar could say nothing to change his father. He turned, went to his room, dropped his bag on his bed and sat down with a grim face.

"Snack." Parvati brought a bowl of *chira bhaja* and a cup of tea. His sister put the bowl on the table and looked at his face for a few seconds. She didn't say anything and left.

Crunching a mouthful of fried flattened rice, his gaze fell on the shelf where Romeo and Juliet leaned crookedly against his other neatly ordered books. Durga's radiant face at the canteen came to him and lifted his spirits. He picked up his math book and began to study.

Chapter Eleven

Boat Ride

It was an autumn Sunday. Both Shankar and Durga had gone on the annual college boat ride on the Hooghly River, a split-off of the Ganges, and called Ganges by local people. They went separately with their friends although they met often in the university canteen and enjoyed being together. They looked forward to coming to school and seeing each other, even if it was only for a few minutes in the library, in class, or in passing. Their furtive looks of admiration, surreptitious meetings in restaurants, and spontaneous nudging were indications they were falling in love, but they dared not be seen going to a public event together. Their growing affection for each other remained unspoken.

The cruise began at ten in the morning, heading south toward the ocean, providing beautiful views of little towns on both sides of the river. Students chatted boisterously with classmates, listened to music, and partook in the bountiful buffet. Shankar and Durga carefully avoided each other except to exchange glances. When the boat returned to Babughat in late afternoon, they both lingered there while most of their classmates went home. Finally, they joined up and walked together along the river among other strollers.

"It was fun," Shankar said. But actually, he wished the trip had ended sooner so he could spend more time with Durga. He looked affectionately at her.

"The girls sang together on the upper deck. I enjoyed that," Durga said animatedly. "Last year I was too timid to go by myself and missed it."

"I'm glad we got back early enough to spend some time together." He wanted to put his arm around her and bring her closer but wasn't bold enough.

"Me too." She cast a sidelong glance at him. "I've already told my mother I'll be late coming home."

When they reached Outram *Ghat*, Shankar bought two packets of spicy puffed rice from a sidewalk vendor. "You can't find this special *Jhalmuri* anywhere else." He gave Durga a packet wrapped in newspaper.

"We must have tea afterwards." She poured some puffed rice into her hand.

Shankar looked at the ghat—the steps leading down to the water, where a few boys were playing. He then moved toward the cemented promenade, hoping to sit on a bench, but no seat was free. They stood against the balustrade. The river flowed a few feet away. Several small, old-style boats with cylindrical covers over the center of the hull moved unhurriedly by a majestic oceangoing ship anchored in the middle of the river. Young couples sat on benches close to each other on the promenade, some holding hands, some men putting an arm over the shoulder of the young woman next to them, some whispering in their lover's ear—all enjoying forbidden moments in the last rays of the sun.

"I loved watching the ghats along the river," Shankar said. He leaned against the balustrade and faced Durga. "But what fascinated me most was when the river widened near Diamond Harbor. I couldn't take my eyes off the huge expanse of water near the Bay of Bengal; I felt a calling to the ocean."

"I see you are reading too many literary books." Her eyes danced, and her voice took on a teasing tone. "Next you will tell me life's nothing but a dream."

"Isn't it?"

"Perhaps it is." Durga nodded. "We all live in our dreams."

Shankar gazed for a few seconds at a strand of hair fluttering by her cheek. How lovely she was. Could he live his dream? His family lived such a constrained life, as if there shouldn't be anything beyond the life prescribed by the scriptures. Was it possible to go beyond their circumscribed world? He knew, from her behavior and her ebullient spirit, her family was not like his—not disconnected from the real world and in tune with the changes happening all around. He lived in one world when he was home and in another outside the house. Durga was watching him. "Someday, you can make my dreams come true," he said softly.

"Ha! I just love to go on boat rides and later eat jhal-muri," Durga chuckled. "That's my dream."

"I guess you need tea now," Shankar said, "to make the day perfect?"

"Yes. Let's have tea. I'll buy." She turned toward a vendor.

After a sip of tea, Durga said, "I've known you for some time, but I know very little about your family."

"They are boring. Listen to this: the first movie my mother saw was when the religious movie *Prahlad* came to our cinema hall in Dum Dum. See why I don't talk about them?" Shankar put the last jhal-muri in his mouth, crumpled the packet, and threw it in a garbage can. "Let's go to the park and sit on the grass. You can then drag out more about my family."

"Good idea."

But how could Shankar tell her about his father, his ideas and attitudes that governed their lives? Especially his feeling of superiority over other castes? Earlier he had wanted to tell her but now he could not bring himself to say anything. How could he tell Durga his family didn't encourage anyone to enter their house if they weren't brahmins? He was afraid of how she would take it. His mother obeyed her husband's wishes without reservation and spent her days cooking, cleaning, and taking care of the family. No non-brahmin could enter her kitchen. This was how Shankar had seen his mother every day—sitting on a low stool in the kitchen, cutting vegetables, cooking, or serving food. The only pleasure she had was when she went to visit her brothers and sisters or went to the temples on religious occasions. But she seemed to be happy to follow her assigned role in life.

"When Muslim workers came to repair or work on our house in Dhaka," his mother had told him, "we were careful not to step on their shadows. We purified the places where they walked by sprinkling water mixed with cow dung and then Ganges water on the floors. So pure is our family!"

"But times have changed, Ma," Shankar told her. "We are in Calcutta. We go out and mix with all sorts of people and go places and eat in restaurants. We cannot keep those rules."

"You do what you have to do outside the house," she said. "Your father makes the rules inside the house."

They crossed the road and found a spot under a tree.

"Your family must be fun," Shankar said. "Think about why I don't talk about my family. You do things for enjoyment. We aren't raised that way. My father lives a strict, old-fashioned life. He is a high school teacher, but he carries his ancient ideals everywhere." He looked away. "I was born in East Bengal, but I don't remember anything about my birthplace. I presume life was better for our family there, before the Partition of India. Partition changed the lives of those who came from East Bengal, but I don't think that has anything to do with my father's strict outlook on life."

"What about your brothers and sisters?"

"I have two sisters." Shankar answered, matter-of-factly.

"I have three siblings—one brother and two sisters. I am the oldest. Yes, we have fun together. We like doing things together like going out to restaurants or to movies."

"I wish my family was like yours." He fixed his eyes on her. How nice it would be if she were around all the time.

Her face flushed. There was romance in her eyes, but she said, "Then you would have fun all the time and wouldn't study hard. What about your physics?"

"All right. I'll tell you when I have the most fun in our family." He took her hand in his and felt a tremor go through his body. "That is when we have Kali puja in our house."

"Kali puja? Very few families do that anymore because you have to follow the rules very strictly."

"We do."

Truly. Shankar knew well Kali puja was serious business, as everything had to be done correctly. Any mistake in the worship service would cast a bad curse on the family. Despite the gravity of the puja, it was festive because many relatives came from distant places. Lots of delicious foods were cooked, and on the night of the puja, the house was decorated with earthen oil lamps on door lintels, windows, walls and the roof, and children could play with fireworks. The auspicious moment came around midnight when a live goat would be sacrificed in front of the Goddess. Big drums beat loudest at that time and smoke from the incense burners suffused the courtyard. When Shankar was sixteen, his father allowed him to hold the goat tightly before its head was chopped off with one stroke by an adult. It had to be severed with a single strike; otherwise, a grave disaster would fall on the family. Shankar felt proud when he held the goat along with others. He didn't feel bad for the goat despite its loud 'maa, maa' screams and struggles to run away. That was a part of the worship service. At the end of the puja, they distributed the goat meat to all guests, who took it home with reverence and devotion as *Prasad*—a gift from the Goddess. Shankar's mother cooked the rest of the meat the next day for a feast. All looked forward to and loved her famous 'vegetarian goat curry.' They didn't eat the head though; they gave that to the man who cleaned their bathrooms.

"Maybe one day you will come to the puja in our house."

"That would be nice. I was never awake to see the worship service."

***

That night Shankar tossed and turned in bed for a long time. He finally fell asleep, but soon woke up sweating and breathing hard. He'd had a dream. He was inside a modern glass palace in a gorgeous country where everything was neat, bright, and beautiful—the flowers, the bushes, the trees, the meadows. People milled around in the courtyard outside the palace, but silence prevailed inside the beautifully kept spires. He was cautiously walking up a wide white marble stairway, carrying a delicate, ornamental china cup containing a sacred liquid. He could not spill a drop. The stairs seemed to go on and on, and he didn't know how far he was going. He climbed slowly, one step after another. Then he noticed the face of a man looking down on him from two floors above with spiteful, glaring eyes. He averted his eyes, and, at that instant, the cup slipped from his hand. His fingers clutched the saucer while he watched the fall of the cup like a slow-motion movie. He observed every detail of the fall, how the cup tilted and passed by each level and finally crashed on the marble floor and broke into pieces. The sound woke him.

Drenched in sweat, he kicked off the sheet. The sound of the crashing cup was so real! Shankar lay in bed and remembered the sequence of the dream. He stared at the dark ceiling for a long time before falling asleep again.

Chapter Twelve

Durga's Mother

I t was dark. The neighborhood had already settled down for the night when Durga walked home from the bus station. Very few people were in the street and dim streetlights made the darkness seem even darker; the silence was forbidding. Durga crossed the threshold of their house with light steps.

"You came late," her mother complained in a low voice from the kitchen. "Did you have a good time?"

"Yes, mother. Shankar and I had tea at the Kwality restaurant on Park Street. Sorry, Ma, it got late."

"Change your clothes and then tell me about your trip."

When Durga returned, her two sisters, Kalindi and Sujata, were also there. They were eagerly waiting to hear about her outing on the Ganges. She described the boat ride in a lively manner—viewing the beautiful scenery on the riverbanks from the middle of the river, the fun of passing underneath Howrah Bridge, observing Belur Math temple on one side of the river and Dakshineswar Temple on the other side, the many ghats they passed where men and women bathed, and small boats picked up passengers. The landscape along the riverbanks was timeless—trees arching over the water; primitive, neglected land on both banks wild with bushes, reeds, mango and banana trees; and the occasional sight of decaying, abandoned mansions. She told them how much fun it was singing with other girls in the middle of the river and the scrumptious food they had.

"I'll go on such a boat ride when I go to college," Kalindi, her second sister, said enthusiastically. "Did Shankar-da also go?"

"Yes, but we weren't together on the boat. I saw him after the ride."

"Go finish your homework," their mother told her two younger daughters. After they left, she looked at Durga intently. "Tell me about Shankar."

Everyone in the family knew about Shankar. But Durga understood what her mother wanted to know. "He is quiet and reserved. He doesn't talk much about his family, but I found out a little more. They are old-fashioned—very conservative and keep to themselves. He said he'll invite me to Kali puja in their house. They sacrifice a goat! Can you believe it?" She inclined her head toward her mother, almost gasping as she said these words.

"I see," said her mother, keeping a fixed gaze on her. "Be careful, Durga. They are quite different from us."

"You're thinking too far ahead, Ma."

"We have to."

"I like him. He is sincere, but I'm not thinking that far yet. My studies come first. Don't worry."

"You know I had an arranged marriage with your father. We will find a good marriage for you. A boy from a suitable family with a good education and good future. Don't do anything in haste."

"I know." She nodded. She knew she did not have to find herself a man to marry. Her family would see to that.

"Jaya's parents found the right match for her and they are happily married now." Her mother exuded a calm demeanor, gazing directly into Durga's eyes.

Durga nodded and went to her room. Her mother was watching over her. She liked that. She also cherished her mother's confidence about her future.

Durga's cousin from her mother's side, Jaya, was older, but they were close. Jaya had confided in Durga when her parents were looking for a suitable boy for her. Jaya was fine with an arranged marriage, even happy. Jaya said she had confidence in her parents—they would select a good man who would be her companion for the rest of her life. She had this trust and grew up knowing that this was the plan. Durga also had trust and confidence in her parents, but she knew that if she loved someone, her parents would allow her to choose for herself. Jaya's family found a candidate from a family culture like theirs—a teacher, like her.

Durga then thought of Shanti, another cousin in Sodepur, who was now married to a college professor in Calcutta. She had 'modern' ideas about marriage and gave her family terrible problems when her father was trying to arrange her marriage. Durga had seen it herself. She remembered what Shanti had done.

***

Bride Selection

I happened to be visiting my uncle's family in Sodepur when, unknown to me, they had arranged a 'Meye-Dekha' or 'look at the girl' meeting for Shanti, my oldest cousin. I knew that was how marriages were decided, but I had never actually been present during a "Meye-Dekha."

On that day, my aunt, and her middle daughter, whom we called Mejdi, were very busy, starting right after breakfast. They spent several hours sweeping, cleaning, and tidying the apartment. They organized the shelves in the room where they received guests, arranging the books and a few display items nicely. I was around to help any way I could. As instructed, I bought a bunch of long-stemmed tuberoses from the market. Mejdi put them in a tall vase in the corner. Those tubular snow-white flowers, always used for weddings, perfumed the room. My aunt dragged a trunk from under her bed and took out a beautiful, thick, golden bedspread and put it on the single platform bed in the room for guests to sit on. The gold color brightened the room like the fabulous Mughal emperor's court my teacher had described. My aunt had transformed the mundane room into an opulent salon, like the ones rich people had in Calcutta. This would impress anyone.

My uncle paced back and forth in the corridor. He read the paper twice, cover to cover, with a pensive look on his face. He came to his wife and reminded her, "They will come at 3 o'clock. And only three people: the parents and an uncle. The marriage broker said they are a well-to-do family."

"I know," she quietly replied and took down a set of fine bone china plates and cups from a shelf above the window. The set was hand-painted on the borders with tiny pink flowers and were my aunt's pride and joy.

"We'll cook luchis with ghee," she told Mejdi. "We serve this on very special occasions, but I decided to make them for this time." She opened a Lakshmi-brand can of ghee bought especially for the event.

I was watching everything with fascination. I saw two packets of sweets from *Rajbhog*, the famous sweets store in Central Calcutta, that Uncle had brought home the day before.

"Where is Shanti?" Aunt inquired.

"I haven't seen her since breakfast," Mejdi said. "She's a little bashful. Probably reading a novel on the roof."

"Let her alone. We will dress her around 2:30."

When the food was cooked, Mejdi went to talk with Shanti but could not find her in the apartment. Where could she be? She asked me to search the roof. I climbed up the spiral stairway, but the flat roof was deserted. The house looked so beautiful and my aunt had cooked such wonderful food. The buttery fragrance of the dishes permeated the kitchen area. All for Shanti's sake! For settling her marriage! But where was she? I leaned on the roof wall and gazed at the coconut palms in the distance.

Mejdi had told me she knew Shanti didn't like the candidate her father was considering for her marriage. The marriage broker said the boy had a graduate degree and had a good position with excellent prospects in the Bata shoe company. When Mejdi had pressed Shanti, she had said: "He has a degree in leather technology. Can you imagine, he works in a shoe manufacturing company! Making shoes!" Mejdi told me they both knew people who worked with leather were not highly regarded in society; this man's family belonged to the industrial 'owner class,' but the taboo was indelible.

"Won't it be better than marrying a clerk who slaves in a government office?" Mejdi had asked Shanti.

"Many will find this man worthy," Shanti had agreed, "but not me. India has been independent for ten years! Isn't it time for us to throw off these antiquated customs of arranged marriage?"

"For the family's sake, please go along with it," Mejdi had cajoled her. "You can reject the boy later."

Mejdi told me she thought she had convinced her sister. Now, she had no choice but to report the conversation to her mother. Mejdi told her mother she had underestimated the intensity of Shanti's objection to arranged marriages, and especially this one.

"Does she have someone in mind?" my aunt inquired.

"No. But she wants to take charge of her own life."

"This is our way—good or bad," my aunt lamented. "I went through the same thing. My father considered all the possibilities and did what was best for me. My mother was also similarly married off. And her mother. We learn to love the man we marry."

"Times have changed, Ma."

"It's been this way for generations in India." After some time, my aunt sighed. "Fate! We can't avoid what's in store for us."

"I understand, but the guests are coming in half an hour."

"Your father is a good man, but he is not a salesman. You don't know how hard and how humiliating it is for him to find a bridegroom for his daughter. He feels as though he is begging. He placed anonymous advertisements in newspapers and contacted several marriage brokers. This candidate was one of the best. Shanti is already twenty-four. An unmarried girl is a blemish on us. If we cannot get her married off, what will happen to you?" My aunt started to cry. She wiped a few tears away with the end of her sari. "What am I going to tell your father?" She slapped her forehead several times.

Uncle's voice rang out, "The guests have come."

Aunt quickly changed her sari, combed her hair, and made herself as presentable as she could. Then she told Uncle that Shanti was nowhere to be found. He stared dumbfounded at his wife.

"She didn't like the idea of being presented for marriage and has walked out."

His face blanched; he was speechless, but there was no time for discussion.

After the guests were seated and introductions were made, my aunt went to Mejdi. "The guests have reason to be bitter; they will spread nasty gossip about us. We will be humiliated."

Mejdi shook her head silently.

"I feel sorry for your father. It breaks my heart." Then she looked at Mejdi and said, "There is one way out, if you are willing."

"Tell me."

"They do not know Shanti. You go in her place. You are only two years younger. Answer a few questions. That's all you have to do. Afterwards, we'll reject the proposal."

Mejdi stared at her mother. "I guess we have no other option."

"It will save your father's honor."

"What will I say if they ask me to sing?"

"Say you love Tagore songs, but you cannot sing before an audience."

Mejdi went to her room to get dressed.

Everything went smoothly. The guests were extremely happy; they said they would let my uncle know their decision soon.

I went to the roof, a little forlorn for all that had happened. What a commotion we had been through in the last few hours. Then I saw Shanti, walking down the street from the train station. She walked in a steady gait as if she were returning after work. I was worried Shanti might have run away and left her family forever, but as I saw her on the street, my heart lifted. I ran to her. "Shanti, I'm so happy. You are alive!"

"Why wouldn't I be alive?" She pulled me close. "Now tell me what happened at the house."

I quickly described how Mejdi saved us.

Shanti and I entered the apartment with our hearts fluttering. She kept her head down, but there was no fuss, and no one blamed her. Everyone understood. Her complaint was against society; she longed for change. Mejdi took her to the roof to talk.

***

Durga could not identify herself with either Jaya or with Shanti. She stared out the window from her desk. There was nothing to see out there; it was all dark—no stars or moonlight. The day had been so nice. She smiled to herself. Then, her mother's cautious words crept into her mind.

Certainly, a girl's life is more complicated than a boy's. She liked Shankar. She did not have any other experience or know any boys outside of their family. She wondered what had prompted her to speak to him the first time they met. There was something deeply sincere about him and he appreciated her sense of humor. Was she considering him as a life partner? She had not thought that far. Besides, they belonged to different castes. She enjoyed being with Shankar and it was nice to spend time with him. A happy feeling spread through her chest. Her studies came first. She would not sacrifice anything for her education, but she would keep on seeing him.

Chapter Thirteen

Diamond Harbor

F our years passed quickly. Shankar and Durga saw each other at college but they did not go out to movies, concerts, or outings by themselves. They knew that privately seeing someone of the opposite sex was looked down upon and to many, considered scandalous. Although boys and girls secretly desired romance, only a few had enough courage to venture out into the forbidden territory. Those who were amorously involved had to be extra-careful not to be seen openly in public. Shankar and Durga met at the library and had lunch at their favorite place, the university canteen. Most days, Shankar and Durga's joy was simply a glance and eye contact or a smile while rushing to their separate classes—the romantic pleasure of just being in the college together. If they did not see each other one day, they felt something missing and eagerly looked forward to a chance meeting the next day.

Studying and doing well in college was of primary importance to both; as a result, they did extremely well in their final exams at the end of two years to complete Intermediate Science and Intermediate Arts certificates. Both stood among the top three at the university. They did not have common literature or math classes any more as Shankar went on to study physics honors and Durga to economics honors. But they continued their meetings at the college in the same way. They were in love, but neither mentioned it.

Two years later, the day Baccalaureate degree exams were finished, euphoria broke out, all relieved that the exams were over. Boys and girls gathered in groups all around the college compound. Many might not come to this college campus again and would go their own ways. Abruptly, Shankar separated from his group, went to Durga and asked her to meet him at the college on Monday.

"Are you planning something?" she teased him with a raised eyebrow.

"Yes. We must start working on graduate school admissions." Shankar told her seriously.

Durga looked at his face with an 'I don't believe it' expression. A wide grin appeared on her face. "What's on your mind?"

"I can't tell you now, but come before lunch, say 9:30," Shankar said in a lower-pitched voice. Then his eyes sparkled.

"Do I trust you?" She asked but her eyes gave a different message.

"You will find out." Shankar walked away to join with other physics students.

Durga met Shankar at 9:30 on Monday. She was jolly and said, "Quite happy to get out of the house." She wore a dark blue blouse and a blue printed cotton sari, with a matching blue *bindi* on her forehead. She looked fresh and sprightly. "So, what are we doing?"

"We are going to Diamond Harbor."

"Diamond Harbor?"

"Yes. Any objection?" An expression of feigned irritation appeared on his face.

"No, no." She said with a bemused but admiring expression. "You planned this for some time?"

"I wanted to spend a day out with you. Away from Calcutta." He wanted to go where nobody knew them.

Her face lit up. "That will be a delightful escape."

"We'll go by train; they are not crowded now. There is one a little after 10. Let's go."

They took a taxi to the Sealdah train station, which was not far. They rushed and found two window seats in one compartment facing each other. "It is a local train," Shankar said. "Slow, but we aren't in a rush. Are we?"

"If I knew we were going on an excursion, I'd have brought some snacks to munch along the way."

"I didn't tell you because I wasn't sure if you would come."

"Of course not." She rolled her eyes. "Going away from Calcutta, alone, with you?" she said with mock horror. "What would my mother say?"

Just then a young hawker entered the compartment. "Spicy, crunchy mix and spicey peanuts," the man stood in front them with a basket hanging from his neck.

"I'll buy," Durga said. "What would you like?" she asked Shankar.

"One of each. We will share."

The train started to move. They both gazed outside, munching. "We will reach Diamond Harbor in one and a half hours," Shankar murmured.

"I've never been there," she told Shankar. "I am liking the idea more and more." She gazed at the panorama outside and started to hum a Tagore song:

My heart's desire is filled today
Listen everyone in the world
My heart's desire is filled today
What beauty I experience, Oh my Lord!
My mind sits on a steady mat.

Shankar quietly listened and watched the scenery outside. When she finished the song, he turned to Durga, "I like your voice – sweet … this one is awfully hard to sing. You must have years of practice."

"My mother insisted that we learn to sing. … What were you people talking about after the exam?"

"The physics students talked about their fear of not having done well and wondering if they would get admission at a graduate school."

"The girls in my class had similar concerns, but they were more interested in what kind of jobs they could get."

"India will need many economists to develop our country; they will find good jobs even if they don't go to graduate school."

"Hmm. I see you don't know much about economists." Durga shook her head and a slight chuckle escaped her lips. "Guess how many economists will be needed in India?"

"Thousands, I am sure."

"The correct answer is it doesn't matter because nobody listens to them."

"I know why. In physics, two plus two is four. If you line up all the economists in the world, they could cover the entire Equator, but no two will agree on a solution. They say this will happen but then I can also see the possibility of a different outcome. See?"

"OK. Tell me, smart physicist, why do people think Einstein is the best physicist in the world, but not Marie Curie who won the Nobel prize twice?"

"Because E=MC2."

"So?"

"Everybody agrees with this equation. E, Einstein, is equal to MC, Marie Curie, squared."

"Now tell me how many economists are needed to change a light bulb?"

"I don't know." Shankar looked at Durga. "Probably many."

"None. The market will do it. If it is dark, it will cause light to come up."

The train came to a slow stop. Being a local train, it halted at all the stations, and many passengers boarded with large bundles. The empty seats next to Shankar and Durga were filled soon after the train left Sealdah Station. The compartment was now filled to overflowing with people. Old hawkers left and new ones came in. A blind man held the hand of a young girl and sang a devotional song. Shankar put some coins in a can she held in her outstretched hand. "God will give you a happy life," the man said as he and the girl squeezed between people on their way through the crowd.

Shankar and Durga kept to themselves, looking primarily outside. When the train stopped at Baruipur, he announced to Durga, "We've come halfway."

"Already?"

Shankar nodded. He looked outside at the disembarked passengers walking by the railway track with bundles on their heads. He suddenly turned and asked Durga, "Do you know much about Buddhism?"

"Not really, but my father admires Buddha very much. Why did you ask?"

"My friend Soumen reads a lot about what Buddha taught and tells me."

After the train started again, Shankar gazed outside. "I love to watch the green paddy fields." He spoke to Durga. "Harvested. All yellow now."

"I'm looking forward to seeing the river," Durga said.

"We will arrive in twenty minutes," Shankar replied.

***

The Diamond Harbor road was next to the station and crowded by trucks, buses, rickshaws, and people. A few minutes' walk brought Shankar and Durga, suddenly, to the wide Hooghly River and they stopped on its bank. They were not sure if they were looking at a river or the sea. It was difficult to see the opposite shore. The muddy brown color of the river in Calcutta had changed to a darker ocean color. Spellbound, they watched the gentle movement of the waves and where blue sky and water met. The sight took their breath away. A huge boat went south to the Bay of Bengal. The waves it created tossed all the little boats near the shore. Several fishermen took advantage of the waves created by the big ship to reach the middle of the river, their destination for fishing. The activities on the river changed as constantly as the clouds overhead, and both Durga and Shankar stayed glued to the view. Although the tropical sun was directly above, the river breeze soothed them.

"Now that we have seen the river," Shankar finally said, "let us have lunch." They walked a little further along the bank and came to a decent looking hotel, Sagarika, and went into their restaurant. Two other people were in the dining hall; they sat at a table with a view of the river. Shankar ordered for both fish curry and tea to be served later. "You can't miss the famous Diamond Harbor fish curry!" he told Durga.

After a sip of cold lemonade and a bite of the fried, battered eggplant appetizer, Durga leaned forward and said, "Thank you for this lovely treat."

"Aah! Finally, I get some credit. Frankly, I wanted to get away with you for some time and get to know you more."

"Really? What do you wish to know?"

"Nothing particular. Just to know you more."

"Here is one. I like to read romance novels," said Durga.

"With good endings, right?"

"Of course. Who will read a romance novel with tragic ending?"

"I like novels with secret lovers, tragic heroines, and joyful endings," Shankar replied.

"Right. Your heart stops and you suffer along with the heroine, but a joy to read the ending."

"Do you have someone secret like in those novels?" Shankar asked coolly.

Durga's expression became playful, "You will never know." Her eyes sparkled.

Before Shankar could reply, the waiter brought food to the table.

"Shad in mustard sauce, I love it." She exclaimed.

Shankar nodded. "Me too," he said and started to spoon rice on their plates.

"Excellent," she said after tasting a spoonful. "My mother sometimes puts a little ground coconut in this dish. Maybe I will invite you one day to our house."

"How will you explain that to your mother?"

"She knows about you."

"I hope it's all good." He said and kept on eating. After some time, Shankar said, "Here is something new about me. I eat almost everything outside the house, but my mother never cooks food with onions and garlic."

"Does she have someone in mind to marry you off to also? To make your life easy," She teased him.

"Are your parents looking for someone for you?"

"No. They will ask me first, but … I should have said yes to see your reaction."

"You want to see my wistful face?"

Durga gazed at his face without saying anything. Shankar took some food without a word. Durga shifted her view to the river, forgetting the food.

"Is your family terribly religious?" Shankar asked her.

She laughed. "The answer is a definite no. We enjoy all the festivals with gusto, but we are somewhat free spirited. My father is perhaps agnostic."

"Good. My family is religious, but I hate conservative, unexamined ideas."

The waiter brought over two bowls of water and lemon slices to wash the grease off their fingers. "We have *khejur gur payesh* for dessert," the waiter said. "After that I will bring tea."

"You selected the perfect restaurant," Durga exclaimed appreciatively. "I am pleased to hang out with you."

"They harvest date tree juice right here and make khejur gur."

The dessert came and both delved into it immediately. "Very good," she said, licking her lips unabashed. "The date sugar flavor is strong; what we get in Calcutta is diluted khejur gur."

After a sip of milky tea, Shankar said, "I don't know what I am doing but I think about you all the time."

She examined Shankar's face and stretched her hand on top of his, "Me too. I could not stop telling my mother and sisters about you."

"You did? I have no one in my family to talk to about you. My family is so different." Shankar wrapped her hand in his two palms. "I'm glad I met you the first day at college. I don't know what is in the future for us, but I hope it will be good." His voice choked a little and he looked away toward the river.

Durga let him hold her hand, murmuring, "I am very fond of you."

They sat there quietly. "I like that you have an upbeat character," Shankar said. "You cheer me up."

"Really? I had no clue." But her expression betrayed her statement. She could not stop smiling with delight.

Shankar finished the last sip from his cup and looked at his watch. "We should return before the trains get crowded."

She nodded. "But I am enjoying sitting here with you. Let us stay a little longer."

On their walk back they saw another big ship, steaming down the river, churning the water's surface. They watched the ship going south where there seemed to be no horizon—the cloudy sky and the water totally blended as one.

"Next time we will take a boat ride to the other side," Shankar said, "then you can really feel the presence of the ocean."

"And buy sweet khejur gur."

"And see the fishermen catch shad fish."

As they started to walk back to the train station, Shankar stretched his hand toward hers, and she took it, accepting the offer of intimacy. Breezes of romance suffused the air in the 'faraway land'.

CALCUTTA

1957

Chapter Fourteen

Finals and Future

Shankar walked cheerfully to the bus stop. He had just finished the final exams for his master's degree. Feeling free as a cloud, he strode along his regular route—a shortcut through a field covered with small bushes and trees. He stopped short at the night jasmine tree. How beautiful! Small white flowers with red-orange stems had covered the ground in a wide circle. Their sweet fragrance filled the air. He played with his little sister Parvati under a similar tree when she was small. His older sister kept these night-blooming little flowers in a flat bowl in her bedroom, their gentle fragrance spreading around the house.

Night jasmine flowers lying on the ground were a common sight at this time of the year, but today Shankar admired the scene with new eyes. How fresh and beautiful they looked! His heart lifted with wonder. He wished he could share this rustic beauty with Durga. He picked up a handful of flowers from the ground and inhaled their fragrance. He put the flowers delicately in his pocket. Autumn was wonderful. If Durga came to this side of town, he would bring her this way. Eagerly he increased his speed toward the bus stop that would take him to College Street—to Durga.

Shankar found Durga cheery, also freed from the burden of her exams. "I think I did well," she told him. Her face was radiant, contrary to the expression of most students after exams when they wished they had done better. Both were satisfied with their exams and delighted to be in each other's company. They walked around the university campus, chatting, and laughing spontaneously with each other. Anyone could see they were joyously in love.

Shankar held her hand, and she let him without wondering who was around. A romantic day for them, feeling carefree like children and dreaming of the future. They strolled off the college grounds and meandered to Gol Dighi—a nearby park built around an artificial pond in College Square. The Buddhist Society temple was across the street, and the University Senate Building, with its imposing colonial style pillars, was on the other side. Benches and a few trees surrounded the square pond.

"I've recently read a story from Buddha's life," Shankar murmured, staring toward the Buddhist temple. "A sixteen-year-old precocious brahmin boy, Assalayan, was goaded by other brahmins to tell Buddha about their claim that they were direct descendants of Brahma and hence a superior class. Buddha convinced him that no one can truly know their lineage from ancient times because so many things might have happened over the years; so that was only a false myth."

"How did the young man respond?" Durga's eyebrows frowned for a moment.

"He agreed with the Buddha and told him he would take refuge in his teachings." Shankar looked away from her. "The more I'm learning about the Buddha, the more I am liking him." he said. "But let's not discuss this today."

They strolled around the pond, taking their time, relishing these moments detached from all the things they would have to do next. Durga talked about the ordinary occurrences of her life, and Shankar rather enjoyed listening to her. She said she liked Sundays best, when she and her siblings were together gossiping, going to movies, or visiting relatives. She so enjoyed her family. Shankar's focus, he told her, was on physics. How he would love to do research on the frontiers of science.

Durga glanced at the Senate building and said, "We are the hundredth-year students at the university, we ought to celebrate. Let's go to Putiram." She proceeded toward College Street.

While munching a kachori at the restaurant, Shankar felt the night jasmine flowers in his pocket. He took them out and looked at Durga's face. He smelled the fragrance. A pleasant smile spread across his face, "This morning when I saw these flowers, under a tree, I thought of you. Such beautiful flowers: the dew drops were still on them. I wished you were there with me."

"I love shiuli flowers with their deep orange stems." She picked one from his hand. "The tree is near your house?"

"No, no. It is in the field on my way to the bus stop. Nature's beauty ... no one even takes care of this tree. It is so exquisite in its natural surroundings."

"Maybe one day I'll see it."

"Why not today?" Shankar abruptly perked up. "Let's go to Dakshineswar! We can go by my house and I'll show you the lovely tree."

"I can go home from there by ferry."

"Right." He nodded.

Elated with the idea of the spontaneous adventure, they walked to the bus stop. "You will not forget this experience," Shankar said, pleased that she agreed to go with him.

As Shankar entered his home, he heard the stirring of the metal spatula hitting against the *karai*, an Indian wok. His mother was cooking.

"Ma, I have brought someone to meet you," Shankar called out to her from the veranda in the courtyard. Durga was behind him. Not much sunlight came to the inner courtyards in the old house, so she was in shadow.

"Come, come inside." His mother came out of the kitchen.

Durga dipped to touch her feet.

"Be happy in life," his mother said, as older women bless younger people. Shankar had sometimes brought home a friend or two, but never a girl. Shankar's mother smiled politely but the smile did not go all the way to her eyes. She examined Durga's face and her dark complexion intently. She glanced questioningly at Shankar as if to say, '*A lower caste girl?*'

"I met her in college, Ma," Shankar told her proudly. "She was in my English class."

Shankar's mother peered at the girl's calm demeanor. "Ah, a scholar! I didn't go beyond seventh grade. I got married . . . You two sit in the Baithak-khana." She motioned them toward the drawing room. "I've cooked halwa," she told her son. "Let me bring two plates for you."

"No, Ma. We will not stay long. I'm taking her to Dakshineswar."

***

His father came out from an inner room.

"Baba, this is Durga. She finished M.A. finals yesterday."

Durga bent down to touch his feet.

"That's wonderful. What did you study?"

"Economics."

"She is a very good student, Baba," Shankar said, glancing at her. "She came first in B.A. Honors in economics and now she has finished her M.A."

"Great accomplishment," his father said, keenly observing her face.

His father's critical gaze on Durga made Shankar nervous. "We're going to Dakshineswar," he told him. "I'll come home in the evening." He turned and signaled Durga to follow him.

As they were going out the main gate, his father called him back. "Shankar, Shankar, come here for a minute."

"You wait here," Shankar warned Durga.

He followed his father into the courtyard; his mother was standing there too.

"What are you planning with this girl?" his father asked him bluntly. His posture had changed in the last few seconds from relaxed to very rigid. His face resembled that of a schoolteacher severely annoyed at his student's behavior.

Shankar hesitated. He had long been afraid of this moment; he knew this would happen one day, but he didn't expect it to be right then. It was such a happy day. He saw his father's hazy figure in front of him and felt weak-kneed. Light seemed to dim around him. He blurted out in a feeble voice, "I ... plan to marry her someday."

His father's face changed to a scowl. "You have decided to marry her without knowing the horoscope and without consulting us?"

"Naturally, I was going to talk with you, but—"

"We do not know anything about her family. Are they brahmins?"

"No. They are not brahmins." Shankar answered hesitantly and looked down at the floor, knowing this was utterly unacceptable to his parents.

"What?" his father shouted at him. "You decided to marry a non-brahmin girl?" His father's eyes bulged out, his nostrils flaring.

A shiver ran through Shankar. He murmured, "We have debated this—"

His father cut him off. "This cannot happen in our family."

Shankar remained silent. His heart sank, his stomach hurt, as if tied in knots, and his mouth felt dry.

"You want to forsake our traditions? . . . Then you cannot be a part of this family anymore." His father waved his hand and shook his head vigorously.

"You are our only son," his mother chimed in. Her eyes, usually so placid, burned with rage. "How could you think like this, Shankar? You know our heritage. You want to abandon everything for this girl and bring disgrace to our family?" She slapped her forehead and howled.

"Hai Bhagavan! Oh God! . . . Your father has raised you so well, with such good hopes that you will carry on our family traditions. And you want to do this?" She slapped her forehead again.

Shankar's face paled, thinking Durga might hear his mother's words.

His father closed his lips and clenched his jaw, fuming. Shankar who had been afraid of this confrontation for years, remained soundless, frightened. His father paced back and forth in the courtyard. Finally, he told him, "If you marry her, you will no longer be my son."

Shankar's fists clenched so hard that his knuckles lost their color. He looked at his father for a second. "Baba, times have changed," he finally spit the words out and unclenched his fist. "The world is different now," he pleaded, but he couldn't keep eye contact with his father.

His father took a step toward Shankar. "Then you are a *tejya putra*. I don't have a son anymore. Get out of this house and don't come back." He turned away and walked inside. The sound of his sandals echoed in Shankar's ears.

His mother cried loudly. "Oh, Bhagavan, what have you brought down on us?" She followed her husband.

A sudden coldness hit the core of Shankar's body. He felt as if all the blood had drained out of him. The earth shook under his feet.

The smell of burning dry red chili and cumin seeds came from the kitchen. Shankar stood there alone. '*Tejya putra – a son rejected, discarded by his father.*' He knew the words very well. '*He does not belong to the family anymore.*'

His shoulders slumped. Completely at a loss, he dragged his feet toward the door, head down.

Durga was standing next to the gate. Shankar looked at her and knew that she had heard the conversation. She grasped his inert hand and pulled him away. He let Durga lead him to the main road.

"I didn't expect this today," was all Shankar could say and looked away from her.

Durga hailed a taxi and they got in.

The beautiful night jasmine tree was completely forgotten.

Chapter Fifteen

Tejya Putra

Shankar huddled in the taxi while Durga held his hand. He silently gazed at the windshield without seeing anything nor hearing the random honks of cars or the non-stop noise of the people on the road. The taxi left them at Dakshineswar, famous for its Kali temple, on the banks of the Hooghly River. They got out of the taxi, but Shankar was still in a daze and simply followed Durga on the path toward the river.

He was confused and despondent. How could his father throw him, his own son, out of the house? Family meant nothing to him! As usual, the path was crowded with people. However, the furious activities on both sides of their route—people buying souvenirs, flowers, and sweets at road-side stalls—passed by his unseeing eyes. The worshippers, carrying small packets of flowers and offerings for the Goddess, thronged around them, but Shankar couldn't identify himself as one of them. He felt completely detached, as if he were not in his body, but floating, looking down on the scene. He saw himself and Durga, just two of the many walking along below.

His mind whirled around his parents. How could they treat him like this? Didn't they care anything for what he thought of or wished in his life? They had no empathy for him. Was his father only concerned about following what some ancient rishis had written down for an ideal Hindu society without any regard for individuals? And why should those rules apply now, a few thousand years later? Alongside the desolation he felt, anger started to grow in his heart.

An event from his youth came to him: *He was crossing the courtyard of their house diagonally to go out to play soccer. His father was standing near the kitchen and called him. "Shankar, here is a test of how well you have memorized the Bhagavad Gita," he told him smilingly. "Tell me the sloka where Krishna says, as we change our clothes when they get worn out, so our soul leaves the old body and takes a new one."*

Shankar's face dimmed and his toes curled. He reluctantly looked at his father and started to recite in Sanskrit, "Vasamsi jirnani yatha vihaha, ..." and then he stumbled and could not remember the rest. He saw his father's happy face become stiff, eyes glaring. Shankar hung his head down.

"You are not devoting enough time to studying the scriptures, Shankar." His father came a few steps closer to him. "This won't do." He shook his head and raised his voice. "I'll let you go this time, but not in future. As soon as you come back, memorize this sloka and repeat it to me. Now go." His harsh voice stung Shankar deeply.

There was no heart there; he couldn't even allow small joys his son might have playing games with friends. He had seen this afternoon that his father had no inclination to understand his own son's wishes. It was beyond his imagination that his son could be seeking happiness in this world, instead of the other world that he was aspiring for. His father did not have any room for their differences. Shankar had always obeyed him as best as he could because he was his father, but his father never reciprocated the familial bond. To him a son was not a son if the son did not follow his beliefs, his ideologies, totally.

Chapter Sixteen

Along the Riverbank

S hankar and Durga reached the Kali temple on the river, but instead of entering the temple, where the worshippers went, they strolled along the riverbank toward an old banyan tree. Only a few people were on this path. The muddy-brown river flowed on their left, and various tropical trees grew on the right, keeping the area wild. The serenely moving wide river, wavelets murmuring against the banks, the primordial jungle, and the gentle breeze soothed Shankar a bit. And all that was in his heart about his life and his family poured out of him. "I wanted to, but I couldn't bring myself to tell you before about my family," he began, fighting the sadness that clutched his throat.

Durga listened quietly as Shankar talked about how stressful his life was living with the rules his father had established for the family and held to so strictly. He confessed how he had wanted to reject his father's rigid ideas but couldn't bring himself to directly disrespect him.

"My father always told me that we are descendants of the ancient sages who heard the original Vedas in the ancient times and have remained untainted for countless generations—thousands of years. We must preserve the sacredness of this line and must not pollute our purity by thoughts and actions. My father was strict about observing every detail of the customs for brahmins regarding food and castes and sub-castes. We have strict rules of what we can and cannot eat. We must not eat food cooked by a non-brahmin or eat in a non-brahmin's house. No non-brahmin can enter our kitchen. My mother always gave my father a home-cooked lunch to take to work.

"A feeling of superiority existed in our family," Shankar told Durga. "Even compared to the other brahmins. My father believed the others had deviated from the ancient traditions in the name of progress and modern times. This is prevalent in most brahmin families to a certain degree, but my father's beliefs are extreme. When I compared myself with my classmates in high school and college, I could never find how I was superior to them. The only things my father consented to do for non-brahmins were performing religious services and explaining the scriptures to them.

"Listen to this: One day, a man came to our house after evening prayers were completed and asked my father if he would conduct the marriage ceremony for his son. My father nodded as that was one of the religious duties he performed. He asked who the boy was marrying. The man said his own family was Kayastha, a sub caste of the Vaishya caste, but his son had fallen in love with a Baidya girl, another sub-caste of the Vaishya caste.

"My father's demeanor changed instantly. His body stiffened and face darkened like thunder clouds. He bluntly told the man he could not officiate at such a marriage. Inter-caste marriage pollutes the entire caste system, established in antiquity. He reproached the man for condoning his own son's marriage, turned his back and left the man standing in the courtyard. His retreating footsteps echoed in the otherwise soundless courtyard. I felt so embarrassed. That is my family. Now you can understand my father's reaction. His son marrying a non-brahmin girl is the worst thing possible for him, worse than death." Shankar glanced at Durga as they both knew their caste differences. "But remember this," he stopped and looked at her, "I will not let him denigrate you." His voice suddenly changed from a thin, melancholy complaint to a vehement force.

"In our family we talk about everything," Durga said. "There is no bar. Did you ever discuss any of these feelings with your parents?" Durga asked.

Shankar had a faint chuckle. "I guess I've not portrayed my family correctly. We never asked questions! That'd be considered disrespectful and disobeying our father—even to ask. When I was in high school, I once asked my mother, 'Why don't we eat onions, Ma? Others eat them.' She had sternly told me that brahmins must not consume food that increases passion and ignorance. They must maintain purity to worship the gods. After that I could never bring up any questions." Shankar looked away toward the river. "You want to know more? We ate fish and goat meat in our house, but never chicken and eggs. And we never ate fish that didn't have scales, never ate snails or crabs, and certainly not meat from mother cow or dirty pigs. My grandmother's food was prepared separately, untouched by utensils used for cooking non-vegetarian food. She had become a strict vegetarian, per Hindu custom, after my grandfather's death."

The monkeys on the banyan tree stopped their play of chasing one another and observed them; all visitors halted to watch the monkeys, but not these two. They were oblivious to the monkeys.

"Did you expect your father's reaction to be this bad?" Durga finally asked when they came to the end of the path. It was a jungle beyond this point.

"I've been afraid of this for a long time." He gazed toward the top of the Kali temple for a few seconds, then turned to her, "But I didn't expect it to be this fierce, and certainly not this afternoon."

"I'm so sorry, Shankar." She took his hand in hers. "What do you want to do now?" she asked in a gentle, loving voice. The concern was clearly hers too.

"It happened so suddenly; I don't know what to do, or even where I can spend the night."

"Come to our house," Durga said.

"I cannot go to your house." His voice was melancholy. "No one knows me in your family—how could I simply show up?"

"Trust me." Durga pulled him toward the ferry ramp.

"Today was supposed to be a joyous day . . . I shouldn't have brought you to our house."

His voice was full of despair.

"Shankar, it was bound to happen. Only, it came too fast. We will deal with it." Her voice was resolute and calming to Shankar's quaking body.

They walked by the small lane between the temple wall and the river. Stall owners on the path called them to buy flower garlands and sweets for puja. Their persistent calls to buy things had annoyed Shankar when he used to come here with his mother. They sounded particularly upsetting today. He wanted to shout at them to stop but said nothing, for fear that he might not be able to contain himself. They waited near the *ghat* where the worshippers were taking spiritually-cleansing dips in the sacred river before entering the temple.

They boarded a small ferry to take them to the other side of the river. The ferry quickly made way, and soon the top of the Kali temple vanished from their sight. The muddy-brown river flowed gently and the scenery of buildings and trees on both banks appeared peaceful. "This would have been a most pleasant trip any other day," Shankar said as he tried to inject normalcy into their situation. But their journey remained mostly silent until they arrived at Durga's house.

Chapter Seventeen

Family Deliberations

When Shankar and Durga arrived at her home in Shalkia, Durga introduced Shankar to her mother. "This is Shankar, Ma." After a short pause, she burst out, "His father told him never to return home again."

"This happened today?" her mother asked, looking inquisitively at her daughter. "I was afraid of something drastic like this."

"Yes. Only a few hours back."

"Welcome to our home," Durga's mother told Shankar warmly. "I'm sorry to hear your father's decree. Stay in our house for as long as you need … Life brings these situations to test you. Either you rise to the occasion and follow what you believe in or you give up." Her voice was serious but kind.

Shankar was nervously waiting for her reaction but was surprised to find that Durga's mother knew about him and received him with such an open invitation. He thanked her.

Durga took him to meet her two sisters. Kalindi was in second year in college and Sujata a senior in high school. They were bubbly and took Shankar by the hands to Kalindi's room. They smoothed the platform bed and asked him to sit. There was a dressing table with a large mirror against the wall. Next to it was a wooden blanket rack covered haphazardly with several sarees and blouses. Below were a few sandals. The sisters quickly tidied up the top of the dressing table. Then they plunked themselves down on either side of him, tucking their sarees under them as they sat cross-legged on the bed. They teased him about many things; did he know their sister fell in love with him the first time she saw him? What did they do to avoid friends who might find them together? Did they go to any movies together? Innocent curiosities, but Shankar enjoyed chatting with them, even asking jokingly if they had secret boyfriends. They simply giggled, falling over each other, without answering. The younger one's bangles made a sweet, tinkling sound. The older one, a little shyer, had a tiny nose ring that sparkled with a small diamond.

"When you marry our sister," Sujata said, "you have to deal with us too. And I'll give you a hint. We love going to movies."

"And you will have to take us to the Kwality restaurant in Park Street." Shankar happily agreed. "That will be our special deal."

They were jolly and made Shankar forget the devastating event of the day. His heart was heavy, but he loved being there with them.

Durga's father was a lawyer at the Calcutta High Court. When he returned home and heard what had happened, he told Shankar, "No one can deprive you of your family assets or heritage; that is against the law. But I know that is not your concern. The problem is that however much you wish, you cannot change society quickly. You have to start from the ground up and build your future yourself." He paused. "What are your plans?"

Shankar admitted he had no definite ideas. The two men remained silent for a while.

Then Shankar summarized his dilemma. He had finished his final master's degree exams and hoped to do research work. He didn't know exactly in which area to concentrates his research—solid state physics, nuclear physics, and the new area of particle physics all interested him. He also wondered if he should put in for a teaching position first or go directly into research.

"I think it will be good," her father said after a while, "if you go away from Calcutta for some time." He kept his gaze on Shankar. "Perhaps go to America for higher studies."

"To the U.S.?"

"After the Russian Sputnik event, U.S. universities are giving scholarships to good students from all over the world. Why don't you apply there?"

It wasn't easy to go to the U.S. for higher studies. Shankar knew of only one physics student, a few years senior to him, who had gone to Chicago for a Ph.D. "What about Durga?" he mumbled, looking at her.

She had been listening to the discussion quietly. "I shall wait for you," she responded quickly. "I could teach at Bethune College or at Lady

Brabourne and join you later."

Shankar glanced at her father and saw him flinch. Perhaps he did not know or realize the depth of their relationship. He had certainly not discussed marriage with his daughter. Shankar's father had reacted abominably, but Durga's father, while taken off guard, didn't appear to feel slighted.

"Don't rush to any decision now," her father urged.

"Right," Durga said. "But I like the idea ..."

Chapter Eighteen

Durga's Mission

What a momentous day! Durga lay in bed, exhausted, but she couldn't fall asleep. Shankar was a sincere, kind, and loving person. She had fallen in love with him. Now she understood why he was always reticent to talk about his family. Shankar had once said he lived two lives, one at home and one outside. She grasped the gravity of that statement. Shankar was struggling all the time—and alone. *In this moment, he had no one but her. She loved him. But what does love mean? Isn't it how much one is willing to sacrifice one's goals and comforts for the loved one?*

Shankar had rebelled against tradition, which he felt was not valid anymore; she had not, but her life did not follow the traditional path either. They belonged to different castes, but that did not stop her from seeing him. Durga looked out the window and gazed at the moonlit sky.

Since ancient times, a woman's role in India has been to help and support her husband. This has also been true all over the world. Women rarely put themselves ahead of their husbands. What should her role be? Shankar had clearly stated his commitment to her when he spoke to his father—boldly. She had no intention of forsaking him; instead, she thought she must help him proceed to the next step in his life. There was no other choice. She had Savitri as an example who chose and married a man knowing he would die in one year. Then she fought for his life and saved him.

***

Savitri

A long time ago, even before the time of the Mahabharata epic, there lived in India a king named Asvapati. For many years, he wished for a child but had none. He was a devotee of Savitr, the divine light of dawn, and prayed to him for a child. Pleased with the king's devotion,

Savitr granted his wish, and a daughter was born to the king. She came to the world glowing like a bright sunrise. The king named her Savitri in honor of Savitr.

As she grew, Savitri became a beautiful and bright princess. When she attained the age of marriage, however, the nearby princes did not clamor for her hand. The king surmised they were intimidated by her intelligence. He sent her on a tour around the country, telling her to find a man whom she wished to marry.

Savitri travelled around, guarded by the king's army, and met many princes. She found no one she wished to marry. But she was not unhappy. *Why marry someone if you don't consider him good enough to love, honor, and cherish?* As she was returning home, Savitri and her entourage camped near a hermit's cottage. There she saw a young man carrying kindling and fruits. He was slim, tall, and handsome. More than that, his steps emanated the glow of devotion to his duties. On inquiry, Savitri found he was Prince Satyavan, who lived in the cottage taking care of his blind father, a deposed king, and his mother. Savitri fell in love with him.

But the blind king asked her, "Princess, can you live with us in the forest with a meager diet of fruits and vegetables and wearing no gorgeous clothes or ornaments? Can you spend your life as the wife of a hermit?"

Savitri replied she did not care for comfort or hardship, in a palace or hermitage, if the members of her family were pure in heart.

The blind king gave his blessings but asked her to consult her father.

Savitri's father was elated his daughter had found a man to marry. He knew when Savitri had chosen someone, he and his family must be worthy without any doubt. But when the king consulted astrologers, the sage Narada, who could see the future, told the king that Satyavan would die in one year and advised against the marriage.

"Father," Savitri said when she heard the prediction, "In my heart, I am already married to him."

Her father had to agree with Savitri and allowed the marriage.

After marriage, Savitri went to the hermitage and lived with Satyavan's family, carrying out the duties of a wife and taking care of her in-laws. Time passed happily for the young couple, but soon the day arrived when

Satyavan would die. She was the only one who knew about it and she did not tell her in-laws. That day, Savitri accompanied her husband everywhere. While he was cutting some dry wood for the daily yagna worship service, Satyavan felt a severe headache and lay down on the ground with his head on her lap. Savitri caressed his head and saw Yama, the God of death, in the distance, walking toward them. Ordinary human beings cannot see Yama, but Savitri was so pure she could see Him.

Yama told her, "The time has come for your husband's death. No one can avoid it. This is the law of nature. Would you please move aside so I can take him?"

Savitri did what Yama asked her.

Yama slipped a noose around Satyavan's soul, turned, and walked away. But Savitri could see Yama and followed him. After some time, Yama noticed her. "Princess, you cannot follow me. I see your distress, but I have to do my duty and take your husband. I am very pleased with your devotion and grant you a wish—you may have anything except the life of your husband. That I cannot give you."

"My father-in-law has suffered from blindness for a long time, please give him eyesight."

"It will be. Now, please go back." After saying this, Yama moved on.

Savitri continued following him. Yama stopped and said, "Please do not follow me."

"I follow where my husband goes," Savitri replied. "That is where my place is." She lowered her eyes.

Yama looked at her. He could not tell her not to follow her husband. "Please take another wish from me, but do not ask for your husband's life."

She did not ask anything for herself. She said, "Let my father-in-law get back his kingdom with its old glory."

"That is done. Now please go back."

But Savitri followed him. Soon Yama stopped again and said, "I am about to go beyond the realm of humans. There you will see only devastation. You should return to your family."

"I shall follow my husband as long as I see the path where you are taking him," Savitri firmly told Yama.

Irritated and lost, Yama said, "I cannot stop you from following your dharma, but please understand my role. When the time comes, I take the dead." He looked at her heart and saw the purity of her soul, love for her husband, and determination. He had never met a woman of such virtue. "Please make another wish. Anything except for the life of your husband."

"Please grant that my children will eat from golden plates."

"All right. That is done. Now go back to your family." He hurried forward.

Savitri could see the tall figure of Yama with his lantern and the noose hanging from his shoulder where he kept her husband's soul. She followed him.

"I gave you three wishes," Yama told her. "No one can get back a loved one after death. Why are you still following me?"

"You have granted me children," Savitri said, "but as a Hindu woman, how could I have children without my husband?"

Yama realized he had granted this boon in a rush. There was no way he could take back his blessings. He had been defeated by the wit of this virtuous lady. Pleased to be defeated by such a pure and devoted soul, Yama returned the life of her husband.

In the next instant, Savitri found herself sitting on the ground with her husband waking up in her lap. They went home and found his father with good eyesight, the house full of dignitaries from the old kingdom and jubilation all around. Savitri's father was also among the guests celebrating the restored king.

***

As an Indian woman, Durga had inherited Savitri's spirit and that was her role in life now. She felt peace and finally sank into slumber.

Chapter Nineteen

Parvati the Traditionalist

Durga's family gave Kalindi's room to Shankar. He laid on the
bed, but couldn't sleep. Many thoughts about his family swirled
through his mind. From the moonlight that shone through the
open window, Shankar saw several framed photos on the walls. He vaguely
discerned a group photo of Durga and her sisters in a restaurant. It was a
cheerful picture. Shankar and his sisters had never gone out together to a
restaurant and didn't have such photos in their rooms. He dozed off late
that night but woke up hearing the heavy voice of his father.

"If you marry her, you will no longer be my son."

His father's resentful face of last afternoon floated in front of him,
so different from Durga's father's calm demeanor. Shankar stared at
a large portrait of Durga's family on the wall. Her father was such an
understanding man. Indignation burned inside Shankar as he thought of
his own family.

Then he remembered the calls of his father just before dawn that began
after his sacred thread ceremony. It was still dark outside, but his father
insisted on getting him up. Shankar would hear the call again and again
until he was up.

He hated those calls . . . and the religious practices he had to do while
he was longing for sleep. His father stopped waking him up only when
teachers complained that he was dozing off in the afternoons. He had
wondered at the time which disappointment mattered more to his father.

Shankar got up and stood at the window. The moon was large and bright and so close he felt he could touch it. He watched the moonlight glow upon the trees, the garden below and the neighborhood houses. His thoughts drifted to the college days, just barely behind him, where he had been free and happy—his true escape from home. Now that home didn't exist, and he was free. But he must stand on his own. Instead of sadness, however, a feeling of determination came to him.

***

Sunlight had already streaked in through the window when Shankar awoke. He quickly got up and realized that he had no toiletries or fresh clothes to wear. He could hear everyone in the house was awake. A few minutes later, Durga politely brought him a cup of tea. After breakfast and after Durga's father left for work, Shankar went out alone to buy a razor, toothbrush, and a change of clothes.

Late in the afternoon, he went to Bethune College on Cornwallis Street to see his sister, Parvati. He wanted to tell her about Durga and ask if she wanted to meet her. Maybe Parvati would understand his love for Durga. One day she might fall in love with someone and face a similar situation. He fervently wished she would support him. He waited outside the gate. Young girls clad in colorful saris spilled onto the street, bursting with energy—chatting and laughing—blooming with great hopes for the future. After some time, Shankar spotted Parvati with her classmates. They were all jubilantly leaving school, happy to go home. He went nervously toward her, calling her name.

Parvati paled when she saw her elder brother. Her face, so happy a moment before, shrank and turned dark. She looked away and did not greet him, but she did separate herself quickly from her classmates, and walked over to him with her eyes looking down at the ground.

Shankar was eager to talk with her and did not heed her changed demeanor. "I came to tell you about yesterday. Let's walk to the Hedua pool."

"Mother told me everything that happened," she murmured as she followed him toward the pool opposite Scottish Church College.

"What do you think?" He inquired nervously.

Parvati stopped abruptly. She raised her head and took a step back from her brother. "How could you marry a girl from a lower caste?" Her words flew at Shankar like bullets. "Violating all that Father and our forefathers have taught us?" Her face was stiff with ill will and disgust.

Shankar was taken aback. He had never seen her eyes burn with such hatred.

"Did Father tell you this?" He asked, stunned.

"No. He did not talk with me. You know he does not talk with me unless he has something to say about what I should do. But I know he is fuming."

"You are in college now," Shankar pleaded. "You aren't a child anymore and can think for yourself. Don't you understand my situation?"

"No, I don't." She almost shouted, wincing as she turned away from Shankar. "And really, I can't. How could you forget we belong to the Brahmin caste?" She paused and looked at him with cold, hateful eyes for a moment. "Mother told me she is not even pretty."

Shankar watched as Parvati's sweet round face shifted to a twisted expression he had never seen before. His mouth gaped and his eyes widened. He couldn't believe the pettiness he was hearing. But mostly, he was shocked by his beloved little sister's callousness. Nothing had prepared him for this. He expected outrage from his father . . . but from Parvati?

He was confused, lost even. Then as the realization hit him, he felt completely alone. No one in the family supported him.

"Alright." He shook his head slowly, barely connecting to the reality around him.

She had turned away from him; he could only see one side of her face with a pouty expression. Her downturned lips and blazing eyes faced off into the distance.

"I am never coming back," he stated.

His sister showed no concern. She stood silently, stiffly, looking away from him.

This was the last time she would see her only brother, who had looked after her and played with her since she was a toddler. He tried to catch her eyes one last time, but she turned and walked away from him.

"Parvati!" he exclaimed, his voice breaking along with his heart. He tried to muster the courage to say something else. But all that came out was "Take care." It was only a whisper.

She fled into the sea of girls on the sidewalk without a word.

He watched as she melted into the crowd, shoulders hunched, as if she were trying to hide.

A profound sadness came over him, hitting deep in his belly. He felt like crying, but no tears came to his eyes. His chest cramped, making it difficult to move. He couldn't help but stare forward vacantly.

Finally, he managed to turn around and move in the opposite direction. He did not look back.

Chapter Twenty

Botanical Garden

In the evening Shankar took Durga to the Botanical Garden across the Ganges from Calcutta and on the same side of the river where Durga's family lived.

"I want to get some fresh air," he told her. The whole afternoon after his visit with Parvati, he had felt altogether small and tossed aside. The only good thing was that the crushing weight of his family's judgmental world was completely gone. The problem was that it took his family with it. He was now all alone, his own man. These thoughts completely occupied Shankar's mind as he entered the vast herbarium.

Silently, they walked at a leisurely pace to the lotus pond, where large circular leaves floated on the water. Shankar, unfocused, contemplated a pink lotus.

Durga watched him for some time. "Did you know," she asked him, "that tea plants from China were first introduced to India right here?" She wanted to change Shankar's serious demeanor, but he kept quiet. "Many also don't know the tea trade was established from this garden."

Unresponsive, Shankar stared at the pond. Finally, he said, "Last night, I thought more about my life and about us." He moved closer to her. "The caste system is too deeply ingrained in our culture. Vidyasagar, the social reformer who fought for and succeeded in legally allowing remarriage of Hindu widows, did not really succeed in changing society. Even now, a young widow has difficulty remarrying . . . I have no choice but to leave this damn place." His eyes flickered with anger, his facial muscles tensed, but his voice was determined. He looked into her eyes desperately looking for acceptance, seeking home within this spritely and steady girl. She was the only oasis amidst his world collapsing into ashes around him.

Durga reached for his hand. "You know I'm with you," she announced, her voice resolute.

"We will emigrate to the U.S., but I do not want to drag a trace of what we went through yesterday into our future. I need to completely forget my family, the nonsense of my heredity, and start fresh in America." He tightened his hand around hers. "I want you to be my partner for the rest of my life, but I wish you would agree we will never talk about my family in America—to anyone. We will build our life without any caste bias, without any bias based on anyone's birth."

Durga gazed at him for a few seconds. "I fully understand your rage and your desire. But do you also want me to abandon my family?"

"Sorry." Shankar blankly stared at Durga, realizing that he had not considered repercussions for Durga. "I was only thinking about me . . . Selfish of me. You have such a wonderful family, you cannot forsake them, and I'll never ask you to do that."

"I understand your position," she said, "and I promise not to bring up your family or mention this to anyone. Even to our children if we have any."

"Thank you," he managed, choking up. He pulled her to him, embraced her, and rested his head on her shoulder. "I am so glad you came into my life."

She held him tight and caressed his back. It was clear she cared for him deeply. After he regained his composure, they resumed walking. He clutched her hand, as if it were the only thing tying him to this complicated world.

Soon, they came to the banyan tree, famous for being the widest tree in the world, and stood under its shade. Shankar observed the huge canopy of the tree; its main trunk had died long ago, but the large number of aerial roots that came down from the branches and ran vertically to the ground had sustained and spread the tree. It looked more like a mini forest than a tree. Simply amazing. The words that came into his mind were: 'It survived.'

After a while Shankar said, "Tomorrow, I'll visit the USIS and start researching what I have to do to apply for admission and financial aid from U.S. universities." He was finding new energy for action. He also thought of visiting the nuclear physics professor who received his Ph.D. from Berkeley. So many things he would have to do.

"And I," Durga said, "shall inquire about teaching possibilities in Calcutta."

They walked to the bus stop by the garden entrance and waited. "I am not abandoning our Indian culture or our ancient wisdom," Shankar murmured to her. "We have many good things, but I must forget my family."

"Do not worry." Durga leaned toward him. "We will build our new world together. We will bring the good with us."

Shankar proposed their marriage to her parents who warmly welcomed him into the family. Durga's father sent a letter to Shankar's father proposing their marriage, but no reply ever came. Somehow, that seemed to hurt Shankar more than a fierce letter of opposition. It seemed he had no choice but to move on, as his family surely had, without him.

They were married a few weeks later because Shankar wanted to marry as soon as possible to affirm his love for Durga.

The wedding celebration was arranged quickly, but Durga's parents did not hold back for their first daughter's wedding. All relatives, loved ones, and Durga's and Shankar's friends were invited. Large wedding tents were erected on the roof and in the front of their house to accommodate many guests. On the night of the wedding, the priest established a ceremonial space with religious symbols, flowers, earthen lamps, and incense. The fragrance of sandalwood from long incense sticks filled the wedding tent creating an atmosphere of auspiciousness. When she was escorted to the sacred fire by her sisters and friends, Durga looked coyly down as if she were being led to an unknown bridegroom in an arranged marriage. Sandalwood paste had been used to paint her forehead and cheeks with an artistic design of tiny leaves and flowers with a huge bright red dot in the center of her forehead. She was adorned with exquisite gold jewelry—necklaces, bracelets, and rings, some of which were clearly passed on as gifts from her mother and grandmother. Her arms jingled with bangles of various kinds—gold, glass, carved conch, and red lac. Her hair, tied in a bun, shimmered with more jewelry. Her lipstick matched the color of her bright red silk sari with embossed peacock designs in gold thread and a maroon border woven with golden flowers. Her palms and feet were painted dark pink, usual for a Bengali bride. She wore an almost transparent light red veil and a white shola pith headdress—the prerogative of brides and goddesses. Durga looked radiant and ethereal.

Shankar wore a white silk dhuti, a beige silk shirt with gold buttons, and the traditional conical shola pith bridegroom's hat. The priest, Shankar and Durga, and Durga's father sat, cross legged, around the sacred fire to perform the wedding rites. Near the end of the wedding, the couple stood and the ends of Shankar's dhuti and Durga's sari were tied together, and they walked seven times around the sacred fire. Many guests, who had been off in corners chatting during the long repetition of Sanskrit mantras of the wedding prayers, quickly appeared for this final moment. Then, Shankar caught a glimpse of his uncle, his father's younger brother, at the back of the joyful crowd. No one else was there from his family.

Shankar's mind was eager to continue planning their future rather than going away on a honeymoon, but Durga's father booked them a bridal suite in the five-star Taj Bengal Hotel in Calcutta for three nights with all expenses paid. Durga felt no trace of worries about the future and floated in the love she had nurtured from the first day she met Shankar, now her husband. Despite his worries about the future and sadness at the loss of his family, Shankar quickly melted in the joyousness of their time together. No thoughts of any concern found a way to enter his mind. Their honeymoon, away from the prying eyes of the world, registered as the most romantic, heavenly time in his mind.

USA

PHILADELPHIA AND ANN ARBOR

1958 - 2003

Chapter Twenty-One

Arrival in Philadelphia

A few months after their marriage, Shankar accepted an offer of assistantship from the department of physics at the University of Pennsylvania. Durga and her family were elated with the news and they, along with Shankar, prepared for his journey abroad. Shankar and Durga didn't tell anyone that Shankar would never return, which was a melancholy undercurrent for them. And their dreamy ideas had no clear path for the future. Shankar was sailing like Columbus, but would they ever meet again? Even if he were able to bring her to the U.S., could they adapt to such a foreign culture? Their hearts quavering, they wondered what the future held for them.

On the day of his departure, Shankar's friends and Durga's family came to the airport to bid him success in the United States. Only when he proceeded to the boarding gate, did he see someone from his side of the family—his uncle standing at the back of the crowd.

Shankar landed in Philadelphia on September 8, 1958, a beautiful autumn day—with no clouds in the sky. He walked out of the airport with two firm goals in mind: first, do what was necessary to settle in the U.S. with a good standing in society, which meant completing his Ph.D., and second, bring Durga over as soon as possible. There was no dormitory for graduate students at Penn; Shankar had no choice but to live on his own. He met older Indians on campus and with their help rented an efficiency apartment on 42nd street, almost ten blocks away from the physics building. Despite his research about living in America, Shankar found he was not prepared for the task of living on his own and attending school. The initial excitement and tribulations of getting settled in an unknown land and culture exhausted him. With guidance from his advisor, he registered for quantum mechanics, electricity and magnetism, and mathematics. He thought his class load was too light, but soon found the classes and the homework kept him extremely busy each week. In addition, he had to grade freshmen papers as part of his assistantship, go grocery shopping, cook, and clean just to live—activities he had never done in Calcutta. However, he was single-minded in his goals—no going out on the weekends, no parties, no sports, nothing except his studies. Occasionally he wistfully looked at the bubbly boys and girls holding hands on campus, and heard music coming out of the dorms or from the Mixers in the campus dining halls on Friday evenings.

Early in the school year, he was invited to a party by a classmate. He told him, "BYOB." Shankar didn't understand and repeated the letters with a questioning gesture.

"Bring your own girl," he winked at him. "Don't worry about that. Just come." He slapped his shoulder.

But Shankar didn't go.

His soul ached for Durga. But how could he bring her to the U.S. without financial security? That meant she couldn't join him until he had a firm footing in the physics department. He wrote her every week, but in those days, it took a month to get a response from India. There was no possibility of a telephone call as it was extremely expensive. He saved as much as possible from his assistantship money of $240 a month for when Durga would come. On the days he got her letters, his heart lifted; he opened them hastily, often tearing the thin, blue envelopes. The onion skin rustled in his hand as he read them slowly. Durga was persistently upbeat in her letters to Shankar. She told him they would face life together – no matter what came along – and they would succeed. Her teaching job at Lady Brabourne College was not fulfilling, but she couldn't start on a doctoral research program, which had been her goal. She was eager to join him and had even secured a passport. She waited patiently for the day when Shankar would call her to him.

Shankar faced severe difficulties with the American system of quizzes, midterms, and finals, which was hugely different from the Indian system of no exams until the final exam. He did poorly on the initial tests, but he did well by the end of the semester. His confidence grew and by the end of two semesters he daringly decided to take the Ph.D. qualifying exam. Most graduate students wait until the end of their second year to attempt this formidable obstacle. But passing this exam was the only way to assure his place in the physics department. It was a rigorous, grueling two-and-a-half-day closely monitored exam near the end of summer. He forgot the world around him—the wonderful summer days, undergraduate boys and girls playing tennis and other campus activities, and even the hot Philadelphia summer nights—and studied constantly, going over the syllabus and the previous five years' questions. The professors watched his devotion, but didn't believe he could do it.

He surprised all who doubted him and passed that grueling exam. He immediately asked Durga to come to Philadelphia.

Finally, a most joyous day came when Shankar met his young wife at the airport. She admitted she had boarded the plane with a tremulous heart. To come to America was a dream for any Indian but leaving her known world forever was frightening. The path they had chosen, permanently abandoning life in India—really, *he* had chosen, and she had agreed—was bold but scary.

"You'll like it here," Shankar assured her as he embraced her like a lost jewel he had found and was not willing to part with ever again. Sweet scented *Jabakusum* herbal oil from her hair and the fragrance of her supple, willing body enveloped him completely. Memories of home returned to him instantly.

She touched his face, examining him. "You've gained a few pounds and look so healthy ... handsome." She leaned her head on his chest. "We're finally here, together."

When they returned to Shankar's 42nd Street apartment, he gave her a tour of the kitchen, the bathroom and the one large bed that occupied most of the space. "I have adjusted to life here," he told her. "Are you hungry?"

"A little." She said and looked around.

"I've food for us."

"You cooked?"

"I cook and eat my own food every night." He was proud to tell her.

She looked around the bare cabinets in the kitchen. "I guess we will live here."

"Dinner is ready," he told her, "chicken curry, rice, and cauliflower!"

"You cooked chicken?"

"My dinner is chicken and rice every night," he told her as a matter of fact. "Each weekend, I buy a whole chicken, cut it into small pieces and cook chicken curry." He told her how he cooked. "I fry onions in a pot with oil, then I put the chicken pieces and fry some more. Finally, I add ginger powder, turmeric powder, salt, and then boil it with water. I often add a little chili powder to make it hot. Sometimes I throw some potatoes into the pot. I eat that with rice over the week. It's quite good." For Durga, he had added a good amount of butter to make the dish tastier.

Durga glanced into the small kitchen. "Do you have lentils?"

"I've already cooked our food." Shankar told her.

"I feel like having some *daal.*"

"O sure! I have lentils." He took out a bag of red lentils he had bought some time back and never cooked.

"Do you have any whole spices?"

"Whole spices?" he asked in surprise.

"You know like cumin seeds, coriander seeds, dried red chili?"

Do they use those for everyday cooking? he wondered and confessed that he didn't use whole spices.

"Then give me some onions. That will do."

They talked about Calcutta while she cooked. Shankar couldn't figure out how she had so much energy to cook after such a long flight. It was late and he was hungry. After she finished cooking daal, they sat down to eat. The daal tasted just like home. It was wonderful to eat this ordinary everyday dish after so many months. She tasted a little of the dishes he had cooked. "So, this is what you eat every day?"

Shankar nodded.

***

How wonderful," she said in a cheerful voice a few days later. "We are going to live here for the rest of our lives."

Shankar saw that Philadelphia had dazzled her. He arranged for another graduate student to drive them to the rose exhibit in Longwood Gardens, 30 miles from Philadelphia. Shankar knew Durga loved roses and planned the excursion to impress her. It was a marvelous trip, a fabulous display of roses from around the world, and a picnic. Durga couldn't stop admiring the large garden and how much care had been given in cultivating the flowers. On the way back, Shankar told her, "We know the U.S. only from what we have read in newspapers in Calcutta and a few books. We should know it now from the inside. Let's explore the country together."

During their Saturday tour of downtown Philadelphia, Shankar sheepishly asked her a question he had on his mind for some time. "Why did you take the trouble to cook daal, a most ordinary dish, when you arrived while I had chicken curry and rice ready to eat?"

"Ah, why I cooked daal?" she considered him for a few seconds. "I wanted to make sure there was something I could eat."

Shankar got his answer. It was obvious to her that his cooking was not edible to others, especially a Bengali woman. He had seen her rearrange his kitchen, stock it with various spices and cook with whole spices, not just turmeric and ginger powder.

Durga didn't want to sit at home and simply watch Shankar finish his degree. But she had a dependent visa and could not work or study. She was more than enthusiastic about Shankar's idea of learning the country and the culture, which gave her a purpose and a goal she liked. She immediately started to learn about Philadelphia, so rich in American history. While Shankar was preoccupied at the University, Durga went to museums, starting with the University of Pennsylvania Museums. And together they visited the cracked Liberty Bell, Independence Hall, Elfreth's Alley, and the site of the first President's house. These trips felt exciting and wonderful like the time they had during their honeymoon. They went with other international students to nearby cities like New York and Washington, D.C. It was a pleasure for Durga to write to her family about their explorations and how happy she was with Shankar in Philadelphia.

Samir came along a year later, bringing a new dimension to their lives. Their travels were put on hold until their son became a little older. Durga had spent hours at the university library reading economics journals. She told Shankar the subjects she would study in graduate school for her Ph.D., but the baby changed all that. She became a full-time mother.

Samir was four when Shankar finished his Ph.D. Shankar and Durga were jubilant. They had passed their first milestone for settling in the country. She cooked many wonderful dishes and invited their friends to celebrate the occasion. They closed their sofa-bed, and tidied their apartment to make space for the visitors. They even had a friend bring Indian sweets from New York City. Nothing was held back for their celebration.

Shankar continued his research work at Penn and was now paid a little more. He and Durga started to enjoy life as they had made it in the U.S. However, after a few weeks, Shankar's professor called him to his office and asked him to close the door.

"I'm sorry to have to tell you that I can support you only a few more months." He looked at Shankar for a few moments.

The light in Shankar's eyes suddenly dimmed and his arms felt limp. "You mean I cannot stay and continue the research?" He could barely speak or look at his professor.

"Sorry. Funding for academic research has dried up all over the country because of the Vietnam War. You must find a job somewhere else. Apply for post-doctoral positions. I'll help as much as I can."

Shankar's heart sank. He hung his head and turned to leave when his professor called out, "One more thing, Shankar. Your student visa will allow you to stay for only two more years unless your status changes."

Shankar nodded vacantly and left.

The reality of settling in the U.S. hit them hard. The joy they felt after his graduation evaporated. Shankar must find a job to stay in the country. He sent out over a hundred inquiries for a post-doctoral research position. He even sent one to Brigham Young University, a Mormon school where the likelihood of a Hindu getting a job was highly improbable, but he had no such knowledge at that time. He received no hopeful responses from anywhere. Would they have to go back?

"Would you consider a teaching position at a small university?" Shankar's thesis advisor asked him after a month. "Eastern Michigan University in Ypsilanti is looking for someone to teach undergraduate physics classes. No research money, but it is in the town next to the University of Michigan. Maybe you could do some research work with the faculty in Ann Arbor."

Shankar consulted Durga.

"Won't this be the end of your research career?" Durga pinched her lips together. "You gave up a research opportunity in Bombay to come here. Now if you take this teaching job—"

He looked at her helplessly. "I can perhaps find a research position in India."

Durga stopped him immediately. "We don't want to go back to India," she said firmly, but in a voice of despair. "We *can't*."

Chapter Twenty-Two

Ann Arbor

Shankar had no choice but to accept the teaching position in Ypsilanti. Near the end of summer, they purchased a little house in the next town, Ann Arbor, home of the University of Michigan. Ypsilanti appeared to be a working-class town compared to academic Ann Arbor. Shankar would teach at the college, but the atmosphere was decidedly different. Ipsi, as the natives called it, seemed to have little going on besides a Spicy Pizza store and movie theater. Ann Arbor, on the other hand, was bubbling with activities and surrounded by many shopping places. It was much smaller than Philadelphia, but Shankar and Durga loved that they could have a house so close to campus where students walked by all the time. They could even hear the band and cheering from the sports stadium during football games. Their lives changed significantly from apartment living to being homeowners. It took them a few months though to feel settled and comfortable.

The physics department at Eastern Michigan had made no guarantee Shankar would receive tenure. Being new immigrants with accents, they both knew Shankar would have to prove his worth more than others, and Shankar couldn't imagine working in the U.S. in any other capacity. From the first day, Shankar focused on establishing himself in the physics department. He taught the classes senior professors didn't enjoy. He carried out committee work other faculty members shunned. He worked on weekends too, grading papers and preparing for the next week's classes.

Durga saw what Shankar had encountered while searching for an academic position. She forgot her career and quietly supported Shankar's efforts to achieve tenure—no bickering, no complaints, no lamentations about his time spent away from family activities. She took care of their house, the daily chores of living and all that was to be done for Samir. Durga learned to drive and ferried Samir around to various activities— soccer, libraries, school—that kept her busy. Although they raised Samir together as loving parents, she shielded Shankar from the day-to-day problems of raising their young boy. She quietly forgot her own aspirations to be an economist.

In the summer, Shankar started research work with the physics faculty at the University of Michigan. That also limited their social life; while people around them enjoyed vacations, summer trips and camping with family, they remained limited to activities around their home. They knew what they were sacrificing and had agreed they would persist until they had a secure future in front of them. Durga only indulged herself with one pastime— gardening. While Samir was in Kindergarten, she took classes at the local Arboretum and transformed their small backyard into a wonderful flower garden. Shankar was genuinely happy that she had found something for herself and he loved seeing her weeding and crooning to herself in the flower garden. In the summer she filled many vases with flowers, something he liked very much. Shankar saw her struggle to grow the sweet, fragrant varieties she had grown in her rooftop garden in Calcutta. One year she planted a rose bought from a gardening catalog. The picture showed large, apricot-yellow flowers that were described as very fragrant and right for Michigan's climate, but it died after the first winter.

Shankar hadn't been able to pay much attention to his son in Philadelphia. Now, when he came home from work, he looked forward to playing with Samir. That was his pleasure and a source of relaxation. There was another motivation for this: he did not want Samir to have the kind of experience he had with his father. Shankar could not remember a time when his father had chased him around the house or tickled him or played with him. He wanted to have an open and loving relation with his son. He bought a tricycle for Samir as soon as they moved and watched him master it. As Samir turned five, he loved spending time with his father going to parks and running around the slides and swings. At home they played with action figures. Both parents talked with him in Bengali, so he spoke the language, but they didn't make a strong effort to teach him to read and write Bengali. Shankar read and told him many of the stories that he grew up with, and Durga worked with him on reading and writing English. They devoted all their free times to their son and, naturally, Samir became lovingly attached to them.

Gradually, however, Shankar became quieter and more self-absorbed. The stress and pressure to perform well at the university was weighing him down. One night, Durga was awakened by Shankar tossing in bed and crying, "No, no, no." His hands were up as if resisting something in the air.

"You are having a bad dream, Shankar. Wake up, wake up!" She tugged his arm several times until he stopped shaking. His eyes opened and he immediately turned to her.

"I was having a nightmare. A monster tried to yank me away." He pulled himself up, disoriented. The bedsheet under him was wet with sweat. Durga brought him a glass of water. After taking a sip, he said, "It started very pleasantly. You and I were in a beautiful place with tall snow-covered mountains in the distance; green valleys below and hilly paths covered by colorful flowers. No clouds in the sky. We were walking, talking, and laughing. A vendor came to us, pushing an ice cream cart. 'Do you have Kulfi ice cream?' you asked. He nodded and I bought two for us. 'Wonderful taste!' you said. We strolled to a nearby purple rhododendron bush. How beautiful the color looked against its green leaves! We were so happy. I noticed the ice cream vendor was looking at us. As I gazed at him, something unusual happened. His face started to become bigger and bigger until it grew into a monstrous head. The sun had dimmed, and the face came closer. I didn't know what was happening or what to do. His eyes were focused on me. I felt I was the target for something evil he planned. But why me? Fear overtook me and then, the face changed and became my father's face distorted with rage. It looked so real. I felt he was coming after me. My heart started racing. 'You are a tejya putra. Tejya putra. Tejya-putra.' He was shouting, but the words came from all directions. And he was coming closer and closer. I wanted to run away but couldn't move my legs. He grabbed my arm when you woke me up."

Durga rubbed his back and spoke in a calming voice. "You feel the burden of getting us settled. You blame your father in your subconscious for our predicament." She paused and quietly massaged his shoulders. "We have come this far, and we will make it together," she assured him. "Lie down and try to sleep." She crooned a Tagore song.

Play your Veena in my innermost being
When I am with loved ones or on my own
In times of delight and joy
In times of peril and woe
Play a blissful strain, my friend, in my innermost being

—*Rabindranath Tagore (Translator Rumela Sengupta)*

***

Shankar fell asleep, but Durga couldn't. She laid still as if frozen, her eyes on the ceiling, but she wasn't seeing anything. No footsteps of anyone returning home late night and no light came from outside. Her family and friends were proud of her; she had come to America. They expected her to go somewhere—to '*achieve*'—something. But where was she going?

Was she fooling them by writing about the wonderful life they had in the U.S., about Samir's progress in school, about her flower garden? Was this the dream life she sought? Shankar had become aloof. Did she make a grave error in marrying him? Was it not more than just feeling sorry for him? But she had always loved him. She felt sad she had no power to wield, so helpless. The idea of her becoming somebody in America made her want to laugh. But instead, water filled her eyes; drops slid down her cheeks. She clutched the bed sheet tightly with all her strength so she would not wake up Shankar.

Chapter Twenty-Three

Samir's Adventure in India

Two years passed and their lives settled in a definite pattern. Shankar never brought up Calcutta in their discussions—true to his vows to forget his family. Durga kept constant contact with her family by letters, but she didn't tell Shankar much news about them, as she didn't want to remind him of Dum Dum.

One late afternoon, as Shankar sat at the dining room table grading papers, Durga told Shankar that her younger sister was getting married.

"Your sister Kalindi?"

"Yes. I got a letter today. My parents have found a qualified engineer for her."

Shankar perked up at this news. Weddings are one of the most important activities in a household in India and everyone – brothers, sisters, parents, uncles, and aunts – get involved in the wedding planning and execution. It is a huge festivity and a lot of fun. "Durga," he said, "you have not seen your family for over five years, and you must not miss this. You go home for the wedding."

Shankar had never mentioned Calcutta since they arrived in the States. Durga's expression was one of utter surprise—eyebrows up, eyes wide; the spontaneous words that came out of her were, "Really?" Shankar wanted her to keep in touch with her family, but his response genuinely surprised her. "Leaving you alone here?"

"That's no problem. The school is closed in summer. . . . yes, you go and take Samir with you."

Durga couldn't believe what she heard. She took Shankar's hand and said, with a catch in her voice, "It will be wonderful to go, especially for the wedding. Are you sure?"

"I want you to keep relations with your family. I like your family. So, go. I'm sure they would love to see Samir."

"I have not mentioned your family since we married." She stared at her husband. "I was thinking when a grandson is born, sometimes parents forgive their fractious son and accept him back."

"My family does not exist," he replied curtly.

Durga saw his face stiffen and eyes turned cold.

Shankar calmly turned toward the stairs and called their son. "Samir, you are going with Mommy on a plane to Calcutta."

Tears filled her eyes, knowing the sadness her husband harbored in his heart.

Shankar devoted more time and energy to his research during his family's month-long absence, but he felt lonely at home and truly alone in this world. He realized how much his life depended on their presence—he longed for the little sounds of Durga cooking or talking with Samir as they talked about Samir's school and friends, or just watching her quietly reading. He had little to do in the house; Durga had cooked a lot of food and kept it in neatly labeled packages in the freezer, ready to heat up. Beside the news, TV didn't hold any interest for him. Sometimes he moved from room to room, gazing out the windows. He spent longer and longer hours at the university. When Durga and Samir returned, he experienced real joy. He realized his melancholy mood had been smothering him—as if he had been holding his breath the entire time they were gone.

**

Mischievous Monkeys

Samir was ebullient and talkative after returning. He told Shankar all about his newly found grandparents, aunts and uncle, the things he had seen, the presents he got and what fun it was. The attention and love he received from his mother's family were clear from his bubbliness. Finally, he said, "*Dadu* showed me monkeys in a tree!"

"Monkeys with black faces?"

"Yes. They chase each other. I love the baby monkeys. They hold on to their mothers' tummies when their mothers jump from one branch to another."

"I hope you didn't get too close to them."

"We were standing back, but I asked one monkey to come down from a tree. He didn't."

"Monkeys are very smart. You need to be careful around them."

"They are in the tree, Baba, away from us!"

Shankar shook his head. "They can come down very quickly and bite you. This happened to someone I knew."

"Really?"

"Yes."

"One monkey blinked at me," Samir said. "What else do the monkeys do?"

"If you put some fruit at the bottom of the tree, a monkey will come down and take it. Sometimes two come down at the same time, and the quicker one gets the fruit."

"I wish I had fruits with me to give to the monkeys."

"I'll tell you what happened to my cousin Chinta. She and I were once watching monkeys in a tree. Slowly, she went closer to the tree and made faces at the monkeys. She was having such fun! But, suddenly, a monkey came down and snatched her handbag away!

"Chinta yelled in a high-pitched voice, 'My bag, my bag!' I rushed to her but didn't know what to do. The monkey ran back up the tree and sat quietly, holding her bag, and looking around, as if nothing had happened. Several men shouted and made gestures at the monkey to drop the bag, but he sat there and did nothing.

"After some time, the monkey opened the bag. He took out an item that glittered in the sunlight. The monkey examined it with some interest. He didn't care for the bag anymore and dropped it.

"Chinta screamed, 'That's my gold necklace!' and she started to sob.

"Her cry brought more people near the tree, but no one knew how to get the necklace back. The monkey remained seated on the branch nonchalantly.

"'My gold necklace!' Chinta wailed. Tears ran down her cheeks.

"The crowd talked about whether to call the police or find someone who could capture the monkey. I saw how sad my cousin was and thought of an idea. I fetched a bright yellow banana and went to the tree. I showed the banana to the monkey. When I saw that he had noticed my banana, I threw it up to him. My aim was perfect. The monkey grabbed the banana, looked at it for a few seconds, and dropped the gold necklace. Chinta picked up the necklace immediately and moved away from the tree."

"Baba," Samir asked, "How did you know the monkey would give the necklace back?"

"Monkeys are smart. A banana is more important to a monkey than a gold necklace."

Samir nodded. "The monkey will eat the banana."

"Right. So next time you're near a monkey, be careful"

"Okay. I'll go and tell Ma about the naughty monkeys."

The sound of Samir's rapid steps on the stairs reminded Shankar how wonderful life is when one was a child! He stared, unseeing, at the oak tree on the lawn. Soon he was transported to his childhood in Dum Dum. How he and his sisters played in the house and prowled around the neighborhood. So many monkeys were in the trees! Many other images came to him: green mangoes hanging in the trees, tall rice plants swaying in the wind, farmers lifting water with a boat-like gadget from the pond to their vegetable plots, the same pond he had jumped in on hot summer days. He released a deep breath. Childhood does not last; he was in Ann Arbor and had work to do. He went back to preparing his lecture notes. He had been working hard but no one had said anything about his standing at the university. Did that mean the permanent faculty members were just being polite, and he wouldn't get tenure at this place?

Chapter Twenty-Four

Walk in the Arboretum

One afternoon Shankar came home early and went around the house looking for his wife. "Durga, Durga, we have been invited tomorrow to a special party at the physics department." She had not seen him in such a happy mood for a long, long time and looked at him questioningly. He put his hands on her shoulders. "I am tenured!"

Durga's face froze; she couldn't say a word. She quietly rested her head on his shoulder and gently caressed his back. It was hard to believe they had achieved their goal. Her long held tension and suppressed emotions gave way and tears poured down her face. Her chest heaved convulsively. "I was starting to feel we were jinxed."

Shankar embraced her tightly. "A long six years . . . but we have made it."

She nodded, wiped her tears and her face relaxed. "I'll cook something special to celebrate."

"No cooking today. Let's go to our favorite restaurant."

Suddenly, the 'future' had arrived. At night Shankar told her, "We will go on travels again, in the summer, as we did before."

Durga made sweets and they giggled while they ate them for breakfast the next morning. "You know the old Indian saying," Shankar said, "foolish children eat sweets in the morning."

"I want to be foolish for a while," Durga said.

On Saturday, Shankar proposed they go for a walk in the Arboretum Gardens. The last time he had asked her to walk together in a garden was their momentous visit to the Calcutta Botanical Garden. Durga looked over her shoulder at Shankar, who was standing near the kitchen door, surprised by the suggestion. She stopped stirring the potato and scallion curry she was cooking on the stove. She beamed as she saw Shankar's relaxed and smiling face. "That would be wonderful. It's such a nice day today. The potatoes are almost done. We'll be ready in ten minutes." She turned to the living room door and called, "Samir, Samir. Stop what you are doing and get ready to go out."

They chose a short, easy trail in the Arboretum along the Peony and Laurel Ridge loop. The Peony Trail was flat and curved through a landscaped garden. It was late May; the peonies bloomed profusely showing a riot of pink, red and white. There were many people strolling through the gardens enjoying the flowers. A few had set up easels and were painting.

Ten-year-old Samir didn't understand the meaning of his father's tenured position, but his mother explained to him that it meant they were going to live in Ann Arbor forever. Unable to stay still, he ran ahead, darting in and out among the peonies. After some time, Durga sat with Shankar on a bench near the end of the Peony Trail. The sun's rays warmed their faces. Looking around at the beautiful scenery and seeing how all were enjoying the gardens, Shankar released a sigh. "It's unfortunate we didn't come here before."

Durga took his hand and said, "We've plenty of time left."

"I hope so. Now that we have become citizens and established ourselves here, we can relax a bit and do more things together as a family."

"We will."

Shankar gazed at the large peony hill, so gorgeous in the sunlight. He turned toward his wife, looked tenderly into her eyes, and spoke softly, his voice cracking with emotion. "You have sacrificed your life for me."

"What do you mean?"

"You have suffered, I know. You can blame the first day we met. If we hadn't met, you could have had a rich, wonderful life in Calcutta."

"Marrying another man after we had met?" Durga tossed her head like a young girl. "Suffering? You can say we have gone through some turmoil, but that is life. Me living with you in the U.S., you call that suffering?"

"You came away with me, left your family, and couldn't pursue your career. You were a better student than me, but you couldn't follow your dreams."

"That's partly true. But girls always leave home after marriage." She waved at Samir, who was running around the peonies with abandon. "Raising a child is also a mother's job."

"But—"

Durga interrupted him. "Men may not understand this: career is not always our highest priority. Women balance their interests with their husband's life and with the needs of the family. It has been this way since ancient times." She stopped for a second and added, "Here it is a little different now. Women are fighting for options—choices."

Shankar always knew Durga was a feminist, but like other Indian women her feminism was internal. He shook his head. "My needs have overridden yours. You sacrificed your freedom, your choice for yourself ... I have an idea."

Before he could elaborate on his idea, she raised her palm. "What does freedom mean? I see here women are fighting, to have a life of their own. I don't know where this will finally lead them. I feel we need a balance in life. Traditionally women provide that balance."

"But your professional career is off track. I know it. Now, can I tell you my idea? ... It is not too late; do your Ph.D. at the University of Michigan."

Durga spun toward Shankar, eyes opened wide and stared at him for several seconds. "When I first arrived in Philadelphia," she said in a low voice, "I dreamed of getting a Ph.D. from a university in the U.S., but now, I have forgotten that dream."

Shankar squeezed her hand. "I've thought about it for a long time." Circumstances had forced her to abandon her academic career, and that happened to many women after marriage. But she had expressed no regrets, in word or deed, with the course her life had taken. That was her character, and she did extremely well, managing their home, raising Samir, and taking care of all the extraneous business of their family. Many in Calcutta had urged her to continue her studies; they had even written to tell Durga a brilliant student like her should not become a mere housewife. The only thing going for her was that she was in America. Living in the U.S. had prestige when viewed from India; that had a pleasure of its own. Shankar also knew the boy in her class who came second to Durga in the master's degree program was now a professor at Calcutta University and a member of the Indian Planning Commission in New Delhi. Shankar knew Durga could have been a hugely successful and influential economist had they remained in India. Her professors had expressed great hopes for her, but she had come to America and forsaken those goals. Her parents expected her to be the first Ph.D. in the family. She had done enough to get him settled in America; now he could give her the opportunity to shine. "I think your parents would love to see you finish your Ph.D."

Durga sat silent for a while, then stood up and grinned. "I'll think about it. In a few years, Samir will be off to college." She nodded. "You are right; I need to do something."

Shankar sprung up and took her hand affectionately. They clasped their hands together tightly and looked into each other's eyes with warmth, as if the old romantic college days had returned. "I feel sorry," Shankar said, "that we wasted your talents for all these years."

Shankar called Samir and they started to walk again. He took Samir's hand and moved ahead.

Durga fell behind, absorbed in her own thoughts. She looked around. The natural beauty of the garden surrounded her. It was clear from her demeanor that Shankar had lit a fire under her feet. She stared at the peonies and the visitors enjoying the day. Then with some newfound enthusiasm, she quickened her pace, caught up with her family and grabbed Shankar's other hand. She didn't say anything but walked in rhythm with them. Anyone who saw them would know what a loving family they were.

They returned home with an increased sense of happiness and delighted with themselves as a family. The future held many possibilities.

Chapter Twenty-Five

Academics and Adventures

Durga visited several professors at the University of Michigan economics department and explored how she could restart her studies. Since she had not been associated with the academic world for over ten years, she found that she would have to find a non-traditional way to gain admission to the graduate school. Fortunately, she met with Professor Weisskopf. He had been a visiting professor who taught economics at the Statistical Institute in Calcutta when she was an undergraduate student. He was familiar with the high standard of economics studies in Calcutta and was impressed with Durga's record. With his support, Durga not only received admission to the graduate school but also an assistantship from the economics department.

The family started the fall semester with a 7th and a 17th grader (their little family joke)—two serious-minded students—and a physics professor. As usual, Shankar had an active schedule at the university, but at home he now carried out all major activities of the household and took care of Samir's needs. Durga was as studious as she had been in Calcutta, but still cooked and tended her garden. When Shankar protested, she smiled and told him, "These relax me." He couldn't say any more after that.

Shankar knew that devotion to studies during the day, cooking for the family in the evening, and gardening on warm days were the only things Durga allowed herself at this time. And he was happy with it, as he found the same Durga of their college days—lively and interesting and fully dedicated to her family and studies. He spent most of his free time at home teaching Samir math and going over his homework. Together, they read Indian epic stories from the Ramayana and the Mahabharata. Occasionally he told Samir some stories from his childhood, avoiding details of his family. By the time Samir was twelve, he had become a studious boy. His teachers told Shankar and Durga that it was a great pleasure for them to have him in their classes. That made them proud and happy.

Now that they were so busy, spending time outside in their backyard on warm weekends was special to them, time to relax a little—Shankar and Samir horsed around and Durga played in her garden. Their life continued with little homey pleasures. And both Durga and Samir progressed through their academic courses. One evening, near the end of Samir's junior year in high school, he told Shankar that his classmates were planning an adventure trip and they would very much like him to join them. He didn't disclose that he himself was one of the planners and asked for his father's suggestions.

"Will these be more difficult than the Boys Scout adventures you went on when you were younger?"

"I think so and perhaps more daring."

"What exactly are you planning?"

"We have two ideas. The first one is going down the Green River of eastern Utah through Desolation Canyon. What caught our interest was that John Wesley Powell described it as a rare journey. The second idea is paddling through a stretch of barrier islands off the North Carolina coast. That area is steeped in pirate legends and history."

"Both seem quite risky to me."

"You know, Baba, our advisors tell us that significant extracurricular activities are necessary for admission to good schools. Just being good in academics is not enough; we will have to show that we are more capable than that." Samir looked at Shankar expectantly. "Baba, did you go on any adventures in India when you were growing up?"

"I grew up in a city and was very much protected. We were not allowed to do anything that had any trace of danger. But when I look back, I think I had more adventures than most Bengalis." Shankar looked out through the window to the pending darkness and remained silent for some time. "I can tell you about an adventure of mine. I didn't know about all the pitfalls when I went with my uncle. One can't really foresee all the risks in advance."

Samir's face lit up. "Now you have made me curious. I'd love to know what you did."

"It is so long ago. I was young, perhaps twelve or thirteen. What led me to go on the adventure was that I had no idea what a forest was. How densely packed were the trees? How could one go through a jungle? Where did the animals hide? So, when I heard my uncle would be going to the Sundarban forest with two friends, I clamored to go with him. 'Sundarban is a dangerous place. Royal Bengal tigers are there,' my uncle told me flatly. 'I cannot take you.' But I kept on bugging him. Finally, he yielded and asked me to promise that I'd not tell anyone because my parents would be angry if they knew he had taken risks with the life of their only son. He would just say he was taking me on an outing on the river, which was partially true. And he said I must be quiet and follow what he tells me to do. I promised immediately.

"Wow! In the Sundarban forest!" Samir's eyes widened.

"My uncle's friends would go there very early in the morning to collect beehives for honey. We met them the night before."

"Baba, bees from the hive can swarm and sting! How could they succeed?"

"Of course, that is a problem. The bigger risks were—other stinging or biting insects, tigers, and snakes. They are all there in the jungle." Shankar paused for a moment. "The honey they get from the Sundarban beehives has a special fragrance, the best in the world. So, it is valuable. It was quite the adventure."

"Now I'm hooked. Please tell me everything."

***

Sundarban Honey

My uncle's friends, the beehive collectors, started the expedition long before the sun was up. They led us in quiet darkness to a small river when dawn was just breaking. Birds were waking up and I heard many birdcalls I hadn't heard before. They had a boat there—an old, ordinary wooden boat with an arched half circle cover in the middle. It didn't have a motor, but the current was strong, so the boat went swiftly as soon as they untied it from the moorings. They steered it with the oars. No one talked, and they went south for an hour.

Many branches of the Ganges River go to the Bay of Bengal through the Sundarban forest. We were on a stream of that river. The jungle grew thicker and thicker on both banks of the river. It seemed to loom over the river. Soon the channel narrowed, and the jungle seemed to close in on our boat. I heard strange animal sounds and a shiver ran down my spine. The surroundings were unbelievably beautiful, though, with different kinds of trees, small plants, and creepers.

It was cool on the river, and I had on long pants and a warm jacket. My uncle also wore long pants and a long-sleeved shirt, but his two friends wore only cotton shirts and the traditional dhuti that men wrap around their lower bodies. They were lean but quite muscular and tanned dark mahogany from the tropical sun.

I put my hand in the stream out of curiosity, but my uncle pulled my hand away. 'There are crocodiles and snakes in the water,' he said. 'Don't do anything and stay quiet. The animals can hear you.'

The forest became denser, and we rode closer to the shore. Soon the beehive gatherers gave everyone a mask with a man's face painted on it. My uncle told me to put that on the back of my head, so the mask would appear as if I was looking backward. He explained that tigers don't attack when they think you are looking at them. That sent a chill through my body.

We moved on and the beehive collectors found a place to land. They tied the boat to a tree. However, before they proceeded on land, they looked around for signs of big animals—marks on the ground or broken branches. Then they marched through the jungle; I stayed in the middle. The man in the rear often walked backward to look around. The sun was up; the forest was gorgeous—many kinds of trees and lush vines twining around tree trunks surrounded us with a shimmering green veil. It was quiet except for the occasional calls of birds. We marched on for about half an hour, but no one talked. When they talked, they spoke in hushed voices. Each quiet whisper sent shivers down my spine, filling my head with terrible images of what danger might lie ahead or behind us.

Their cautious movements frightened me. They listened to the sounds from the forest and carefully looked around as they proceeded. Once the man in the front stopped short, spread his hands out for us to halt, and pointed out a tiger footprint on the ground. It was dry, about six inches wide. They could decipher the claw marks. They decided those were old and continued.

Suddenly, there was a loud thud. I leapt. Something fell from a tree in front of us. It was a rather heavy man who pointed a rifle at us. He looked scary with a dark, round face, small, penetrating eyes, bushy eyebrows, and uncombed hair.

'What are you doing in our territory?' the man growled, and a few more men appeared from behind other trees.

'We're looking for beehives.'

'Hmm. Beehives! Sure, you aren't hunting for tigers?'

'No, no.' One beehive gatherer said. 'See we have no big guns.'

But the sight of the big gun had made me anxious and I blurted out, 'Isn't tiger hunting illegal?'

The man looked at me angrily. 'Who's this boy?'

'Don't worry about him,' the first beehive hunter told him. 'We won't tell anyone.'

The man's eyes seemed to burn fiercely. His yellow teeth shone on his dark face. I didn't know they were poachers.

'Shall we keep the boy here with us?' one of the poachers asked his cohorts. 'He needs to learn a lesson.'

'He'll be good bait for the tiger,' another man with a big belly said with a laugh, frightening me. I hid behind the beehive hunters.

'You know what we will do to you if you squeal?' the man asked me. 'We'll find you and burn you alive. Right at this spot.' He pointed his finger to the ground. 'Go for now.'

He then told the beehive hunters, 'Get lost, but don't go this way. Find another place to hunt for beehives.'

Our men changed their course, but there was no clear path. The man in the front cut the branches with a big, machete-like knife to make a path. Soon we noticed one or two bees buzzing around. 'We must be close,' one man said. They walked looking up at the trees. Finally, they saw a beehive hanging from a branch, about fifteen feet off the ground—a beige sac, almost two feet long. I thought it was a bird's nest and wondered if bees were in the hive who might sting us.

The beehive hunters knew what to do. They collected kindling and quietly started a fire under the hive. A large plume of smoke rose, and bees started to come out of the hive. They formed a cloud and moved away. We stayed low on the ground. When no more bees came out, one man climbed the tree, cut the hive free, and put it in a burlap bag. It was so simple. We left the place immediately; they knew the bees would soon return.

As we came closer to the river, we heard loud cries. I thought a tiger had attacked the poachers.

One of the beehive hunters at the rear murmured, as if talking to himself, 'The bees got them.'

***

"Baba," Samir said, aghast. "That was really dangerous."

"Yes. But I was thrilled to go and didn't realize how perilous it was until I was in the middle of the forest." He looked tenderly at his son. "You are an Eagle Scout, so I know you will handle your trip well. I am proud that you included me in your planning."

"Now I want to taste Sundarban honey," Samir said. "Can we buy some?"

"I've never seen it here. I guess they don't get enough to export."

Durga came over, telling Samir, "Go to your room and study or go to bed." She looked at Shankar, "What were you telling him?"

"Nothing special. We talked about an adventure he's going on with his buddies." He glanced at her, with an 'I think we should change the subject' look on his face. "It is time for bed."

Chapter Twenty-Six

Graduation

With Shankar's support and their strict, disciplined life, Durga finished her Ph.D. in five years. The day she received her degree, she sent a telegram to her father and took the family out to a fancy Japanese restaurant, Kamakura, in Detroit. Soft Koto music floated in the air as they entered, and kimono-clad Japanese women with lacquered bowls on trays added to the ambiance. A subdued light filled the restaurant. It was a joyous day for Durga and Shankar. "Samir, you can order any dish you like," she cheerfully told her son. "Don't worry about prices tonight." Shankar ordered a large plate of sashimi as an appetizer for all. "I like Miso soup. Any of you want it?" Both nodded.

After tasting a spoonful of Miso and expressing his pleasure, Shankar said, "I do not know how to say this, but I am so glad your Ph.D. is over. No more stress, dear wife."

"You tell me." Durga said. "At one point I thought I could not finish it. I had to struggle on so many levels—from being the oldest student in the department, studying for the qualifying exam, feeling guilty about neglecting you two, to disagreeing with my advisors."

"I know." Shankar nodded.

"When I saw younger students give up, it broke my heart. They didn't have the emotional support they needed to carry on. You two were gems in that regard."

"You had to fight with your advisors, Ma?" Samir's eyes widened.

"You know what energy conservation is," Durga asked Samir. "I studied economics impacts of energy conservation. I used matrices to handle several factors like energy needs, availability, demands, gas prices and futures, etc., at the same time. My two advisors in the finance and engineering departments didn't like the idea and they resisted it from the beginning. My economics thesis advisor encouraged me, but he was away on travels and not available when I needed him. I was pretty much alone. So incredibly stressful."

"The important thing is you finished it," Shankar said. "Let us be happy."

Halfway through dinner, Samir said, "You know, you two have put me in a difficult position in life."

"How?" Durga said, with surprise in her voice. "Are you kidding?"

"You see, when both of my parents have doctorate degrees, it is hopeless to strive to be a peon now?"

"Right," Shankar said and laughed out loud. "We did this just for you."

Then father and son raised their glasses for Durga. Time passed in a wonderful mood with excellent food and wine—no worries, no stress, only loving moments.

Durga's thesis title was *Economic Impact of Energy Conservation*. Her thesis dealt with academic analysis and future implications in all spheres of life from jobs to economic health of the country. The subject was political as well. After the oil embargo of 1973, this had been a major concern in the U.S. Once her thesis was published, Durga was in high demand to give talks. One morning their telephone rang just before she was about to leave. She heard a strong male voice on the phone. "May I speak with Dr. Durga Lahiri please?"

"This is she."

"I am Dr. Aaron Meyer, Vice President, JPMorgan Investment Bank. We wish to offer you a position with us as a Principal for our energy conservation investment sector."

Astonished, Durga blurted out, "How did you come to know of me?"

There was a quiet laugh in the background when Mr. Meyer replied, "We try to keep on top of things relevant to our business."

"Thank you but could you please tell me a little more?"

"Certainly. We believe energy conservation is going to affect all businesses in the world. We want to be abreast of future possibilities. If you join our team, you will have sufficient research money and several bright analysts working for you. We pay excellent salaries and will pay for all your relocation costs, including selling your house and buying a new one here. You will work at our Wall Street Headquarters. You will also receive special stock options."

Durga was stunned and didn't know how to respond. This would give her an opportunity to explore her ideas. She could only say, "Please give me a few days to think about your offer. I will get back to you." Mentally and physically shaken, she dialed Shankar, but no one answered.

When she reached her desk in the economics department, the secretary gave her a slip with a name and a telephone number. "You just missed a call. The man wants you to call collect."

She glanced at the paper: Jeffrey Blair, HSBC, and an international telephone number. She was aware of HSBC being a colossal British bank known for international trade for over a century with offices in important cities around the world. She called and was immediately connected to Mr. Blair. They offered her a senior position in their San Francisco office with an incredible salary and perks but said that she would have to make frequent international trips to London, Zurich, and Hong Kong.

Durga couldn't wait to go home and talk with her husband. "You won't believe this," she told Shankar, and explained the two job offers she received without even applying.

"That's incredible," Shankar exclaimed with pride. "What do you want to do?"

"I don't know. These are fantastic opportunities for economists. We can test our ideas with real applications."

"Samir will graduate soon and go somewhere," Shankar said. "I can handle his last year here if you wish to take one of these good jobs."

"I don't know. Both are great opportunities."

Over the next two weeks, she received more jobs offers from well-established Wall Street companies, like Exxon and utility conglomerates to non-profit Institutes in Washington, DC.

"You know," Shankar told Durga, "we can live well just with your salary. And I can find a part-time teaching position anywhere we go."

"I am torn," Durga confided. "It's like receiving a 100-million-dollar lottery but feeling lost after the initial excitement."

She struggled and fretted. She was forty now. If she were to pursue her career seriously as an economist, she would certainly have to live in another city. And most of these jobs meant living separately, at least part time, from Shankar. After a few days, she told Shankar, "You know why you and I left India and came here?"

Shankar simply stared at her.

"We did not leave India for money or fame, rather to charter a life without the constraints of society." She paused for a few moments, looking at his face. "And you know many lottery winners die miserable."

Shankar came closer. "You have sacrificed so much—family, friends, all the enjoyments of life in Calcutta. How can I stop you from the pleasure of success? Please follow your heart. I'll be with you."

"This is like the golden deer Sita wanted in the Ramayana."

"What are you saying?"

"I'd rather be happy together." She surrendered herself on her husband's chest.

"I'll be happy with whatever you decide."

Durga accepted a faculty position in the economics department at Wayne State University in Detroit. It entailed an hour-long commute, but she didn't mind. Soon she established herself as a valuable faculty member. Both students and faculty admired her, and she whole-heartedly made Wayne State her professional home.

That was Durga, Shankar thought, shining in whatever she endeavored. Their focused efforts to make emigration to the U.S. a success had, in a sense, ended. Now they could simply carry on with life. He was happy, but the pent-up emotions that Shankar hid behind his work at the university, behind his support for Durga and Samir in their success, behind deliberately avoiding any news from Calcutta found a fissure. His father's last words came to him one night, opening the floodgate of memories he had wished to obliterate completely. An unmistakable pain surfaced like the emergence of a foreign submarine periscope. All their accomplishments weren't enough to extinguish the misery his family had caused him.

Chapter Twenty-Seven

Joy and Pain

S amir went to Columbia University. The first few years Durga and Shankar passionately watched over their son's needs, his progress, and looked forward to his visits home. They vigorously engaged themselves in their individual teaching and research, which kept them busy, but soon home felt empty. They sensed something missing in their lives; it was like missing one's younger days—the spontaneous laughter and wonders one dreamt about under the blue skies. They pined for the leisurely culture of life in Calcutta, a large part of which was chatting with friends over tea and snacks, going to movies, and celebrating the various festivals together. They knew they could not go back to the rhapsody of youth. But a wistful desire for some cozy little thing to look forward to at the end of the day or weekend came to them often.

They started traveling, something they enjoyed very much when they were new to the U.S. And Shankar encouraged Durga to visit her family often. Durga pleaded with him to come along.

He'd only say, "I have seen enough of India. You go for both of us."

"My family and your friends would love to see you."

But Shankar would not budge. One time he'd remind her, "You know, I have vowed not to return to India."

Durga saw his impassive face and did not mention it again.

Their son graduated from college, went to medical school, specialized in heart surgery, and got married. Samir's marriage was a significant event for Shankar and Durga. Their marriage was a 'love' marriage as opposed to an arranged marriage: they chose their own spouse and even violated Indian caste dictates. At the time, they had not thought of their own child's marriage, as children were nowhere in their minds. They hadn't discussed anything about marriage with Samir. They were mostly concerned with his future in the sense of his career and providing him with a good education. When Samir brought Julie home to meet them, they had to accept that his and their world was moving on.

They knew they could not oppose who Samir chose as his partner in life. To many Indian parents, they understood that having an American girl as a daughter-in-law meant putting their son on a boat to a foreign land. That was what they had done. *Gone to their own world.* When Shankar and Durga first came to know about Samir seriously dating Julie, they were neither surprised nor conflicted; they had their own experience, and they had both taught and advised young men and women in college. They had observed them closely. They were fine youngsters as any in India—only they grew up in American culture, as did Samir. Certainly, there were all kinds of boys and girls with different characteristics, but if their son found a suitable girl, they had no reservations and no problem with his choice. They only hoped that he would choose someone agreeable to them.

"My family rejected you outright," Shankar told Durga, "not because of who you were, not because of your misdeeds, but simply because you were born in a non-brahmin family. We cannot let that happen to our son."

Durga nodded. "Even if we wished to have an Indian daughter-in-law," she said, "it is not possible for us to arrange such a marriage."

"We did not raise him with such a concept." Shankar chortled.

"I only wish he marries someone he cherishes." After a little pause, Durga murmured, "Our marriage cost you your family."

"We have not told this to Samir," Shankar moaned.

"We must not," Durga asserted, "make it that Samir will have to choose between us and his wife."

"Let us think positive and wish him the best for his married life." Shankar went to the kitchen and brought a bottle of wine and two glasses.

Julie turned out to be a pleasant surprise. Both Durga and Shankar had been relieved when they met. She was pretty, pleasant, and accommodating beside being part of their academic world. She would be teaching university courses in New York, where Samir was working.

Then they became grandparents. And their hair color started to change. But they paid no attention to the signs of aging. They followed their routines unaffected. In the beginning, Shankar thought teaching was his job and his duty, but now he felt something more, a calling to see young students learn and do better in life.

One evening in May while they were strolling in their favorite place, the arboretum, Shankar murmured something that jolted Durga. She stopped abruptly. "Did you mention your father?"

Shankar nodded.

"What made you think of the old days?"

"It's a long story. There is a student in my freshman class, Lenny, a quiet student. He was always attentive in the class, keeping his eyes on me the whole time. But he never asked any questions. Every day he sat at the same place, away from other students. There was something in his gaze that drew my attention. I told him to feel free to come to my office if he needed help. He didn't take me up on it for some time. One day about two months ago he came to my office hesitantly and mentioned that he was having some difficulty.

"I thought he was finding homework difficult. 'Would it help,' I asked, 'if we go over the problems together?'

"His face lit up. I think he liked that I offered to spend time with him. We worked together for several Thursday afternoons. He was quite intelligent; I found he could do the homework himself. But we continued our meetings. After a few weeks, he said, 'Thank you for spending time with me. I don't know anyone to discuss physics or anything else.' After a pause, he added, 'I feel you care about me.'

"His tone and demeanor were melancholy. 'I enjoy working with you,' I said.

"He looked outside for a few seconds. Then in a low voice he said, 'I can't study or do anything at home because I don't have peace there. My relationship with my father is bad. When he comes home from work, he gets irate with anything I do or say. He screams at me with little provocation. He is just mean. It is unbearable in the house. I often go out and walk alone in the neighborhood.'

"'Oh my! Why is he unhappy with you?'

"'He is an alcoholic,' Lenny said and remained silent for some time. 'It started about five years ago when I started high school. I don't know why he began drinking but it has gotten worse since then.' Lenny stared out the window. Then he continued, 'Initially Fridays were worse. Now it's every day. I walk on eggshells when he is home. But still, I can't avoid run-ins with him. Sometimes I am awakened at night by his obnoxious and slurred yelling at mother. My mother screams and tries to get away from his abuse, but where would she go in our small house? One day I saw deep hatred in his bloodshot eyes. I lost any respect that I had. I went up to my room and closed the door. Since then, I can't stand him, neither can I afford to move out of the house. I've no one to talk to. No place to go. I don't know what to do.'"

"I didn't know what to say or how to console him." Shankar looked at Durga for a few seconds. "I have no experience of what happens when one becomes alcoholic. He reminded me of my situation with my father. My father was also drunk—not with alcohol, but with the extreme conservative ideas of our religion. Our situations were analogous. I had only emotional abuse; but Lenny faced both physical and emotional abuse. I found comfort outside the house—in college. He was seeking solace from somewhere." Shankar looked away in the distance.

"I see," Durga burst out, "those painful memories are back and hurting you."

"Today was the end of final exams for this semester," Shankar said without commenting on Durga's reaction. "I was eager to see how Lenny had done in physics, especially after my tutoring. The physics exam was on Monday. I graded the papers today and was shocked to find all the pages of Lenny's exam book empty. He came to the exam but didn't answer any questions." Shankar looked at Durga with a blank stare.

Durga took his hand, saying, "I thought you would say he did well."

"I thought so too. I was lost, wondering what might have happened to him. I couldn't concentrate on any work. I paced in my office and after some time, I went to the department office and found that Lenny hadn't shown up the next day for the math exam. I was about to return to my office when the secretary said, 'Lenny is in the hospital.'

"'What happened?'

"'We got a call from the University of Michigan hospital in Ann Arbor inquiring about him. An ambulance brought him to the Emergency Room from his home. He was savagely beaten up and shouting incoherently. It seems he tried to stop his father from beating his mother and took the brunt of it. But he was raving like someone having a bad trip. He blamed his father for ruining his life, wanting him dead. They said they couldn't find any evidence of alcohol or drugs in him. The doctors were inquiring about his past behavior on campus and if we had observed anything unusual.'

"'When did this happen?'

"'Lenny went to hospital yesterday. The doctors have stabilized him; now they are trying to figure out the root cause.'"

"What a tragedy!" Durga pulled her husband closer, saying, "You must not blame yourself."

"I tried to help Lenny, but he didn't need help with physics. I should have been more sympathetic, especially knowing my own situation. He had no one to go to." After some time, he said, "I had you."

"There's so much hurt in this world," Durga murmured. "I didn't grasp why you never wanted to talk about your family, until I met your father.

I felt your sadness, anger, and the feeling of helplessness when your father told you never to return home."

"I don't know what Lenny should do. I have survived by sheer determination and your love. If you were not there, I do not know what I'd have done."

"Lenny's problem," Durga said, "has clearly originated from his father's deplorable behavior, a feeling of no one caring for him, and nowhere to vent his frustrations."

"Yes." Shankar nodded. "His misery is deep. He was crying for help, for acceptance and empathy, not rejection or indifference. And that's why he came to me, but I didn't realize it." Many emotions erupted in him—anger at Lenny's situation, anger against his own father, sadness because he hadn't been able to give Lenny the help he needed; feelings of vulnerability overwhelmed him.

"Perhaps you can do something now," Durga said when they started to walk.

After some time, Shankar said, "I'll visit him in the hospital."

"You must." Durga laced her fingers tenderly with Shankar's.

ANN ARBOR TO BELLPORT

2004

Chapter Twenty-Eight

Move to New York

S hankar thought he would reside in Ann Arbor and teach at the university in Ypsilanti for as long as he lived. But he became isolated in the physics department as the 'old professor' and didn't have the dynamism he once had to keep going with the same vigor. After thirty-nine years, he finally retired from Eastern Michigan University. Samir immediately called and insisted that Shankar and Durga move in with them. He had been telling his father for some time that they should follow the ancient Indian tradition: when parents grow old, they live with their children, and grandchildren grow up with grandparents. And his wife, Julie, had agreed it would be wonderful, even though this had not been part of her own upbringing.

Despite their enthusiasm, Shankar told Durga, "I have strong doubts about how Samir and Julie will manage living with us. We must recognize that Samir was born in the U.S. and raised with American culture. There is an unwritten streak of independence that is absorbed when growing up here. We don't see it but that must be within him too."

"I know that." Durga replied with irritation in her voice.

"Please don't cloud your eyes. There is no tradition in America of Indian style 'joint family living' and there is no shame about moving far away from parents or putting them in an old folks' home."

"Won't it be nice to live with our own son?"

"Maybe, but we should not move in with them or depend on Samir and Julie for support in our old age. We have made the choice to live here and should follow the customs."

Durga turned away from Shankar.

One night before falling asleep, Durga told Shankar, softly, "All your life you have kept yourself busy and haven't allowed any time to yourself. That has helped you push aside the sadness of rejection by your father. I know it is always at the back of your mind—the unspoken resentment and sadness. If we move in with Samir, we can turn our story around."

Shankar was silent for a while. "But Durga," he said finally, "this is not India. I worry about the long term. What if it doesn't work?"

"It can bring a happy closure to our situation." She said and clasped her fingers with her husband's affectionately. They remained in their own thoughts until sleep came over them.

Their son persisted, insisting it would be a wonderful experience for the grandchildren; and he reassured Shankar that Julie was more than agreeable. During her graduate research work, he pointed out to his father, Julie had lived with a joint family in Vizag, India, and had seen how harmoniously a family could live together. Anyway, Samir argued that as a first-generation immigrant family they were not typical. But if it didn't work out, they could buy a house or build one within walking distance. But under no circumstances could they remain so far away.

That night Durga caressed her husband's arm and said, "We can make a happy ending of your father's rejection of us. We make our own happy extended family, a family that you wished for but never had."

Shankar sat up abruptly. "It's not that I don't like the idea . . . , but Durga, we can't. I don't want to take a chance that might ruin Samir's marriage and life. My answer is no."

***

The 2004 winter was mild in Michigan. The roads were dry and ice-free by March. So, early one morning during Julie's spring break at Stony Brook University, Samir and Julie showed up on Shankar and Durga's doorstep with a moving van. Durga's face radiated joy immediately. But she turned aside to hide the happy tears that sprang to her eyes.

Surprised and shocked, Shankar stared at them and his wife. Why were they here?

Samir bent down for pranam and touched his father's feet. "Baba, trust us."

"It's not just Samir, I also want you two to live with us," Julie told after her pranam.

Shankar realized their plan. "What about the house and all our stuff?" Shankar protested with some resentment.

"Don't worry, Baba," Samir told him. "We know what to do. We've already contacted a real estate agent and hired some help with moving."

Shankar looked around the living room—the sofas, chairs, bookshelves full of his books, the pictures on the walls. His shoulders slumped. He had planned and prepared for years to spend the rest of his life in this house. He stared vacantly out the window. He felt melancholy at the thought of leaving all this behind; there were so many happy memories in this house. But he had seen Durga's face. He knew how happy this move would make his wife. Hadn't she made an even more difficult transition for him, all those years ago? She had sacrificed so much for him, wholeheartedly supporting him all this time even when he wavered. Durga never once complained or expressed longing for the life she could have had in India. He could at least do this for her.

Samir organized the sale of the house with the agent they knew and who would also help make the house ready for sale. "Downsizing is a formidable task," he told his mother, "but you have at least two months to decide what you wish to bring to Bellport. I have contracted World Van Lines who will help you in this regard. Bring as much as you wish. We have a storage place. You can then take your time to decide what you don't need. We have brought this van to take valuable items that you shouldn't give to the moving company." He then gave her two one-way tickets from Detroit to McArthur airport in Islip, New York, for Friday, May Fourteenth.

Shankar was gradually adjusting himself to the idea of the move, but the tickets brought it to a sharp reality. He didn't know how to react or what to say. His eyes widened. "Well," he looked at Samir with equanimity, "you are really taking us, then."

"Yes, Baba. I want us to be happy." He held Julie's hand and smiled.

Durga couldn't conceal her excitement and embraced her son and daughter-in-law in a bear hug.

Chapter Twenty-Nine

Bellport

It didn't take long for Shankar and Durga to settle in with their family in Bellport. They did not live in the basement or in a separate part of the house; they all lived together and ate together. Shankar was happy seeing Durga's joy in Bellport; she was reliving the family life she had in Calcutta.

Shankar was uncertain in the beginning as to how Durga and Julie would get along. He didn't expect harmonious living to develop immediately. It was Julie's house, her kitchen, her laundry room, her style of folding laundry and keeping things where they should be, and it was *her* house to entertain *their* friends. They were the intruding outsiders, and especially, mother-in-law and daughter-in-law living together as one family is unusual in the U.S.—an uncommon practice for at least a hundred years. Shankar had another concern. In India, the daughter-in-law plays a special and significant role with the parents-in-law, obeying and being respectful, and there is an expectancy of her taking care of the in-laws as they grow older, but not in America. Shankar and Durga did not expect her to meet the 'Indian daughter-in-law requirements,' but Julie clearly understood the Indian expectations of a daughter-in-law from her experience of living in India. And she had willingly and sincerely welcomed them into her life. This lifted Shankar's anxious heart.

A few days after they had arrived in Bellport, Julie returned home from work to find food cooked and the dinner table ready. A little frown crinkled her face. "You don't have to cook and serve dinner because you live with us," she told her mother-in-law. She put her hand on Durga's shoulder. "Ma, you are our guest."

Durga, thin and short, glanced at Julie tenderly for a few seconds. Julie stood there slim, energetic, and beautiful in her teaching clothes. "This is what mothers do in India," she told her.

Her voice was so affectionate and sincere Julie couldn't protest. She knew the role of Indian mothers from her own experience in India. Then, without showing any feeling of being usurped, she helped Durga rearrange the kitchen, so it was easier for her mother-in-law to reach things she needed. Together, they separated Indian from Western spices and organized the cabinets and kitchen tools.

Another day, Shankar saw the two talking in the kitchen.

"My rice never comes out as loose and fluffy as yours," Julie told Durga, "How do you cook rice?"

Durga laughed. "People think it's easy, but you have to know how to do it."

"I've seen in India, they put so much water in the pot to cook rice – much more than we do here."

"That's how they did it in my house too," Durga said. "They drain off the water when the rice is cooked."

"But then all the vitamins are thrown away."

"Right." Durga nodded.

"Samir never mentioned it, but I knew from his face my rice wasn't right."

"His mother never taught him cooking!" Durga chuckled. "You cook the rice the next few times with me; you will get it."

"How did you go to conferences when Samir was young?" Julie asked Durga another day.

"It would have been wonderful to follow my profession the way people do here," Durga said, "but remember we came as immigrants—alone. We didn't have family around. I didn't feel as free as I'd have been in India. Besides, the logistics of two academics pursuing professional goals would have made our life miserable."

"So, you chose family over your own profession?"

"Yes," she murmured. "That's why we came here."

"Yeah, I see you did; you wrote papers and sent coauthors to present them. You also wore a sari everywhere. That says a lot!"

Both giggled.

Shankar was pleased that Durga and Julie got along so well. He thought Durga's motherly and affectionate nature paired with Julie's wholehearted acceptance of them made this possible. Shankar was also a little uneasy about them constraining spontaneity between Samir and Julie—they might not be able to freely express their feelings to each other. He did not observe any significant changes in their life pattern.

One night, Shankar hadn't been able to fall asleep and had come down to the living room to read. He heard Samir come home late and go to the kitchen. Some nights, Samir came late from attending his patients at the hospital in Stony Brook or if he had meetings at Mount Sinai Heart Institute in New York City. Shankar heard some noise from the kitchen but didn't pay attention. Soon he saw Julie come down in her robe. Samir and Julie chatted in the dining room. Shankar went back to his reading but, after some time, his ears perked up.

"You're eating these now. You'll gain weight like last time, eating cookies every night before going to bed," Julie said.

"It's okay, my mother made these."

"Those are meant for the children."

"I won't finish them."

"I needed you this evening to go to the PTA meeting with me."

"I couldn't help it. You know these emergency things happen with patients."

"Do they have to happen every time there is a parent teacher conference?"

There was silence for some time. Shankar went back to his reading. Then he heard Julie's voice again, a little terse. "Your mother is doing a lot of work with the children—feeding them, and working with them when I can't. You ought to chip in sometimes."

"She's happy with the children. What do you want me to do?"

"She's your mother. You should know."

There was silence again.

"I heard so many complaints today at the hospital and then when I come home, you are bitching. Gently, but that's what it is. I get it. Now let's go to bed. I'll try to be more available."

Julie followed her husband upstairs. Shankar chuckled to himself. "A normal life, after all." He closed the book and went upstairs.

Though the house and all within it seemed to get along better than Shankar hoped, he still had a little concern about the longevity of their abundant peace. One aspect that he never questioned though was the delight he took in his grandchildren.

Shankar bonded with them immediately. From the first day, Raja and DeeDee were intrigued with him. There was no end to their curiosity and questions about his life when he was young like them. DeeDee was so bubbly and beautiful. And Raja, always active, often reminded Shankar of himself as a child. These two had made Shankar's life wonderful in Bellport and brought him some peace. He thanked his son for this, a thing that he couldn't do for his own father—his father hadn't allowed him the chance. Shankar always came to the door in the morning to see the children off to school and, when they returned, he was there to receive them. The house, so quiet during the day, filled with new life when they came home. After the children ate the snacks their grandmother provided and before they began their homework, it was a special time for them— time to listen to stories from Grandpa. These were stories from Shankar's own childhood in India as well as stories he was told or the stories he had read as a boy. Some were stories of princes getting lost in a forest while hunting, stories of ghosts, and ancient Indian tales. Sometimes he told them stories of *rakshashis—female demons* who ate human flesh—scary but captivating stories, that always ended well—the demons thwarted and heroes triumphant. DeeDee and Raja loved best when Shankar told them stories from his own childhood. That's what they craved most. And he came to enjoy sharing his life with them. Sometimes, he left a little of the story for the next day or finished it after their homework was done.

***

"How are the schools here for DeeDee and Raja?" Durga asked during Sunday breakfast soon after their arrival.

Samir looked at Julie whose face dimmed.

"That's an ongoing debate between Samir and me," Julie said. "They attend the public schools, whose records are bad. The school's standard test results have been consistently low."

"I went to public schools and turned out fine," Samir interjected.

"I thought New York public schools would be better than Michigan's," Shankar wondered.

"Nope." Julie asserted. "Bellport school district includes North Bellport, a much poorer and neglected section, which pulls it down. We want to educate all children, but I don't see a way for DeeDee and Raja to continue in this school district." She shook her head slowly. "We don't have the time necessary to look after their proper education. They'll have to go to a private school soon."

Shankar and Durga became a team—looking after their grandchildren's education. Durga read books with the children and she insisted they learn spelling. After they read a story, she asked them to tell her what the story was about. This was her way of teaching. Shankar supervised their math homework. Each week, the children went to the library with Durga. Sometimes Shankar also went along. He accepted that this was their role now; that was how children learn—at home from parents and grandparents.

Samir was extremely busy during the week, but he made a routine of spending a leisurely breakfast with his father every Sunday. The first few Sundays were a little stiff, but gradually, father and son became more at ease with each other. Shankar enjoyed these breakfasts and intimate talks with his son, which had never happened with his own father.

That was how Shankar and Durga made a new start in Bellport. And, in general, it was a smooth and happy transition, thanks to Samir and Julie. For the first time in his life, Shankar had free time. He felt no motivation to seek part-time teaching positions in nearby colleges or to connect with the physics faculty at Stony Brook. Instead, he decided this was his time to engage in things he was interested in, one of which was studying cosmology. He had long wanted to delve into the origin and evolution of the universe but had always postponed for other, more urgent matters.

And every evening in good weather, he and Durga went out for a walk. They began their walks to explore the area when they first arrived and continued as they enjoyed the time walking and talking together.

LIFE IN BELLPORT 1

MAY - SEPTEMBER 2004

Chapter Thirty

Royal Bengal Tiger

"G randpa," DeeDee came running from inside the house, "did you know that people in India put masks on the back of their heads, so tigers won't attack them?" She sat on the edge of her grandfather's lawn chair. "I'm reading about India for a class project and writing a report."

Shankar stroked DeeDee's hand with affection. "They put on masks in the Sundarban Forest because man-eating tigers live there. Show me what you have written so far."

As DeeDee ran back into the house, Shankar contemplated the garden. He loved the fluffy pink and purple flowers of the astilbe plants Julie had planted. Irises were poking up their heads, getting ready for a late spring show.

DeeDee brought a ruled paper with three sentences written in careful longhand. "I just started."

Some tigers are man-eaters in Indian forests. They are very dangerous. But people still go to forests to collect wood.

"Good," Shankar told her, but he kept on staring at her handwriting. Some characters were so eerily like Parvati's. He was startled. He had taught Parvati to write the alphabet on a slate in their youth. Shankar sighed. Parvati was so obedient and cheerful, but how she changed when she went to college. He tried to forget what she told him at their last meeting.

"Have you seen a Royal Bengal tiger in a zoo?" he asked DeeDee.

"Grandpa, did you hunt tigers when you were in India?" Raja was playing soldiers on the porch and came over with his GI Joe doll.

These two grandchildren, born in New York, had no idea about life in India. "Oh, yes," he replied with a playful smile. "I shot one."

DeeDee rolled her eyes. "You don't have a gun ... and we've never seen you go hunting."

Images of Shankar's youth rolled through his mind like a motion picture. How he wished he could take these two to Dum Dum, back to the time when he was a young boy. He could run around with them and play with homemade toys. "It was a long time ago," he sighed with a grin. A playful smile came to him. "I'll tell you how I shot a tiger."

***

Tiger Hunt

Before my family settled in Dum Dum, we lived in a small village, Joynagar, forty miles south of the city. The village was very green and surrounded by small farms and ponds. Narrow dirt roads lined the space between houses. In the morning and evening, bells sounded from bullock carts rumbling down the roads . . . very peaceful. And in early mornings in winter, cranes came to a marsh at the edge of the village. I loved to watch how they stood so quietly on one leg, their white feathers shining amid tall grass. From a distance it looked like they only had one leg. But I knew birds had two legs. I wanted to capture one to see that they did indeed have two legs, but one cannot capture a crane; they are very smart. So, I decided to shoot one and bring it home.

I mentioned this to my father, but he shook his head and sternly told me, "We are brahmins. Our job is worshipping God, not killing living beings."

I looked at the floor and stood there glumly unable to get away from my father's glare.

He admonished me further. " . . . And no one knows when a tiger will show up. It's unsafe for a boy to go out alone to the marshlands."

The Sundarbans forest was several miles away, so wild animals didn't usually come to the village. But once every few years a tiger would appear and kill a goat or a cow. It would come very quietly in the early morning and kill it with one strike. The animal didn't even have a chance to cry for help. The tiger would drag it to the edge of the village and eat it there. Only its bones would remain. Then people would beat large drums continuously for several days to scare the tiger away and no tiger would come for some time. My father's words disturbed me, and I remained dejected for a few days, but I was captivated with the idea of getting a crane. I decided I'd do it quietly so no one would know. If my family owned a gun, which they didn't, no one would have allowed me to take it. I decided to make a slingshot, but I couldn't ask anyone for help. My mother would have been terribly angry if she knew because she believed boys with slingshots caused accidents.

I needed a Y-shaped tree branch to make the slingshot. The mango and lichee trees are big but not strong, so I decided that a guava branch would be the strongest. I climbed a large guava tree in our backyard and found a Y-shaped branch, just the right size for my hand. I carved the wood with a pocketknife and kept it hidden under my bed.

I needed three more things: a strong elastic band, a piece of leather, and something to shoot with—the ammunition. A piece of leather was easy to get from an old sandal, and I cut out an elastic band from the rubber bladder of a soccer ball. I tied the two ends of the elastic band to the two sides of the Y and tied the leather piece in the middle. That was my gun, the slingshot. I tried it out with small stones, and it worked fine. But my aim wasn't good; I practiced and practiced improving my skill.

Finally, I needed pellets for bird hunting. I collected clay from the bottom of a pond and made round balls of many sizes—big ones for big animals, and little ones for birds. You can't shoot all creatures with the same size balls. I dried the balls in the sun for several days. Then I created a small fire in the field behind our house and burned them until they were glowing red. I covered the fire with soil and went home. The next day they were like rough red marbles, hard as rocks. Absolutely perfect. I then practiced shooting every day after school.

Our school ended in December when exams were over; then we had two or three weeks of no studies. I waited for the first day of the school break to carry out my plan. I got up early in the morning, grabbed my slingshot and quickly walked to the edge of the village and along a narrow path through the rice fields. I was alone, enthusiastic but a little nervous. The sun was not yet up. I tried out one ball; it went a long way, and my aim was now excellent.

Near the marshland I saw two or three cranes, but they were beyond my range. I slowed down and moved quietly. In the early winter there was always a fog lingering there. That made it especially mysterious and adventurous. I felt I was truly a hunter in a lonely place. I would surprise everyone by bringing a crane home!

I crept forward. Suddenly a few cranes landed near me. I crouched and watched intently. They were so beautiful standing on one leg. This was my chance, and I mustn't make a mistake. In my excitement, I took a large ball instead of a small one, loaded it, and pulled back the elastic. I aimed through the tall grass—very carefully. I saw the white crane move and a faint orange-yellow color came into view. I was confused. I let go of the shot, the clay pellet flew, and a loud roar filled the air. The yellow-orange color rose in the air and fell. I was frightened, not knowing what I had done.

I heard people running through the tall grass. A man shouted, "We got him."

I tiptoed forward. I didn't have to go far before I saw the yellow-orange thing lying on the grass—a large Royal Bengal tiger, almost eight feet long.

Soon several men with tall guns surrounded the area. I was afraid that I had done something wrong. I quietly backed out and went home. I couldn't tell anyone that I had shot a tiger.

***

Did you really shoot the tiger?" DeeDee touched her grandfather's arm, admiration in her gaze.

"It must be. What do you think?" His eyes shone with excitement.

"But then, what were those people doing there?" She stared at her grandfather, eyebrows up. She then jumped to her feet, "Ah ha! I know what happened. They shot—!"

"Shh ..." Shankar shushed DeeDee.

"I'm glad you shot the tiger," Raja said in a satisfied voice. "One day I'll go tiger hunting in India."

"When you're ready, I'll go with you." Shankar clasped his hands behind his head and leaned back with a satisfied smile. He looked out at the backyard, as if he could still see a tiger lying in the marshland. His white hair fluttered in the breeze.

DeeDee suddenly pulled Shankar. "Grandpa, your father said you are brahmin. Does that mean we are brahmins too?"

"Yes. It depends only on your birth. Your father is a brahmin because I was born in a brahmin family. So, you and Raja are also brahmins."

The children gazed at him studiously, feeling slightly proud of their newfound knowledge.

DeeDee and Raja went back to what they were doing, but Shankar reflected on whether his tiger hunt was the most rebellious and sly act he had done in his childhood. He saw, in retrospect, that his independence had been developing all along. If only he had been able to be a "good" boy, obeying his father without question, he would not have suffered this much.

But then, he never would have shot a tiger, either.

Chapter Thirty-One

Breakfast with Samir

Putting down his newspaper and looking at his father affectionately, Samir asked, "Do you remember, Baba, you didn't know anything about lashing and tying knots when I was in Boy Scouts?" His eyes danced a little and his face revealed an innocuous chuckle.

"Yes, I remember it well," Shankar nodded and gazed affectionately at his son. He knew Samir was teasing him, but he liked it; he could never have had such a conversation with his own father. "Before you joined Boy Scouts, I had never done any camping either." He brushed a wisp of white hair from his forehead and looked at his son with a tender smile. "You don't know how difficult it was for me."

"You managed it well though." Samir sipped from his cup and looked at the kitchen. Julie was busily stirring eggs in a bowl. "I thought you were just like the other dads," he told Shankar. "I didn't feel anything unusual and didn't know how hard it was for you, not growing up in this culture."

Indeed, Shankar thought. He had barely managed to raise him.

Samir shifted his view to the plate of biscuits on the table. "I never thought about your difficulties."

"Children never do," Shankar said. His bright, black eyes gazed calmly from a smooth brown face. He had worked with Samir seriously on his studies, especially math and science, and had always encouraged him to do well. He attended his extra-curricular activities but perhaps not with the same degree of enthusiasm. Though, Samir was always happy that he went to his events. It was unfair to Samir, Shankar thought, that he couldn't actively lead him into extra-curricular activities because American culture was so foreign to him. He had tried the best he could. But Samir had naturally grown up as an American, absorbing the culture as he went along.

Shankar took a sip of tea. He turned to the backyard. How it had changed in the last few weeks. Nature had woken up. The tulips and daffodils were gone but had been replaced by phlox and Julie's roses. He loved the single fragrant white rose blooming on one plant. The asparagus plants in the vegetable garden looked silky and feathery with fronds of soft green. His son's words came back to him: *I never realized how hard it was for you, not growing up in this culture.*

How right he was. Shankar had no experience of raising a son in America and he had no one to guide him. Raising children in India was easy; one moved along with the strong current of an old society. In his time, fathers didn't participate in activities or take their sons out for fun. No catching balls, no little league. Fathers took care of the family and guided children from a distance. Fathers were loved and respected and obeyed, but they were never close to their children the way American fathers were. Shankar's father, who died long ago, had done everything in life based on his proud brahmin identity and his belief that they were the guardians of an ancient culture. His father's primary emphasis was on maintaining their life as high caste brahmins and leading his son along that same path.

Thinking about his first days in America, how ignorant he was about everything, he chuckled loudly drawing his son's attention. He kept on laughing for a few seconds and finally said, "You wouldn't believe how little I knew about living in America when I first arrived. It's a wonder I could raise you at all."

Samir waited for his father to tell him what was so funny. Shankar kept on laughing, remembering his first semester in Philadelphia. When he finally controlled his laughter, he said, "When I first arrived, I was so ignorant and unprepared! I can laugh now at the things I did. You will too."

"Well let's hear it."

"They aren't flattering. Okay, since I brought it up, I will tell you some."

***

First Semester

I had just arrived in Philadelphia and rented a furnished apartment in a large brick building where other graduate students lived. I was so tired the day I arrived I did not meet any other residents and went to bed. As I came out of the apartment in the morning, I met an older Indian.

I introduced myself as a new student and learned that he had almost finished his Ph.D. thesis. He gave me some advice.

"Never go beyond Market Street after dark," Mr. Deshpande told me, raising his forefinger, and gently wagging it.

I gave him my utmost attention and respect. "Very kind of you to tell me this, sir."

"You aren't in India, my friend." He smiled broadly. "Just call me Ganesh."

"Thank you, sir."

He stared at me for a second. "You'll learn. We live on the second floor; drop by if you need help." He hurried away.

I went to my orientation class in a building covered by ivy leaves. Afterwards, I walked to the cafeteria for lunch. The fragrance of cooked food floated in the air. I had not eaten much that morning, just two slices of bread with scraped-off frozen butter, which wasn't enough to sustain me through the long lectures. I picked up a tray and rushed to the line. But when I reached the food counter, I did not know what to order. I just blurted out, "Is there any spicy food here?"

A thin, black man wearing a tall white hat said, "You'll like the soup today."

I nodded. "Okay, I'll have soup." Then I saw a chubby white man behind the counter wearing a similar hat and carving a big chunk of red meat. I was aghast. *Is that beef?* I wondered.

The black man gave me a bowl of soup. "Bon appetite."

My face shrank, and I could feel nausea rising in me. "Does it have beef in it?" I mumbled, pointing to the bowl of soup.

"No. It's vegetable soup," the man said confidently. His eyes calmly appraised my ignorance.

I looked at the soup again. "What vegetables are these little dark brown pieces?"

"Oh, meat."

"Beef?"

"Yeah, it adds to the flavor."

"But you said it's a vegetable soup."

"It is. Very little meat. You won't even notice it."

I returned the soup. My stomach was roiling. I took roasted chicken that I could identify, boiled potatoes, and rolls and butter. I was here to get a degree, I told myself, not to hanker for rice and curried fish. I sat down at a table with another Indian student. Boiled carrots, broccoli and potato filled his plate; he was obviously a vegetarian. I asked him how he had survived the weekend.

"No problem," he said, moving his head from side to side. "I eat bananas, milk, and Rice Krispies for breakfast and dinner."

When I returned to my apartment, an overwhelming smell of Indian food surrounded me. It was everywhere—in the foyer, on the stairs, and in the hall. I followed the aroma to Mr. Deshpande's apartment, as if I were hypnotized.

"Here's Shankar, the new fellow." Ganesh introduced me to his wife, Kamala.

"Could you teach me how to make some Indian dishes?" I asked her.

"You had your first day at the cafeteria?" Her large, black eyes sparkled. Kamala had long black hair, like my sisters. I liked her immediately.

"Yes. The food was boiled or broiled, not spicy, and had no flavor."

"You'll survive. We've all gone through this. Eat with us tonight, and I'll tell you how to prepare a dish."

I sat down on the sofa. The TV talked about the arrival of more American soldiers in Vietnam.

"Do you want a drink?" Ganesh asked me.

"Yes, that'd be nice."

"Gin or Scotch? That's all we have."

"Alcohol?" I gasped. In India, only bad people and movie stars drank alcohol. And in Indian movies when a man drinks, he misbehaves and often falls asleep in the wrong place. If a woman drinks, she is either a prostitute or so depressed she wants to end her life.

Ganesh winked at me, "When in Rome, behave like the Romans."

My head started to spin. What would Durga say? Then I thought: how could I survive in the West without learning their ways? I was about to say, "Yes, gin and tonic," because I had heard those words in the movies, when suddenly, my left brain kicked in. "No, not tonight. We'll celebrate after I finish the semester."

"Okay, that's a deal."

The classes were another experience altogether. Just three days of classes kept me fully occupied throughout the week. In Calcutta, the students didn't study seriously until two months before the yearly exam; then they crammed like hell. Their whole lives depended on it. I was shocked when, after six weeks at Penn, the electricity and magnetism professor wrote October 22 on the board in big letters. He then smiled broadly and said, "This is the date for the midterm test." I couldn't believe that he was talking about a test in such a jolly manner.

I asked the student sitting next to me, "What test? We just started."

His small pink face, topped with curly red hair, stared at me blankly. "Don't worry, everyone gets a B in grad school."

"Really?"

"Only the top few will get an A."

That student had come from Princeton and had no fear, but I started to have nightmares. The more I thought about the professor's jolly countenance, the more severe my anxiety became. My apartment remained unclean; I ate only rice and boiled chicken with salt and pepper. After dinner, I went back to my office in the physics department to study—every day. I studied hard, memorizing the topics that were taught in the classes, as I would have done in India. Yet I was totally unprepared for the midterm exams. The electricity and magnetism exam was my first test. Unlike an Indian exam, the questions were brand new; none of them resemble the examples in the books I studied. I did the best I could. Then came the quantum mechanics exam, which was open-book—a big surprise. I had never heard of open-book exams. It was unthinkable in India. Students would simply copy answers from the book! What kind of an exam would that be? With some trepidation, I went to the exam with my book and study notes under my arm.

When Dr. Schrieffer came into the room, I had never seen him so cheerful. He scanned the students' faces and flashed a wide and toothy grin. My anxiety skyrocketed. The professor said something in a low voice, and everyone laughed, except me. I sat all serious and wondered how they could take it so lightly? Finally, the professor distributed the test questions.

I searched through the relevant chapters in the book, but there was nothing I could find to copy for answers. I glanced at the student next to me, a graduate from Columbia. He had a pencil in his mouth and stared at the blackboard. I was sure he was adrift and would flunk the test. I saw another student with one foot up on the next chair. Don't they take the exam seriously? I wondered. Anyway, I had wasted a lot of time going through the book. I started to work out the problems. I did what I could.

It was strange—I didn't have to wait for months for the results as we did in Calcutta. The professor returned the test to us at the next class. I got 69 in quantum mechanics. Any mark above 60 was excellent in Calcutta—a first class mark, and exceedingly difficult to achieve. Only a few would get above 60, so I was elated, but only for a moment. The professor explained how the class had fared. I was in the middle of the class. There were probably ten students who had done better. A student from Taiwan got 95.

"It's a C," Peter Hakim, the boy who sat next to me, told me, "bordering on D."

I was devastated. I barely heard the professor's consoling words: "It's only the midterm. You still have a quiz and a final. If you haven't done well, you can make it up. Don't sweat it."

That was easy for him to say. My grades in the other classes were similar. If I didn't do well, I would lose my assistantship and would have to go back to India completely disgraced. The best student from Calcutta couldn't make it in the U.S.!

I remained dazed for a few days. Finally, after a week, amid huge homework assignments, I told Durga in a letter that I got 69 in QM. She wrote me immediately to convey her elation.

I was so depressed I stopped visiting the few acquaintances I had. No weekend get-togethers, no parties, no movies. My friends thought I was studying hard for the final. Well, I was. I studied and studied and studied. Fortunately, I did not have a TV!

Thanksgiving came and everyone left the campus. My host family invited me to celebrate Thanksgiving with them, but I refused. No turkey until I got decent grades! My chicken 'curry and rice' would have to do. I heard there was a wonderful parade downtown with many floats. I asked an American man in the apartment building what a float was. "Will it be something floating in the air?"

After staring at me for a few seconds, he said, "They are decorated exhibits on a rolling platform pulled by a truck and are beautiful to look at."

I kept my eyes on my books. I relaxed only after the semester grades were announced. I did okay. I got one A and two A minuses. Peter got one A minus and two Bs. He was from Cornell, a more prestigious school, certainly deemed much, much better than Calcutta. We did homework together and we had become friends, but Peter was a little miffed. "We'll see how you do next semester."

Exhilarated, I went to Ganesh's apartment. "We can have that drink today."

Kamala was happy to know my semester grades and said, "Let's have dinner first."

"But I'll have to go back to my office after dinner," I told them.

"After you drink?" Kamala asked, smiling, and rolling her eyes.

"Oh! No problem, I can handle it."

Ganesh gave me a gin and tonic.

We sat around and chatted. I loved the gentle lemon flavor of the drink and finished the glass quickly.

"Another?" Ganesh asked.

"Don't give him another drink," Kamala told her husband. "He's not used to drinking."

But I was having a good time. When Ganesh brought me another, I took it greedily.

Suddenly, I understood why this was the favorite drink of the British when they were in India. Then I talked about the freshman girl who came to the coffee machine near my class and said, 'Hi' to me. I talked about the X-rated movie that another foreign student had taken me downtown to see.

"Another drink?" Ganesh asked, but before I could speak, Kamala said sharply, "That's enough."

I got up after dinner. "I must finish my homework for tomorrow."

"Are you sure you want to go to school now?" Ganesh asked me.

"Oh, I'm fine. I'll walk and save the bus fare."

I scuttled straight to my office, laughing all the way—they thought I couldn't reach my office after a drink. What a wonderful evening! I felt like singing.

I opened the door and sat down at my desk. Everything looked bright and gay.

I looked down at the paper on my desk. The words appeared small, so I bent my head down closer.

Then I heard a click. The door opened and the student who shared my office entered, saying, "You're early today!"

I saw bright morning sunlight streaking through the window, and the voices of undergraduate students heading to their first class floated in from the corridor.

I blinked my eyes and tasted gin at the back of my tongue.

***

This is a gem of a story," Samir said, laughing loudly.

"See why I was laughing?" Shankar said and chuckled. "But it wasn't a laughing matter then."

Julie came into the room with a tray of scrambled eggs, bacon, and toast, asking her husband, "What's so funny this morning?"

"Oh nothing," Samir replied. "Baba was just sharing some stories about adjusting to life in the States."

"I'd love to hear those too," Julie told her father-in-law. "Next time please wait for me."

Durga joined them and they directed their attention to eating breakfast and reading the paper.

Chapter Thirty-Two

Night Adventure

"Today I am going to tell you a story when I was very young." Shankar told Raja after his snack. "You know I grew up in Dum Dum, a suburb of Calcutta. In those days, there were fewer houses there."

"Dumb . . . Dumb?" Raja giggled.

"Sounds funny, doesn't it"

"Isn't there something called Dum Dum bullets?" DeeDee asked. She had quietly entered the room and was standing behind the armchair, listening.

"Yes, the British built a factory in Dum Dum to make those bullets. That's how the bullets got their name. Those bullets were awful. If one hit a man, it didn't simply go through his body—it whirled around inside him, causing much pain and a miserable death. Those bullets were banned after a time. No one makes them anymore."

"Good." DeeDee agreed.

"When we first went to Dum Dum, there was nothing much for us to do. We, children, were bored, but a few days later our cousins came for the housewarming celebration. We had lots of fun. I'm going to tell you something we did."

***

Throwing Stones

After we moved into our house in Dum Dum, my father performed the worship service appropriate for entering a new home. This was supposed to bring good luck and happiness for the residents. The house was not complete, but my family wanted to move in. My parents invited all our relatives for the occasion. It was fun for my sisters and I because we got to see our cousins.

The neighborhood was new to us and we roamed around. There were only a few houses. We went by ponds, rice fields and big mango and litchi trees. At night, all the cousins talked together and didn't want to sleep. The adults slept, but the children were still awake. I heard two older cousins talking; one said, "Why don't we go up on the roof of the next house and look around?"

Naturally, I jumped up from my bed and followed them. The house was empty and still under construction. It was supposed to have three stories, and they had poured concrete for the walls and roofs but work on the top floors had not started. We climbed the unfinished stairs, and the rest of the cousins also joined in because they were all awake. Everyone was excited because we were doing something we weren't supposed to do! It was rather dark outside and new construction is always unreliable, though that aroused us even more. Following the oldest cousin's lead, we went on the roof and stood there.

The moon was still low on the horizon. The houses in the neighborhood were cloaked in shadows, and a strange quietness prevailed. Tall coconut trees nearby cast a mystic spell over us. Silence and faint moonlight emerging through the clouds made the atmosphere eerie.

Soon, one house caught our attention—a one-story, square, brick building. Only a small lot separated the house from this one. What fascinated us was it was built around a square opening, with a courtyard in the middle. That's how many houses were built in earlier days, but we didn't know that. The opening allowed light and wind to come in and kept the house cool in the summer. In the half-darkness of the night, the hole looked scary. The oldest cousin, who was 17, said, "That's an ideal place for a ghost to live."

Then, another cousin said, "Look, something is rising from the hole."

All eyes turned to the space above the square opening. Soon we were convinced something was coming out of the hole. The oldest cousin said, "It's a spirit, and it can sense we are here."

I clutched the shirt of the oldest cousin. He said, "I read in a book that ghosts search for openings and go from one house to another."

We looked back at the staircase through which we had come on to the roof. No door had yet been put in place to close it.

I discovered a small mound of bits of bricks on the roof, left by the construction workers. "Can't we drive the spirit away by throwing stones at it?" I asked.

Then the oldest cousin said, "Let's see who can throw a piece of brick right into the hole."

We started to throw bits of brick at the building, but some of us weren't good at throwing, and our stones went all over. We were having such fun we forgot we were trying to scare the spirit away.

Then a light came on in the square house.

"Oops, they are up," one cousin said.

We stopped throwing rocks and stood there quietly to see if someone came outside. The front door opened, and a man came out in the dark. He stared at our roof right away. The oldest cousin quickly said, "Get down the stairs before he finds us here."

We hurried down the stairs, back to our house and our beds, pretending to sleep as if nothing had happened. In the morning, as soon as breakfast was over, the older cousins gathered all of us quickly and took us out for a walk. They were afraid the man from the square house would come over to complain. They didn't want to face him.

When we returned, my uncle asked if we had seen any strange activity during the night. We kept silent and looked at each other. He said, "Our neighbor from the square house came this morning to welcome us. He was pleased we brought children to the neighborhood . . . He invited you all to visit him. Go over there and introduce yourselves. He's quite a nice fellow." My uncle smiled with half of his mouth, as though to stifle a laugh, and went away.

We were dumbfounded and weren't sure what had happened. "It's a trick to punish us," the oldest cousin whispered. "He will force us to apologize."

We decided to avoid the square house and not talk with anyone about their nighttime activity.

Over the next few days, no adult mentioned anything about rock throwing. They seemed to be unaware of it, and we children, almost forgot the event.

After our cousins left and the rock-throwing incident had slipped my mind, I was chasing a ball that had rolled near the square house. As I approached, the neighbor cornered me as if he had been waiting. "Hey, come here." He motioned for me to approach him.

I raised my eyes to a tall, heavy-set man with unkempt bushy hair, and froze.

"Aren't you one of the boys who threw rocks at my house?"

I simply stared and shrank.

"Don't be afraid, I'm not going to punish you. I was awake and watched you boys throwing rocks. A fine job you did." He considered me for a few moments. "You know why?"

I shook my head, only thinking how I could get away.

"See, I never liked the design of the house, but my wife liked it. It's a waste of space and a problem during the rainy season. Birds fly in and out and we get their droppings. Now, because of you, my wife doesn't like it. She says, 'Boys throw stones, and we can get hurt.' See how you have helped me? I can now close it up." He laughed hard and gave me a slap on my back. "Come again and I'll tell you what else you can do for me."

I slowly walked back with the ball, a little dazed.

***

"I can throw stones pretty far, Grandpa," Raja said. "I could have helped him a lot."

"Caught in the act," said DeeDee, laughing. "You're lucky he didn't tell your parents."

Shankar also laughed. "You know, sometimes the temperature gets quite high in India. Your body suffers during the day, and you feel stir crazy. When it's cool at night, your mind thinks of all the naughty things you can do."

"Really? Grandpa!" DeeDee scolded him with an exaggerated eye roll.

Shankar grinned without answering DeeDee.

DeeDee looked at Shankar for a few seconds and asked, "Did Baba know you threw stones at a neighbor's house?"

"Of course not."

"I want to hear about daddy when he was little like us," she said. "Was he a good boy?"

"Your daddy was the best in the world. Ask Grandma, she will tell you. He never did anything bad." Shankar glanced at Raja and said, "Except this one thing. But that is nothing compared to all the things I did in Dum Dum."

DeeDee came closer.

"He must have been bored. I don't know where he got the idea. He cut out the outline of a spider and painted it black and brown. Looked very real. He then bent its legs and made it stand up, big eyes staring as if at prey. He kept it in his school bag. When he saw a girl he knew, he put the spider on his head and casually went closer to her until she noticed it. At first, she stared at the spider, then she screamed loudly, drawing the attention of teachers. But before they came out of their classrooms, your dad put it in his pocket and walked away."

"Very naughty." DeeDee declared.

"Yes." Shankar nodded. "Your Baba has forgotten it now, but I remember when he told me this. He knew girls are scared of spiders."

"I want to do that, Grandpa," Raja clamored, but could not convince his grandfather to help.

The children went away, but Shankar's mind churned. He never told his family that they had thrown rocks at the neighbor's house, but the memory remained with him vividly. His mind lit with an inner revelation. Right from childhood, he had done things that were unusual or inappropriate for his conservative, brahmin family. He had always ventured out beyond the boundaries, even if only a little bit. And he had always kept it to himself when he did. These inclinations were probably borne out of necessity in his father's suffocating household.

***

Samir and Julie read bedtime stories to DeeDee and Raja, but Julie had told Shankar the children would remain wide awake and animated as they recounted what he had told them that day and often retold the stories to her before falling asleep.

One morning Julie told Shankar about the lasting impression he was making on the children. "Last night," Julie chuckled, "DeeDee told me, 'Did you know, Mommy, Grandpa didn't tell his mother all the things he did and shouldn't have done?'"

"Hmmm?" Shankar felt a little bit embarrassed and didn't know how to respond.

Julie's head nodded a bit as she considered the mischievous child who was now her rather-reserved father-in-law. She left with a naughty smile on her face.

Chapter Thirty-Three

Fate

S hankar found Samir quite lively at their next Sunday breakfast. His mood seemed to match the early summer sunshine pouring through the dining room windows. He thought Samir must have saved a patient from the jaws of death. But that was not it. Samir told him he had hired a new pediatric cardiologist from Johns Hopkins for their group. He had been looking for someone to complement his practice in that specialty for some time.

Shankar looked around. Durga had taken the children to the living room. Tea and biscuits were on the table, as well as the Sunday *New York Times*.

"This business of medical practice is a different challenge," Samir said. "Not like teaching at all."

"Your grandfather was a high school teacher," Shankar reminded his son in a playful tone of voice. "I was raised with the ideals of a teacher, like being a guru." He chuckled at the thought of considering himself a guru.

"America is different." Samir poured more tea into his cup and took a biscuit. "I never thought about what life was like for you in a work environment in this culture." He raised his head. "Did you feel at ease . . . I mean comfortable in Ann Arbor?"

Shankar lowered the paper to the table. "At ease in America? . . . Even after I got tenure, I couldn't rest and take it easy. In my time, everyone worked hard for job security and to earn respect from colleagues. I'm sure it is no different now. Work at school, and at home—that was my life." Shankar had almost forgotten those days—rushing to go to work on weekdays, teaching, advising students, preparing the next day's lessons, and grading papers. He often went back to the university on the weekend to stay ahead. Then in the summer, he worked with the faculty in Ann Arbor. He never asked what normal life was in America.

"Baba, people move around here for better opportunities, but you stayed in Michigan. I liked Ann Arbor, but I wonder."

"Sometimes I wonder if it was fate." He took a deep breath and slowly exhaled. "I had to accept what came to me—no choice. I wanted to continue my research in physics, but there were not many opportunities for me." His lips tightened into a hard line. He shifted his view to the backyard, unable to forget that stressful time in life.

Samir's voice brought him back. "We like Bellport. We plan to stay here."

"That would be good for DeeDee and Raja," Shankar agreed.

"It was great that you stayed in one place. Good for me, at least."

Shankar did not believe in predetermined destiny, but he thought that some people appear to have better luck than others, somehow. This is what Indians describe as fate.

While Shankar was absorbed in how much fate had played a role in his life, his daughter-in-law entered the room.

"What do you want for breakfast today?" Julie asked, emanating cheery energy. She was wearing navy blue jeans and a white blouse with embroidered pink and red flowers with a draw string at the neck.

Samir gazed at her appreciatively. She surely had a good night's rest and looked lovely.

"Sit with us and have tea first."

She sat down, took a Britannia tea biscuit from a plate in the middle of the table, and stirred some milk into the cup Samir handed her.

"The weather seems to be getting warmer every day; it makes me happy." She savored the flavor of the milky tea and noticed a pensive expression on her father-in-law's face. "What has you two looking so serious this morning?"

"Samir and I were talking about how we ended up where we are . . . you know, fate, if you will."

"Fate?" Julie raised her eyebrow, tilting her head.

"What comes into your life—despite all your attempts otherwise—is your fate. So, if your strivings fail, you accept the situation, saying 'It was not in my fate!' and carry on. Blaming the result on 'my fate' gives you a little solace."

"Here we like to challenge and master our destiny," Julie said confidently. Shankar didn't reply. The face of a water carrying man came to him, dark and shiny from staying in the sun. "When I was a child," he said abruptly, "one man delivered drinking water to many houses in my maternal uncle's village. He was supposed to be a farmer. In his youth, he tried to get away from farming, but when he failed, he accepted what came to him."

Samir quietly observed the budding conversation between his wife and father. Julie gazed at her father-in-law's weary expression for a moment. "What made you remember this man now?"

"I was wondering," Shankar murmured, "if I've done almost the same thing as the water carrying man."

"What happened to him?" Julie asked.

The image of the man came to Shankar again. "I might as well tell you his story."

***

Water Carrying Man

As a young boy, I was fascinated by the muscular physique of the water carrying man. He didn't wear a shirt—only a cloth around his waist. He carried water pots on both ends of a bamboo pole on his shoulder and delivered water from door to door. Darkened by the sun, his muscles glistened. I asked him why he carried brass pots instead of clay pots. 'Babu-sahib,' the man said, looking at me, 'they won't break if I slip and fall down.' His face didn't show any sign of sarcasm or a smile; he simply stated the fact.

One day the man rested a little longer at our house and I asked him how he had become a water carrying man.

"It's my fate, Babu-sahib." He gazed straight into my eyes. "It's all fate." He looked at the ground. "I was born into a farming family, but I did not want to be a farmer. My family struggled too much. The government demanded more and more taxes, and if the weather was bad, we were doomed. All our labor was gone for nothing. Right from my childhood I wasn't fond of working on the farm. I wanted to go to the city."

"Did you go to Calcutta?" I asked.

"Yes, Babu-sahib. When I was eighteen, I ran away." There was a peculiar glint in his eyes, and he glanced up with a jerk.

"My uncle used to take me to Calcutta on the tram, and I liked it. Didn't you like the big city?" I persisted.

"The city was fine. But it didn't like me." The water carrying man stared at his pots on the ground. "The city is cruel, Babu-sahib." He lifted his pots and walked away to his next customer. I was a young boy at the time and didn't understand what he meant. How could the city be cruel?

A few days later, he told me more. The water carrier's name was Satish. When Satish went to Calcutta, he hadn't known anyone there. He wandered about the city, looking for work. He slept at the train station, but soon his money ran low.

It was early summer, and a man suggested he could sell green coconuts. People love to drink green coconut water, and the man told him he could make good money. The same man sold him green coconuts at 30 paisa each and told Satish he could sell them for 50, even 60 paisa or more. He gave him a bunch of straws and a heavy knife to cut the green coconuts. Satish sold a few immediately. He found he could make enough to buy his daily food. Then one day it was hot, and he moved to a street lined with trees in the center of the city and stood in the shade. He thought he was lucky to find the spot. Another man was also selling green coconuts, but that man stayed out at the corner under the blazing sun. After a little while, Satish saw the man pack up his green coconuts and run away. Before he knew what was happening, a policeman was standing in front of him.

"No selling of green coconuts on this street!" he shouted at him. "Didn't you see the sign at the corner?"

Dumbfounded, Satish stared at him. Then the policeman asked him in a lower voice, "Are these sweet?"

"Yes, sir. I sell them for 50 paisa."

"Fifty paisa! Are you asking money from me?" He gave him a blow on his shoulder and took out his baton to beat him. "Out of here!"

Satish pleaded with him. "Sir, I have spent all my money to buy these green coconuts. I have no money left. I'll starve."

The policeman only shouted at him. "Get out of here, or I'll put you in jail."

Another policeman started loading his green coconuts in a van. Satish got a severe beating when he tried to protest.

He wandered in the streets—hungry and tired, looking for work, any work. After a few days, he found a job in a sweets shop. It was a big outfit and he eagerly agreed to be their deliveryman. They had several stores in the city and catered sweets for weddings and other occasions. The storeowner was mean and paid him little for the huge amount of work he asked Satish to do. He gave him one rupee a day, and that was fine with Satish, but then the storeowner kept half of the money as a deposit, to be given back later. A large part of the other half he charged for giving Satish a corner of the store to sleep in (and guard the store) and for the leftover food he served him.

One-time Satish asked for some of his money. The owner looked at him angrily. "Do you want this job or not?"

"Yes, sir," Satish told him humbly. "I want the job."

"Then go back to work." He cast a contemptible look at Satish. "You should thank God I have given you a job at all."

Satish didn't know what to do. The work was hard. He carried sweets to different stores from morning till night. At night he was so tired, he had no energy left, and he simply fell asleep. He dreamed of the green fields and the ponds in his village—how nice his life had been back on the farm. But he couldn't think of going back because he had little money, and it would be such a disgrace to return empty-handed.

The owner gave him a few pennies once in a while, but then if he made a mistake or was late in delivering sweets, he deducted money from his account. And Satish was often late because Calcutta was crowded, day and night, and the buses, trams, and traffic had no mercy for a sweets-carrying man.

Once he was an hour late and the owner slapped him. "Never goof off again."

"A procession held me up," he muttered, hoping for a little sympathy, but the owner only growled.

One day he was carrying a delivery, eight earthen pots of sweet yogurt for a wedding. The pots fit snugly on the two ends of a pole on his shoulder, but it was drizzling, and he slipped in a puddle of water and fell down. The earthen vessels hit the ground and two broke. Yogurt spilled onto the footpath. The air became heavy and sweet with the fragrance of it.

A crowd gathered around him. One man said, "That poor man should've been more careful carrying these earthen pots." Another man said, "So much good yogurt wasted!" But they could do nothing for him and left. A dog came and started to eat the spilled yogurt.

Satish sat where he had fallen; his throat was choked. Tears came to his eyes. He knew the store owner would beat him to death. It was an accident, but there was no way he could explain this to the store owner. Sitting there, he gazed at the moving trams and buses. The traffic was monotonous—trams, buses, cars, rickshaws, and streams of people. As if in a trance, he observed the hurried feet passing by—thin, fat, fair, olive, dark. After some time, he looked around and saw only faceless people. He searched his clothes and found a few rupees. He got up and started to walk, away from where he was supposed to deliver the sweet yogurt, and away from the store. He walked in a daze and eventually reached a train station. He bought a ticket to a place as far away as he could get from the city.

"So, is this where you wound up?" Shankar asked him.

"Yes, Babu-sahib."

"How far is your village from here?"

"I don't exactly remember." He picked up his water pots and started to walk toward his next destination.

***

That's so sad, grandpa." DeeDee said from behind him. Shankar didn't notice she had come to the breakfast room. "Couldn't the man go back to his village and be a farmer?"

"He said he didn't know his village anymore." Shankar told her. But he knew that this was the man's way of saying he didn't really want to return.

"He didn't finish school, that's why." DeeDee's words brought Shankar back.

"Right." He pulled her closer, impressed with her comment. "If he had finished high school, he could have gotten a better job, and wouldn't have ended up like that." Shankar looked tenderly at his granddaughter. "What does that tell you?"

"Study hard." She giggled and left.

Shankar chuckled. That was exactly what he wanted her to say.

Julie Looked at her father-in-law's face for a few seconds. "Baba, you aren't like the water-carrying man at all! You've done so much in your life. You didn't give up and accept what came to you."

"I've always done the best I could with the opportunities I had. I wonder if I could have done more but didn't try."

Julie shook her head. "Coming from such a different country as India, establishing yourself in this culture and retiring as a respected, tenured professor of physics is a lot to be proud of."

"Thank you, Julie," Shankar said but he couldn't get rid of a wish that his life were different. He took a sip of tea and turned to the backyard. He knew the water-carrying man endured his life in a sort of stupor. He didn't have energy left to take on another challenge.

Reality had trained him. He could have been a respected professor at a more reputed Indian university and have done his own research, in whatever meager way possible there. But, no, like the water-carrying man, he had accepted his life as a 'nobody' in a foreign place. Fate! He could not have gone back to the society dominated with conservative ideas like his father's and let Samir grow up in that environment. Julie was also right. He was not like the water-carrying man. He had learned and adapted from each incident of his youth since the time he had defiantly cut off his tiki. He began to chuckle remembering how calmly he had dealt with a childhood predicament because of a beautiful kite with a mossy green parrot picture and won a kite fight.

Chapter Thirty-Four

The God of Engineering

S chools closed for the summer and the children kept Shankar fully engaged, even dragging him to the backyard to work with them on their gardens. Raja wanted Shankar to participate in all his activities. He brought out his baseball bat from the basement and asked Shankar to throw him balls. He wanted to practice for the Little League tryouts. DeeDee wanted him to throw softballs. And they both asked for stories during the hot part of the day when they were inside. Shankar insisted they work on math with him regularly, although he knew American children usually didn't study much during summer. He welcomed all these activities as they kept him fully occupied.

One day, Samir told him, "Baba, I like it very much that you tell DeeDee and Raja stories from your childhood. You told me some when I was growing up, but not all that much." Shankar listened but didn't say anything. After some time, Samir said, "I guess most fathers are more reserved with their children. Same thing with me. I cannot tell my children stories of my childhood as I probably would with my grandchildren."

Shankar agreed. "I want them to know how we grew up without fancy toys. We played with everyday things around us and made up our own games, but we were happy. It was a different world."

"I hope you'll tell them more of your stories. That way they'll learn about their heritage."

That Saturday afternoon, Shankar and DeeDee sat in the garden in the shade of the walnut tree. A perfect summer day with a few silvery clouds drifting in the azure sky. Shankar read a book while DeeDee threaded a necklace of sea glass beads. Raja, in dark blue shorts and no shirt, played with a fire truck near the rose bed. Flower hung around him, sometimes running around the backyard chasing rabbits or birds, but then came back to Raja. Shankar heard the humming of an old Bengali tune and saw Durga crooning in the flower garden. She weeded the flowers blooming profusely in Julie's garden. Shankar thought the sweet Bengali song was the result of her joy in the rose garden. Gardening was her hobby in Ann Arbor. She loved roses, but few species survived the harsh winters there—two zones colder than Bellport.

DeeDee interrupted his reverie. "Grandpa, did you have radio-controlled planes when you were young?" She was gazing at the sky, her glossy black hair falling on her back.

Shankar turned his gaze toward the jet overhead.

"We had not even heard of radio-controlled planes. We flew kites."

"Two boys in my class go to Fire Island to fly planes!" She held the sea glass necklace in front of her, looking at the arrangement of colors. "Jimmy says he'll show me how to fly his plane, if I want to."

"You can learn a lot about planes and electronics. See what Jimmy does and if you want to do that. We had lots of fun with kites.

"Kites are no fun," DeeDee murmured. "It's just holding a string."

Shankar shook his head, "No, no. We could manipulate our kites very well; we could make them go up and down, or sideways." His shiny brown face glistened in the sun. "We even had kite *fights*."

"Fights in the air?" Raja abandoned his truck and came over. His eyes shimmered with curiosity.

"Yes." Shankar turned to Raja and noticed how prominent the collarbones in his bony frame were. "In kite fights, we try to cut the string of the opponent's kite. I was particularly good at it. I was the champion among the boys."

Raja interrupted Shankar, "Grandpa, are those kites like ours?"

Shankar paused, realizing the children had no understanding of what he was telling them. "Indian kites aren't like the sturdy plastic kites people fly in America. They are diamond shaped, flat, about two feet by two feet, and made of thin, lightweight, colored paper. They have little tails like a fish; a big tail would spoil its maneuverability in a fight. Two thin bamboo sticks hold a kite flat: one runs vertically straight and the other, a little longer stick, runs side to side, arched between the other two corners."

"Where do they attach the string?" Raja was now concentrating intensely on Shankar's words.

"A kite comes with a short string attached at the crossing of the two sticks and at six to eight inches below it on the vertical stick. We tie our line to this short string, forming a triangle," Shankar told Raja.

"They are flat and rather plain," Raja said.

"But they look beautiful when they are up in the sky. Many had fantastic designs on them, a peacock, a rainbow, a fat candle with a flame, and many others." He looked up in the sky as if looking for one.

"Grandpa, can we fly a kite here, and have it fight with other kites?"

"People don't do that here." Shankar looked at Raja tenderly. How different his life was at Raja's age!

"Tell us about kite fights, Grandpa," Raja pleaded, hugging his grandfather's arm. "It sounds like fun."

"Let me tell you how a boy tried to steal my secret for winning kite fights."

DeeDee set aside the beads and pulled her chair closer.

***

Kite Fight

There's a special day in Calcutta when all men—young and old—fly kites, filling the sky with color. That is the day of Vishwakarma puja. Vishwakarma is the god of engineering. The day has never been spoiled by rain, or even clouds. We knew it as the day for kite fights.

Flying a kite is easy, but flying it well is an art; it requires good science and engineering. And you must practice a lot. I used to long for this day when we could have kite fights—all day long.

Kite fights have no rules. If there is a kite in the sky, you can fight with it. If you don't want to fight, you take your kite down. When a kite gets its string cut, no one can complain. It then falls and the boys run after it. A good kite flyer can sometimes catch a falling kite with the string of his own kite while the loose kite is still in the air. He maneuvers his kite toward the falling kite, tangles its string with his string, and reels both kites in. Most of the time, though, the kite falls to the earth. Then whoever catches the kite, it's his—the kite and the string that comes with it. The owner can't claim it back. Running after a falling kite is as much fun as flying one. Sometimes the falling kite gets stuck in a tree or on a roof. One of the boys climbs up and gets it.

One day I was running after a falling kite, a gorgeous one with a picture of a moss-green parrot. I got ahold of the string first, but Jiten, who was a little taller than me, caught the kite. Jiten said, 'I'll give you the kite if you tell me how you prepare your string. Otherwise, I'll punch a hole in it.' The parrot was so beautiful; I really wanted it. Jiten's long, thin face was serious. And I saw his fingers rolled into a fist. I told him he could watch how I did it. He agreed and I took the kite home.

Kite fighting isn't a casual business; great care goes into its preparation—from selecting the perfect kite and string, to finding the perfect reel, the lattai, to hold the string. However, the outcome of a kite-fight depends largely on the quality of the string. When a kite fight takes place, the lines of the two kites cross and the string that slices through the other string wins. We buy a fine, strong string, and glue glass powder onto it. The sharp glass grains will cut the other string. The glass powder must be perfect, the grains not too large and not too powdery. That's the trick. Everybody does this, but it must be done very skillfully. If the line is too heavy, the kite won't fly smoothly; if we don't apply enough glass powder, it will lose in a kite fight.

During a fight, you pull your string very fast so your line will saw through the other kite's string. Sometimes we cut our fingers on strings covered with glass powder. At that time, we don't think of our fingers. We think about winning.

Jiten came over to watch my preparation. I had already collected plenty of broken glass from medicine and soda bottles, broken glasses, and such. I put all this in a heavy iron mortar that looked like a large beer mug. I used an iron pestle to carefully smash the glass, covering the mortar with a cloth so glass bits wouldn't fly around.

After watching me for some time, Jiten thought he had made a discovery. 'Ah! Blue glass, eh?' His small eyes opened wide, making his narrow face appear funny to me. He gaped at the glass powder.

I told him, 'Thin glass is better than heavy bottles,' as if I were giving him further tips. I kept on grinding the glass until it became a powder. I let him help finish the grind.

'So, this is your secret!' Jiten chuckled because he now knew how to defeat me. I asked him, 'Do you use freshly cooked, soft rice?'

'Yes, I know all that.' He chortled. 'Now we'll see who wins this year.' He raised his forefinger at me. 'I shall cut all your kites.' He went away.

Cooked rice is the glue. You mix rice with glass powder until they make a smooth paste, and then you apply it on the string very carefully. You tie the string between two posts or trees and first apply the paste with your hand. You squeeze out excess with your thumb and forefinger. Your fingers hurt because you do it for such a long string, often 500 yards or more. You then let it dry in the sun. As it dries, it becomes very sharp and can cut your skin easily.

Jiten told everyone he knew my secret and he was going to sever everyone's strings and win that year. He soon had a few boys with him collecting blue glass from all around. When they had a good amount, Jiten was confident of winning and came to tell me, 'If you win this year, I'll give you five kites. And if you lose you give me five.'

I said, 'Accha! Fine.'

Jiten went away happy.

When the Vishwakarma puja day arrived, I went to the roof of our house early in the morning. There were only a few kites in the sky. I flew several kites to test them out. Slowly the kite flying gathered momentum and by midday everyone was involved.

On this day, young and old gather on rooftops, in parks and on the soccer fields. Everyone is agitated. The sky becomes colorful with kites everywhere. They will shout 'Bho-Kattaaa,' an expression of victory when they cut the string of the opponent's kite. The person who loses the kite reels his string back in and launches another. The afternoon sky is an aerial battlefield with shouts of 'Bho-Kattaaa' coming from all over.

I spotted Jiten flying his kite from the roof of his house. I had been waiting for this moment. Before Jiten could recognize my kite, I maneuvered my string under his in one swoop, then pulled my string very fast, raising my kite high in the sky and cutting through Jiten's string! 'Bho-Kattaa,' I shouted with joy. Jiten stared back at me incredulous.

I raised my lattai in one hand and danced a little victory jig on the roof.

***

"I don't get it," Raja said. "What was your secret, then?"

Tapioca!" Shankar shouted with a laugh.

"Tapioca?" DeeDee repeated with glee. "Instead of boiled rice, you used tapioca? That's smart, Grandpa. Tapioca is gross, but I bet it's pretty hard when it dries."

"Thin glass or blue glass has nothing to do with it. What counts is how finely you put the glass powder on your string. And he never knew it." Shankar laughed contentedly.

Durga came over to find out the origin of Shankar's belly laughs. Raja told her, "Grandpa was telling us about kite fights."

"Boys from Calcutta get overly excited about kites and fireworks," she said and grinned at Shankar as she went back to her garden.

Raja returned to playing with fire trucks and DeeDee went back to her necklace, leaving Shankar alone with his thoughts.

Shankar found he was happy during kite flying seasons because his father showed no interest in kites and left him alone. Kite flying and fights had no barrier of caste, religion or whether one was rich or poor. His dilemma with Jiten taught him a great lesson about how to carry on without giving in to immediate circumstances. He didn't want to disclose his secret to Jiten and he didn't know how to outsmart him at the time, but he kept his cool. Jiten had simply provided the opportunity! Shankar had learned from the instance that people with fixed ideas often stumble because of their pride and hasty judgment. Their family lost a fine teacup because his father had thought his guest, Saurabh Ranjan, was not a brahmin. Shankar's mother had to throw away the cup. The lesson of the kite fight must have remained in his subconscious during his forbidden romance. A warm feeling radiated in his heart.

Chapter Thirty-Five

The Bellport Library

Shankar had become acquainted with the Bellport Public Library after he first went to consult the librarian about the latest books on cosmology. Shankar loved the library's peaceful atmosphere, cozy padded armchairs, and the large collection of science magazines. One day, as he walked to the library, he thought of DeeDee's question and chuckled.

"Did Baba ever do anything that you didn't want him to do?"

Sure, children were always curious about their fathers, if they ever did naughty things like they had done or were contemplating. *"No, not that I know of,"* he told her.

She pressed harder, *"Never?"*

He remembered his careful answer. *"No, not really. Your Baba was a good boy. He listened to us. The only incident I remember was when he got ahead of himself. Once, on a field trip to a hilly, rocky area, instead of keeping close to the group, he enthusiastically ran to a rocky cliff face and climbed up high, like a little monkey. He did that on his own. But then realizing how high he was and how dangerous a fall would be, he was afraid to descend. He was stuck. Luckily, an experienced climber was with the group and he talked your dad through it. We held our breaths—afraid he might fall and hurt himself."*

"That was not mischievous." DeeDee had said. *"Did Baba ever get into a fight with anyone? Like I see some boys do."*

"Nope. Not that I know of."

She was satisfied and went away, but Shankar knew she would return with more queries, especially when he told them the things he did in his own childhood. Was it wrong to tell them his mischiefs?

He should take caution in future over how to tell them, but those came out spontaneously and he felt so inclined to share with them. Memories of his early childhood activities flowed through him easily and fondly, and the children loved to hear them too. The thing was those memories also made him melancholy as they reminded him of what happened later in his life. He wished to forget that part completely, but he could not stop those bitter memories from rising. The sadness and anger that he had suppressed for many decades were coming out. The library was pleasant. Here he did not think of his past—only new frontiers of science. He started to spend more time in the library during weekdays.

"You must be very interested in the progress of science." He heard a man saying, with a hint of a foreign accent.

Shankar turned around from the magazine shelf and saw a well-dressed man, about his own age, perhaps a little older, grinning at him.

"I've seen you here several times, so thought to introduce myself. My name is Jacco Bruin."

Shankar shook his hand and introduced himself. It turned out Mr. Bruin lived nearby in Brookhaven Hamlet. He was a retired businessman.

"A physicist! So, you read science articles," Jacco said. "I come to read about WWII, especially the human stories of the 40's from Europe."

Jacco had a gregarious spirit, and they became good companions, exchanging stories from their lives. He was from Holland originally and was rescued by the Americans from a German camp in his teens.

"We have both kept a little of our accents," he joked the next time they met. "I tried but couldn't get rid of my Dutch accent."

Shankar asked him casually, but full of curiosity, "Do you visit Holland often?"

Jacco's face took on a grim expression. "I have no one left in Holland. My entire family died during the war."

Shankar quickly apologized. "Sorry, I didn't mean to recall your past tragedy."

"It's all right. My father was shot by the Nazis, and we weren't very close with our other relatives. I'm not sure what happened to them, though, I'm afraid to find out."

"I have also not gone back to India . . . but for a different reason." Shankar admitted, but didn't elaborate.

Jacco became another reason for Shankar to visit the library. They both had a plethora of immigrant experiences to share and stories to tell about their own lives. Jacco became a pleasant addition to Shankar's life—two retired men commiserating in one corner of the library.

No one was alone with their memories of suffering from the past.

Chapter Thirty-Six

Eating Chicken

DeeDee was marking capitals of countries on an outline of the world map. When she came to India, she lifted her face and looked toward her grandfather on the porch, enjoying the warmth of the sunlight. She addressed him a little loudly, "Grandpa, the Himalayas are so tall. Could you see the peaks from your home in Calcutta?"

"Oh no." Shankar turned toward her. "They are far away from Calcutta. I saw those peaks only when I went to visit my aunt in North Bengal. I was in college then. The Himalayas were still 50 miles farther north, but I could see a long range of white peaks from my aunt's place."

"They look so close on the map."

Shankar went back to reading the paper. He was pleased that she was studying diligently.

After a while, DeeDee came to the porch through the French doors. "Mommy said we're going on a picnic tomorrow." She beamed.

Shankar put the *New York Times* aside, allowing the sunshine to warm his face. He looked at his granddaughter, her black hair shimmering in the light. "A picnic?"

"We're going to the Cold Spring Harbor State Park – she says it's never as crowded after school starts even if the weather is still nice. We'll go on a hike too."

"I guess this is a nice time for a family picnic—not too warm but just warm enough. I'll take a book. I can't go on steep hikes."

"Daddy said he'll bring goodies from the bakery near his office," she reported, bouncing up and down on her toes. "And Mommy said she'll bake chicken with almond coating—my favorite!"

Shankar raised his head and looked for a minute at the backyard, verdant with bright autumn flowers, chrysanthemums, asters, and especially bright velvety blue Veronica flowers and the little white Autumn Clematis flowers in Julie's garden. He remembered a picnic he and his high school friends had hurriedly organized one autumn. A smile spread across his face. It was undertaken solely for the purpose of eating chicken; there was no hiking or going to a nice park. "You know, we never ate chicken in our home in India."

DeeDee frowned. "Why not?"

"My family wouldn't allow it. We ate fish, goat meat, lamb—but never chicken. Chickens were not even allowed near our house. 'They aren't clean,' my mother said."

"So, you never even tasted chicken?"

"No, no," he laughed. "I ate chicken in restaurants when I went to college, but never in our home." A fond smile came to his lips. "They cook excellent chicken cutlets—crunchy and spicy."

"Never at home?" She put her hand on his shoulder.

"Well, my friends and I went on a picnic once and cooked chicken at someone's house. At first, I was a little afraid. I wasn't sure what would happen if I ate it! I also worried about the reaction from my parents."

"Your mother didn't mind?"

"She didn't know." Shankar pushed back a wisp of white hair from his forehead. "You see, it isn't forbidden in the Hindu religion. It was that the Muslims raised chickens; so, the Hindus wouldn't let chickens in the house. The Muslims came to India as invaders. Even though that happened centuries ago, the Hindus wanted nothing to do with them—although some ate eggs."

"Funny, you have to go away to eat chicken." After a few seconds, she asked, "Is that what you do during a picnic?"

"Yeah, that's what we called a picnic. It is like an adventure!"

"Weird. Tell me more about your picnic." She plopped herself down onto the wicker patio chair.

***

Indian Picnic

One Saturday afternoon, five of us, high school friends, had no plans for any activity. Bikash, Debjit, Shibu, Soumen and I sat in the small neighborhood park, eating peanuts with green *tetul chutney* and longed very much to do something interesting. We were about fifteen years old. Debjit said his uncle had a second house in Barasat, twenty miles away; we could go there. That caught our fancy.

"We can go for a picnic," I said.

"I always wanted to cook chicken." Shibu's face lit up in anticipation.

"We haven't done this before; it would be great fun." Bikash clapped his hands.

I also liked the idea. Once Shibu cooked goat meat curry for us—so wonderful we never forgot it. I looked forward to his cooking.

"My aunt would be mad," Debjit said, alarmed, "if she knew we cooked chicken in her kitchen." His face became pensive. He was the first among us to develop a distinct mustache; now this made him look somber.

I was the only brahmin among these friends. I wanted to do it, but only if I could be sure my family would not find out. I said, "But no one should know about it, especially my family and Debjit's aunt."

"You said your aunt and uncle rarely go to Barasat. How would she know?" Bikash asked Debjit.

Shibu promised Debjit they would clean the place so completely no one would even know they had been there.

"I'll be in big trouble," Debjit said weakly, "if my aunt even suspects it. She may not let me enter their house again."

"Don't worry," Shibu assured him, "there won't be a trace of chicken anywhere."

"I'll make sure about it," Soumen added.

Debjit's uncle gave him the key without hesitation. He was happy knowing we would check on the empty house. "My uncle would have joined us, but he had to attend a meeting to organize the local Durga puja." We were relieved. Our plan remained intact.

We started early in the morning. The train journey was wonderful because few people traveled on Sundays and we found empty seats. As the train chugged along, densely packed houses gave way to green villages. I loved looking at banana trees at the back of houses and green rice fields waving in the wind. Shibu and Bikash sang Tagore songs. Debjit played drums on the wooden seat. Time passed by quickly till we reached Barasat.

We went straight to the market near the station. There were vendors on both sides of the narrow road and shoppers everywhere. We saw many vegetables on the street; all appeared freshly brought for the market. A cow ate green leaves discarded near the edge of the market. Fish and goat meat were sold inside a tin shed; a fishy smell surrounded the area. But no chicken anywhere.

We walked along and finally found live chickens at the very end. Two sellers kept them in round cane baskets—about a foot high and four feet in diameter—covered with loose nets. The thin, middle-aged vendors had unkempt goatees and wore checkered lungi that we associated with Muslim men. Their grayish undershirts seemed not to have been washed for several days. We hesitated for a few seconds, then quickly diverted our gaze to the chickens. They were of many different sizes and colors. Their round eyes appeared alert, and they moved their heads constantly to look around. Strangely, they made little noise.

"I guess," Soumen said, "we will have goat curry. That's fine with me."

"After coming this far, we cannot give up now," Shibu said. "We can cut chickens."

Soumen agreed. "That will be another experience for us."

We bought two of the largest—one mottled yellow and brown and one dark red. The seller tied their legs with a cord to carry them, feet facing the sky. Initially they cawed and flapped their wings, but they soon quieted down. As we walked along in the direction of the house, we saw a sweets store and bought the best sweets the place had. Then Bikash slowed down when he saw a well-kept restaurant, *Mughlai Khana*, and said, "Why don't we buy Mutton kababs for tea?"

Shibu glanced at the restaurant skeptically. "Are you sure they don't serve beef there?"

"It's a restaurant in Barasat, a Hindu town," Bikash said. "They wouldn't dare." He walked straight in and bought kababs. We were in a good mood and excited because everything we did felt like crossing a line we weren't supposed to cross. We were also cheerful because Shibu, our great cook, was with us.

When we arrived at the house, the sun was already high, but we were in no hurry. The one-story stucco house was whitewashed and had many green shutters. We entered through the main door and opened all the windows to remove the musty smell. The vertical iron bars over the windows were thick and painted green. The red cement floors of the drawing room and the kitchen felt cool and pleasant. After we examined the rooms and the kitchen we went to the backyard where we would kill the chickens. The large walled garden had several trees; the grass hadn't been cut for some time, but we didn't care.

Shibu brought out the chickens and left them outside the door, plainly in our view. Bikash took out badminton rackets, and Debjit and I rushed to select our rackets immediately. It was clear: everyone wanted to delay the killing.

We kept playing badminton. When we couldn't postpone the killing any longer, no one wanted to do the job. Debjit and Bikash were quick to claim they didn't know how.

"Cowards," I called them in an annoyed voice. "Give me a big knife, and I'll show you."

Debjit brought the chickens to the middle of the backyard where they immediately started to squawk and thrash about violently.

Bikash held down the red chicken and ordered, "Don't take too long."

"As if you know what to do!" I shot back. I held the head and started to cut the neck, but the knife was not sharp enough. My hand trembled. The chicken moved frantically. My heart beat fast. I became nervous and felt I couldn't do the job. But then Soumen, who was standing next to me, shouted, "Press hard." I closed my eyes and pressed hard. Blood squirted and Bikash let go of the chicken. It flew twenty feet while I had its little red, wet, slippery head in my hand. More blood came out of its throbbing body all over the green grass. It was unbelievable. I felt bad and fatigued; remorse washed over me. I had deliberately killed a living being. My father would be furious if he knew. I couldn't cut the second chicken. Shibu had to do it.

Plucking feathers was another job. We didn't know how, so it took a long time. Feathers flew all over the backyard. Exhausted, we all agreed we must have tea now.

"And kababs," Bikash added.

We'd clean the garden later.

Shibu gutted and cut the chickens in the kitchen. We admired his zeal. He was a little heavier set than us, and with his shirt off and long black hair and heavy eyebrows, he looked like the chefs who cook at weddings. We felt he was perfect for the job. I stood near him, ready to help, but really to watch. Debjit sipped tea and furtively glanced at the door. Only Bikash got involved with Shibu, handing him utensils and spices. Bikash was the smallest among us, but he was quick on his feet and always helpful.

Shibu sautéed onions with fresh ginger, garlic, and whole red chilies; he put in the chicken pieces and then stirred in turmeric and a little cumin and coriander powder. He kept on frying the pieces. He added cinnamon sticks, whole cardamoms, and a few cloves. When the chicken pieces turned brown, he filled the pot with water to boil the meat. A spicy aroma filled the room.

We stood around chatting and waiting for the meat to be cooked. Shibu remained busy; he started rice and cleaned the stove area. We expected the chicken to take a long time to cook, as it takes for goat meat, but the chicken was done quickly. We had hoped for a dry, spicy chicken curry, but to our astonishment the water level in the pot didn't reduce much. It seemed more water had come out of the chicken and the dish became a soup—a yellow broth with chunks of white meat. Not appetizing at all.

Shibu sighed. "I guess you don't cook chicken like goat meat."

We each took a little chicken curry and rice, but as I looked at the pale white meat on my plate, a feeling of revulsion arose in me. Then I noticed tiny bits of onions from the gravy on my rice. Alarm bells went off in my head. Somehow, I controlled myself, tasted a little and found it pretty bad. Bikash, Soumen, and Debjit didn't like it either. The meat was tasteless, and we couldn't mix rice with the watery gravy—the way we like to eat. We quickly finished what little we took on our plates and didn't go for seconds.

We relished the sweets though and went out to play in the backyard.

Debjit suggested we should clean the backyard first, but we ignored him and started to play badminton again. The sun slid down the sky, but we kept on playing.

We forgot about time, heard a knock at the front door and were surprised. Who would come to visit now? We rushed to the door and saw a short, stout man with a round face. It was Debjit's uncle. We couldn't speak for a few seconds and stood there in front of him.

He broke the silence. "Ah! How do you like the place?"

Debjit quickly pulled him inside the house, while the rest of us rushed to collect the chicken feathers. But we weren't fast enough; his uncle saw us and came out. We avoided his gaze but saw the shocked expression on his face. He walked around, surveying the mess in the yard. His face became grim. "Where did the chicken feathers come from?"

We didn't answer him and kept on picking up the feathers.

"Hmmm, you boys cooked chicken?" He turned to Debjit. "You know what your aunt would do?" His annoyed voice sent a shiver down our spines.

Debjit avoided his eyes and meekly said, "They wanted to try out a new dish."

"I don't know what to tell your aunt," he said to Debjit. "She wants to spend some time here next week, so I came to fix a few things." He then turned toward us. "You fellows clean up the backyard. I don't want to see a trace of chicken here."

Bikash was quick to respond. "We'll remove all the feathers; no one will ever know a chicken was here."

His uncle stooped down to see how tall the grass was. "You guys can help me cut the grass. Then we'll be sure." His voice softened slightly. "I've never had home-cooked chicken. How does it taste?" he asked Debjit.

"Not good," we all told him almost in unison.

He went inside and Shibu followed him.

Debjit looked disheartened and glum. He started to gather the feathers as fast as he could, but Bikash and I were slower—we felt so sorry for what might happen to Debjit we couldn't focus on cleaning. Bikash collected the feathers near the house, but I took a bag and followed a trail to the farthest part of the garden. I wanted to stay away from Debjit's uncle. We all did. We were caught and didn't want to face him. I even looked under the flower bushes. We stayed out as long as we could. Finally, when we couldn't find any more feathers, we went inside.

The three of us stopped short at the door, staring at the scene. Debjit's eyes almost bugged out of his head and his mouth fell open. His uncle was sitting comfortably in a chair with a brass plate in his hand, happily eating. Shibu stood at his elbow with the pot of chicken in one hand and a serving spoon in the other. "Quite good," he was saying to Shibu. "You said you put in a lot of garam masala?" A convivial grin spread over his face as Shibu nodded.

"Shall I give you a little more?"

"Well," he said, looking at Shibu, "don't you want to leave some for your friends?" But he passed his plate for more.

"No, no," Shibu told him emphatically. "They had plenty. Please finish what's left in the pot." Shibu gave him all he had.

Debjit's uncle held the plate near his chest, crossed one leg over the other, and continued savoring the chicken curry.

"I've never seen my uncle enjoy a dish so much," Debjit murmured. He leaned close and whispered in my ear, "My aunt is a vegetarian."

***

"Grandpa!" DeeDee stared at Shankar for a few seconds. "You ate chicken knowing your family thought it was bad?"

Shankar's face betrayed him, and he blushed.

"My daddy would never do that," DeeDee stated confidently.

"Your father was very good," Shankar agreed. "The teachers and everybody praised him."

Her eyes narrowed a little. "Did he ever do naughty things like you?"

"No. never. But he did one thing that surprised me very much. He created a brawl in his last year at school. You know, they do outrageous things in senior years because they will not return to school anymore. What your dad and his buddies did was organize a big ruckus at the school compound. It was a quiet day in the morning but suddenly a big uproar started in front of the school. Imagine 200 teenagers agitated, screaming, and shouting on the front lawn. Some were madly rooting for their fighters, hollering, 'punch him,' 'hit him hard,' and even saying, 'get his blood.' All were in a frenzy—talking at the same time. Many were taking pictures and some girls asked others to call their parents to take them home. All tried to get to the inside where this fight was taking place, but it was so crowded no one could get in and see what was going on. The teachers were alarmed and came out of the building, but they could not get inside either and didn't know who was fighting whom. The security guards arrived and, finally, pushed the students out and led the principal and the teachers to the center. There they saw a boy and a girl calmly playing chess."

"No fist fights or anything going on?" DeeDee gasped.

"Nope. The whole thing was staged to fool the staff at the school."

"Very clever, Grandpa. Baba was smart."

Shankar nodded. "You got good genes from your father."

"But Grandpa, I got some of your naughty genes too."

That gave Shankar a good laugh.

Chapter Thirty-Seven

Walk Along Bellhaven Road

F all transformed Bellport. It was already like a wonderful, quiet New England village—white houses with dormers, green and blue shutters, clean black roads, and small shops on the side of the town toward the Bay. Now the stunning yellow, orange, and red autumn colors of the trees lining the streets added a picture postcard dimension to the place. The fragrance of crisp autumn air promising apple pies and beach plum jam permeated the community. The summer sailboats and beach crowds of cheerful young boys and girls had left. Shankar loved the quiet, calm atmosphere, so different from Ann Arbor with hundreds of students always on the streets.

Fall brought sweet melancholies from the distant past. But his son's recent words crowded Shankar's mind: *'I hope you will tell them more of your stories. That way they will learn of their heritage.'* Samir would like DeeDee and Raja to be aware of their Indian heredity, which Shankar had clearly not acquainted him with. Shankar enjoyed Sunday breakfast chats with his son, but they were digging up his life, churning up the dregs he had vowed to forget. The memories gnawed at his mind. He was living two lives: one with the children and the other with Samir and Julie. He amused DeeDee and Raja with some of his childhood deeds. He could laugh now at those acts of his youth, and they were interesting to the children too. The anecdotes also brought him back to his past in Dum Dum—his youth, his room, his family relations and how all had ended.

He had purposely portrayed a playful childhood to DeeDee and Raja, and they loved that—their grandfather hero. That was a life that could have stayed so, but it didn't. He had deliberately not given any hint of his sufferings and his sorrows to the children.

It was a delight to chat with Samir and Julie as adults, especially because he had never had any discussions with his own father. They also ushered in difficult memories of his life that he wished to forget. How long could he sustain these two lives—one of happy, carefree youth and the other of hiding the past painful separation from his family?

For their evening walk, Shankar decided to explore the next neighborhood, Brookhaven Hamlet, along Bellhaven road. He led Durga to South Country Road going northwest. Durga followed his lead, enjoying the fall colors of the trees on both sides of the road. The tall oak trees had turned deep red. She picked up a sugar maple leaf with five taper-pointed lobes and looked up at the heavy crown of yellow, orange, and red leaves. "The maple trees make the town so festive," Durga said.

Shankar looked up but said nothing.

They found several old horse-chestnut trees that had turned yellow. Both sides of South Country road were ablaze with color and looked so pretty. "The colors are much better here than in Ann Arbor!" she exclaimed. But Shankar was mostly silent, self-absorbed. They reached Bellhaven road and Shankar turned right, toward the bay.

A quiet neighborhood of beautiful homes with wide lawns separating the houses and trees in glorious fall colors lined the road. No people or cars were out. There were no sidewalks either, which probably discouraged some from walking. "All nice houses," Durga murmured. "A well-to-do coastal community."

"It's a surprise that we hadn't come here earlier," Shankar said, finally relaxing from analyzing his existential struggles.

They saw a couple coming along the opposite side of the road. The woman recognized Durga when they came closer. "Durga, this is my husband, Scott," she announced.

"Hi Susan, this is my husband Shankar," Durga said. "Susan is a longtime member of the women's group I've joined here," she told Shankar. They stopped and chatted for a few minutes. Before leaving Susan said, "We're very happy that you joined our group." Durga's face lit up with the compliment. "Thank you. See you Thursday at the meeting."

"It's nice that you are breaking into the community," Shankar told his wife and briefly stopped in front of a white house with green shutters and two dormers on the second floor. A typical 1930's construction. A clump of birch trees was at the corner of the lawn—their yellow colors tarnished, and small serrated leaves spiraled down in the gentle wind. The other side of the road looked like a dense wilderness of pines and shrubby oaks.

Shankar turned to Durga and abruptly said, "I've come to know a fellow in the library, Jacco Bruin, a first-generation immigrant from Holland. Quite friendly. I was thinking about what he told me. We must guard against living in sad memories."

"Glad you're making new friends, but how did this come about?" She stopped and gazed at her husband with curiosity and surprise.

"His father was killed by the Nazis. I realized we both are trying to deal with aching memories from childhood. His case is vastly different, even opposite, from mine, but I saw that I was not alone in suffering from childhood traumas. He works hard to forget his fearful memories of WWII. I asked him if there was a way to suppress bad, haunting memories. He has given me hope, at least some inspiration that perhaps I'll be able to dispel my bad memories."

"Hmmm. Memories unsettling you so much?" Durga's face creased with concern.

"I haven't told you, but I am recently more troubled by those," he confided. They started walking and he said, "An old man in my neighborhood in Dum Dum told me, *most unhappy is the man who has no work to do.* I didn't grasp the depth of his words then."

"But you have kept yourself quite busy," Durga said.

"I have, but, you know, I have time on my hand now. Difficult to keep one's mind off negative thoughts when one has a lot of free time."

Durga chuckled. "Are you having devilish thoughts?"

Shankar wasn't in a playful mood. "In Ann Arbor," he said, "I didn't think much and was able to suppress my feelings of how my family had rejected us. They flash through my mind more often now." Shankar, intent on expressing his turmoil, didn't notice how Durga flinched and or the sad look that came over her face. "These memories come at random and overwhelm me when I think of something from the past, a little incident, even a childhood story. Then, my Sunday chats with Samir bring back difficult memories. And I guess Samir wants to know more about me and our family. Memories, so powerful, oh, I wonder if I will ever be free of them." There was a tinge of sadness in his voice. He looked at Durga but didn't know what to expect from her.

"That's a bad sign." Durga whispered. In silence they continued their walk. "I was hoping those memories had receded by now."

"I thought they would too."

"Let us be positive," Durga said after walking a few steps. "You regret that your family constrained your upbringing and didn't give you any freedom, not even freedom to laugh."

Shankar looked at her without knowing where she was going. "Yes. My life at home was like walking on a tight rope."

"But your actions have given Samir what you longed for in your past—personal freedom. He has what you wished for. Isn't it nice you were able to do that?"

Shankar looked at her affectionately, agreeing.

They passed by four narrow roads on the left and came to the end of Bellhaven road. The Bay was before them. Gentle, rhythmic sound of waves filled the air. Durga affectionately picked up her husband's hand, caressed it and interlocked her fingers with his. After some time, she said, "You have become quieter recently—hardly talking during the day—not commenting much at meals with Samir and Julie."

"I think this will go away when we are more at ease in this place and have friends in the community."

"I used to think," Durga said quietly, "that every generation goes through one severe adversity ... WWI, WWII, droughts, famines, calamities, etc. What would that be for us? I came to accept that rejection by your family was it. Our albatross." She gazed at the tides coming to the shore. "But we have crossed the storm," she told her husband. "We're over the tsunami. If we take it this way, we can be happier for the rest of our lives."

"I like that." Shankar said, nodding his agreement and scanning the colors of the setting sun. "My friend Jacco said," he murmured, "one can get beyond emotional hurt when one can forgive the person who hurt him."

Durga gently nodded without saying a word.

They stood there, watching the wavelets. When the sun dipped closer to the horizon, Shankar pulled Durga's hand, and they started to walk back.

LIFE IN BELLPORT 2

OCTOBER 2004 - JUNE 2005

Chapter Thirty-Eight

Fond Memories

S amir and Julie had gone to a dinner party in Huntington. At home, the rest of the family spent their after-dinner time quietly. Durga browsed through her economics journal and Shankar sat quietly in his blue chair, reading a book on cosmology.

"Can a typhoon come here?" DeeDee asked, raising her head from a book.

"Typhoon?" Shankar asked. "No. They are hurricanes in the Pacific."

"I'm reading an adventure story where people got lost on their way to the Philippines."

"I like storms, Grandpa," Raja said from his corner of the room. "I want to run around wild when the winds blow hard."

"When I was young, I loved that too." Shankar said, looking over his glasses. "But we had to come inside when a storm came. I wanted to stay out, but my parents wouldn't let me."

Shankar remembered how he and his sisters ran around in the blowing wind. Then the face of his older sister, long absent from his thoughts, floated into his mind's eye. Uma got married when he was a senior in high school. He didn't remember now if she finished college or not as their father married her off in a rush to a Sanskrit scholar from Allahabad, a faraway holy place at the confluence of the Ganges and the Yamuna rivers. How thrilled their father was to have found the groom from this ancient-lineage family who strictly followed the old brahmin traditions. After her marriage, unfortunately though, he didn't speak of Uma anymore, because he had fulfilled his duty as her father; now she was the responsibility of her husband. Shankar never saw her again.

A stab of regret hit him. He had spent so many years reviling Parvati for not supporting him, but he had not bothered about his older sister being cut off from their family. What fun they had together searching for green mangoes blown about by a storm. He looked tenderly at his grandchildren. "I'll tell you what I did once after a storm."

***

Koel Bird

I was playing outside when the wind started to blow. It was a cool wind, and it felt good. Earlier, I had seen a little black cloud in a corner of the southwest sky, but now it had spread over the whole horizon. Soon the wind picked up and trees started to bend and jerk in a frenzy. In the distance, the tops of tall coconut trees swayed. I ran around the field joyously, sometimes stretching my arms out like the wings of an airplane. I wanted to stay out in the rough wind, but as always, someone called me to come home. They were afraid branches would fall and hit children. Sometimes tin sheets from roofs would be blown off and people killed if the sheets hit them. I always lingered as late as I could, until a few raindrops fell on my body. It was such fun to be out before the rain, especially when it was the first of the monsoon season.

Storms often lasted throughout the night, but the morning was usually calm. Then we went out and looked around. First, we ran to the big mango trees to search for fruit that had been knocked to the ground. My sisters liked green mangos; they are sour but have a delicate flavor. They ate those with salt. I looked for anything I could find.

One morning after a storm, I found a bird's nest. It had fallen off with the branch. I was looking for a nice piece of wood to make a slingshot, but I lifted the nest.

"Look, there's an egg in the nest," I shouted to my older sister.

She wasn't interested. She said, "A crow's egg. Throw it away."

Crows were everywhere from early morning till evening. They ate leftover food and garbage, but no one liked them. People hated their harsh, croaking *kaah, kaah* sound. I picked up the egg and examined it carefully. Crow's eggs are white, but I noticed this egg was not pure white; it was blotched with brown. That aroused my curiosity. I became convinced it was a koel's egg.

Koels have the sweetest voice of all birds. Their beautiful tu-wu, tu-wu calls are heart-rending—joy and sorrow blended. But they hide so well in the branches that you rarely see them. They have striking red eyes and their beaks have a greenish-yellow tinge. The male koel is almost the size of a crow—glossy black, sleek, and he has a long tail. They hardly ever come to the ground. You know one is around only when you hear its voice—so sweet, so melodic.

"It's not a crow's egg," I told Uma and started to walk back home with it.

"Let me see," she commanded and looked at it carefully. "Hmm. It has some spots. Maybe it's not a crow's egg. What'll you do with it?"

"I don't know."

"Wouldn't it be nice if we had a koel in our house?" Her eyes sparkled for a moment, then she went back to searching for mangos.

I brought the nest and the egg home. But I didn't tell mother; I was afraid she would throw it out. I kept it in my room. The next day when I awoke, sunlight was pouring in through the window, and I heard the sweet tu-wu calls of a koel in the distance. That reminded me of the egg, and I sat up immediately. I noticed the gaps between the iron rods in the window to stop thieves from breaking into the house, but what disturbed me was when the egg hatched, the bird could fly away through these openings.

I consulted my older sister and told her the problem. She was three years older, so I was sure she would know what to do. "How can we keep the bird in the house?" I asked her in a pleading tone.

"First," she asked, "who's going to incubate the egg?" She cocked her head and seemed to mock my ignorance.

I stared at her.

"You know eggs don't simply hatch. The bird sits on them for days to keep them warm." She went away.

I couldn't study that morning. I was thinking and thinking, *what can I do to make the egg hatch?* I went to my mother's room and got some of the cotton wool she used to make wicks for earthen lamps. I put it over the egg in the nest. Then I hid it away from the draft of the window. When I returned from school, I arranged my pillow, quilts, and all my books around the nest and brought a hurricane lamp to supply heat.

I wanted to consult Uma again, but during breakfast my sisters talked about what they wanted to buy in the coming puja season. My oldest sister pleaded with mother for a silk sari from South India and my younger sister wanted a dress from Calcutta. They had completely forgotten the storm. They asked me what I wanted. "Puja is so far away," I told them. "I don't know." I remembered how I had badgered them the year before for a leather soccer ball. This time I could not think of anything; my mind was occupied with the koel egg. How could anything be more important than having a koel in our house? But no one else seemed interested. They went back to their discussion of the coming puja festival.

I came back from school with the great idea of hanging a light bulb above the egg. It gave good heat, and I was satisfied. For the rest of the week, I didn't go out to play and read loudly in my room, so everyone would know I was studying hard and would not disturb me. In the meantime, I kept a close watch on the egg and didn't really study.

Two weeks passed by and nothing happened. After a few more days I observed a little crack on the egg. I was beside myself with joy, as if I were the egg's parent. Indeed a few hours later, a little bird came out. The most amazing thing in the world! The skin of the nestling was yellow and pink, its abdomen was swollen out of proportion to the rest of its body, and its eyes were shut. It had only an outline of wings. I was thrilled, and, at the same time, I didn't know what to do next. I rushed to Uma and shouted, "A koel, a koel!"

But she only looked at me. "What nonsense are you talking about?"

I pulled her to my room, closing the door behind us.

"Oooh, how cute the baby is!" She picked it up in her palm.

"Imagine, we have a koel in our own house," I cried out. "Thanks to all my hard work! What do we do now?"

"You go and get some worms."

I ran out and dug up a bunch of worms. I put a few in front of the baby bird, but it sat there. "It's blind," I exclaimed hopelessly. "The worms are crawling away."

"The mother bird chews them first," my sister mumbled.

"Do I have to do that?" I asked in horror.

"Go get a knife," she commanded.

We finely chopped a few worms on the floor and gave them to the newborn, but it didn't make any attempt to eat. It lay like a small pink lump in my sister's lap.

"Shall we feed it some soft rice?" I asked her.

My sister had no idea. I stole some from the kitchen and put it in front of the baby bird. It didn't want the rice either. What could I do? I was afraid to force food through its mouth. It was so tiny and weak.

"We've got to figure out what to do." She put it on the soft cotton on the nest.

"Don't tell anyone," I told her.

"I won't." She gave me an annoyed glance and walked out.

I fretted the baby would die without food and water. Then I got an idea: I could feed it water with a medicine dropper. I borrowed one from my mother's store of remedies. I opened the chick's mouth and put a few drops of water in with the dropper, and that worked. I ran to my sister and reported my success. Her eyes opened wide, and her face lit up. She put her hand on my shoulder and jumped for joy. She cried out, "We can do it," and pushed me to my room. "We can mix mashed worms, a little soft rice, and water, and feed the chick with a dropper." She was thrilled and ordered me to get those, while she got ready with a bowl to mix them. Her idea worked and I was so relieved.

For the next several days my sister and I nurtured the nestling and saw it grow. Its dorsal skin blackened in a few days, its eyes opened, and feather quills started to emerge. In two weeks, it developed black feathers. Uma and I became closer than we had ever been; we talked in hushed voices and discussed often what we should do next.

We were together on the idea that we must keep it a secret and that we would surprise everyone when it started singing melodious songs. We were frenetic—to feed the bird, clean the room, and keep it hidden. Every day we ran to the room as soon as we came home from school. I started to feel like the chick recognized us and freely came to us for food. I imagined soon it would wake me in the morning with its sweet voice. Perhaps I could teach it to call my name. How proud everyone would be of me!

Then my sister said, "It's pooping all over and I can't keep cleaning all the time. We must get a cage."

"My friend said he'd give me one. I'll get it tomorrow."

However, our uncle came, so I couldn't get away, especially since I was quite fond of him. One good thing was his visit kept my mother's attention away from our project.

When my uncle left a few days later, I walked a long distance to my friend's house and brought back a cage. But as I entered our house, I found my mother near my room. She saw me with the cage dangling behind me. "What are you up to?" she asked and pushed my door open. The creaking sound ran a shiver through me. My bed was in complete disarray—the quilt jumbled with the pillow, the bed sheet up on the window, and newspapers on the floor. She saw the little black bird and gasped, "Raising a crow in your room?"

"It's a koel, Ma," I told her confidently, and looked to her with pride.

"Is that what you've been doing the last few weeks?" She glared at me.

I nodded shyly.

She ignored me and looked around at the mess in my room.

"I have a cage now; I'll clean up the room. When you hear its sweet voice, you'll like it, Ma."

She frowned. "I guess you'll have to figure it out yourself," she told me and hurried away. Her key chain at the end of her sari made tinkling noises from her back; I thought she liked the idea of the koel, and I was glad.

I worked hard for the next two days, cleaning my room. Now that my mother knew of the koel, I announced it to everybody, proudly showing the beautiful little black bird in the cage. But I didn't let anyone get closer. It was mine.

Sunday morning sunshine streaked through the bars in my window as I awoke and looked outside. The sky was blue with no clouds. What a beautiful day it would be. Then I heard a faint 'Kaaah, Kaaah,' sound in the room. I turned and found the sound came from the cage next to my bed. I gaped at the little bird and saw its black, conical beak—my crow.

***

"You raised a crow after all?" DeeDee exclaimed.

"Koels lay eggs in crows' nests and let the mother crow hatch and feed their baby, but I never thought the egg I found could be a crow's egg."

"What did your sister say?" DeeDee inquired with a knowing smile on her face.

"She told mother she was helping me because I loved the idea of having a koel bird."

"What happened to the baby bird?" Raja asked eagerly.

"I took the bird to the mango tree and left it there."

"Grandpa, you saved a bird, that's good." Raja patted grandpa's arm.

Shankar remembered how sad and embarrassed he was for several weeks. But Raja was right; he had done something for nature and shouldn't have been ashamed.

DeeDee and Raja left but Shankar kept on thinking about his older sister. She did not belittle him for his foolishness. She was such a sensitive girl. That night, he remembered another event with Uma when he and other kids reveled in the magic of a bohurupee, but how sad, fearful, and helpless her face was in the end. Did she welcome the wonderful-but-troubled bohurupees where she lives now?

Chapter Thirty-Nine

Magic Show

Shankar's escape was watching variety shows on TV with all their glittering performances, songs, and dances. Today he sat engrossed, watching a magic show from Las Vegas. A beautiful, shiny, carmine convertible with the top down was on stage. The magician in a black tuxedo and tall Lincolnesque top hat selected a handsome young couple from the audience, and they got into the luxurious car. The magician leaned forward and whispered something to the couple. They laughed as a door far above the stage opened and a ferocious tiger came out. The tiger looked at the stage below and a few seconds later leaped down! The audience screamed in horror. However, the car, with the couple inside, vanished in the nick of time. The tiger fell onto the empty stage and growled. What a relief! The audience burst out in cheers and clapping.

"You like magic shows, Grandpa?"

Shankar, startled, turned around at the sound of his granddaughter's voice. DeeDee's dark eyebrows came together as if the eleven-year-old had caught her grandfather in a naughty act.

"Yes, it's fun to wonder how they do the tricks." Shankar's face brightened. He brushed a wisp of white hair from his forehead and looked at her with an amused smile.

"They can do anything on TV, Grandpa. Probably all fake." The girl shook her head wisely and rolled her eyes.

"I like magic, Grandpa," said Raja, coming in from the hall with a toy plane in his slim hand. "I wish I had a magic wand. Then I could make things vanish." He waved the toy like a wand in front of him. He pointed his hand toward his sister. "Poof and you'll vanish." It looked like the idea cheered him.

DeeDee gave him the look.

"I've seen real magic performances in India," Shankar said, pulling Raja toward him.

"On stage?" DeeDee asked.

"No, not on stage," Shankar shook his head. "Real magic. Without any trickery." He paused and gazed at the children.

"When I was young, a man would sometimes come to our house. He went from door to door and performed many tricks. We called him bohurupee. They ask for a little money at the end of their act."

"Bohurupee?" DeeDee raised her eyebrows.

"It means 'one who has many forms.' Often many panels of cloth hung from his body. He would whirl round, and round, and all the loose cloths would fly out displaying many colors. It was wonderful and mystifying at night in the flickering light of hurricane lamps. Sometimes he would act out a drama. That was for the grownups, and they liked that."

Shankar looked toward the front yard. He saw a robin. It stared motionless at the ground with its head cocked on one side, hoping to find a worm. The sun flashed on its red breast.

"Grandpa, what magic did he do?" Raja said, his eager expression tinged with impatience.

Shankar shifted his eyes to Raja. "He could pluck some fruit from the air, right in front of us. That's what we children liked most. Sometimes he gave us candies. Then he would bring out so many other things from his hair, arms, and legs! You wouldn't believe it!" Shankar looked affectionately at his two grandchildren and drew them toward him, one arm around each. They had no experience of life in India. How could they? Perhaps, nowadays, those experiences don't exist even in India. He stared out toward the garden and sighed.

DeeDee perched on the armrest as Raja, on the other side, tugged at Shankar's hand. "Grandpa, tell us more about the bohurupee man."

Shankar took a deep breath, sorting the memories. He felt exhilarated and sad simultaneously.

"When a bohurupee came, we always ran toward him and crowded around him. But we were also afraid of him."

"Afraid?" DeeDee exclaimed, her face betraying her pleasure.

"You know, we were little. And he was a stranger who could perform magic we had never seen before."

"Sometimes he chased us and scared us, but we always laughed and ran away. And other times he would come inside our house, even to our rooms, and do magic right there. He didn't need a stage."

Shankar saw that the robin had pulled a worm from the ground. Its head bobbed two or three times and it was gobbled up. A strange feeling of inevitability struck Shankar deep in his gut. He turned back to the children. "I'll tell you when I last saw a bohurupee."

***

Bohurupee

When I was eight or nine years old, a bohurupee came to our house. He was the best bohurupee I'd ever seen, going from door to door, performing many tricks. This bohurupee had very colorful makeup on his face, like the clowns wear here, but a quite different design—more like a Native American dancer. And he had rough, long black hair. When he first came to the courtyard, he stood silently and moved his head from side to side without moving his shoulders, like the dancers do in India. His enormous eyes rolled from one side to the other. I was the first to look out the window and notice him. "Bohurupee! A bohurupee!" I burst out. My sisters immediately came running toward him.

My older sister waved her hands and cried, "Show us a magic," and we all repeated in a chorus, "show us a magic, show us a magic."

My cousin Chinta was visiting from the city. She had never seen a bohurupee. At first, she was scared, but soon she also joined in our frenzy.

The bohurupee played with us and chased us around the courtyard. He gave me a peacock feather from the sleeve of his shirt. Like magic. He then gave Chinta a small rubber ball that came out of her own ear. She laughed and laughed, and her curly black hair swung around her shoulders. She was slightly darker than my sisters, and her deer-like eyes glittered in excitement.

Chinta asked, "Can you give me a doll?"

The bohurupee rolled his eyes and moved his hands and body in a rhythmic fashion, and then he took Chinta's hand and closed her palm. When he let her hand go, there was a bonbon! She screamed in excitement; the doll forgotten.

The bohurupee gave each child a toffee. And those came out of his hair. Chinta wanted one more and he gave her another toffee—from the air! Chinta shrieked, "This is the *best* part of my visit!"

The bohurupee then performed a dance for the adults. It looked like a combination of tribal and folk dances. His hands moved up and down around his body, fingers coming together in different and beautiful forms. His feet tapped on the ground in a rhythmic beat. Sometimes, he put his thumb and forefinger together around his eyes, and his head moved from one side of his shoulder to the other. How gracefully he glided around the courtyard.

Then suddenly Chinta started to cry, saying, "Where is my bracelet? I can't find it." Her face became sad, and tears ran down her cheeks.

People give solid 22 karat gold bracelets to girls in India. It is their way of saving money for them. So as soon as Chinta said the bracelet was missing, my mother came over and questioned her.

"When did you wear it last?"

"Right now, as I was playing. I wear it all the time."

This worried everyone, and the adults gathered around Chinta. The bohurupee stopped his act and everyone searched the house, but the bracelet was nowhere to be found. We also went to look at the places where we had played during the day. Soon, suspicion started to grow around the bohurupee. Had he played a trick on her? Had he taken the bracelet from the naïve city girl?

"I gave her the bracelet," my mother lamented, "now it's lost because of the bohurupee."

My uncle mumbled, "We were all watching him, how could he take it?"

"Thieves are very clever," my father asserted.

Heated discussions erupted inside the house. I didn't understand everything that was going on, but I remember my father saying the bohurupee couldn't be trusted. He was a magician. He could easily fool the girl. "They come from the lower echelon of society; they have no regard for what is good and bad. Scripture teaches stealing, lying, killing, and deceiving others are all bad. Do they follow the religion? *No.*" He vehemently shook his head and paced the floor.

The bohurupee finally said he must move on. Then my father told him he would give him good money if he returned the bracelet.

"But I don't know where her bracelet is."

"You are a magician," my father told him with contempt. "You could easily take it from her hand." I remember my father was agitated, his voice rising, but my uncle's face became darker. I now think he was not in agreement with my father, but he couldn't say anything contradicting his much older brother.

"Sir, I am a performer," the bohurupee told my father, "I don't take things from children."

"I've seen many performers," my father retorted. "Temptation is hard to resist."

"Please trust me," the bohurupee told everyone, "I love doing my act. I am not a thief." But everyone ignored his words and kept on discussing what they could do.

Someone said, "Once he is gone, no one will know where he came from or where he went."

I had no idea who the bohurupees truly were or where they lived. They always appeared unannounced. Their sudden appearance was a fun part of it.

It was growing dark and the bohurupee said he should leave. But my father said threateningly, "You can't go until you give back the bracelet."

"Honestly, I haven't taken it," the bohurupee pleaded. He folded his hands in prayerful submission and bowed. "Please trust me; I have no idea where the bracelet is."

"We'll call the police then," someone from the house shouted.

Chinta started to cry loudly for the bracelet. I was sad Chinta lost her gift. I stood near the mango tree in the courtyard and watched my father accusing the stranger. Now I moved near the veranda where my sisters were. We stood close to each other, frozen with fear.

The grownups were convinced the bohurupee had taken the bracelet. Neighbors heard the commotions from our house and came over one by one. Soon, a crowd formed. No one knew the bohurupee, so no one said anything good about him. Everyone was suspicious of him, but no one knew what to do.

"If we give him a good beating, he'll give it back," someone said.

Then my father suggested they search him. Two strong men from the neighborhood grabbed him and said, "We must search you."

The bohurupee was frightened and said, "Please, I have never taken anything from a child. Don't destroy the only costume I have."

They pulled off his costume and searched him. He was a middle-aged, thin man. In the dim light of the lanterns, the shadows of people moved around him menacingly. I still remember his scared and helpless look, his downcast eyes in his bony face.

Tears ran down the cheeks of my older sister. I felt a lump in my throat. We huddled together silently, frightened by what was going on. Chinta sobbed on our grandma's shoulders while she tried to comfort her.

The two men searched the bohurupee's costume thoroughly, each pocket and each fold. They found many little items, toys, and candies, but no bracelet. Finally, one man pushed him so hard he almost fell. "Go, get out of here," the man shouted, "before we thrash you." A murmur arose from the crowd. The bohurupee collected his clothes and a few other items from the ground and walked away from the courtyard. The men followed him and chased him out of our neighborhood, some shouting at him, "Thief!" Some shouted, "Never come back here."

That's the last time in my life I saw a bohurupee.

The commotion continued in the house for some time. No one knew what had happened to the bracelet or had any idea how they could recover it. I can still hear my father's voice as he cursed the lower-class people: "No hope for them."

We were all sad. Uma kept on mumbling, "He didn't take it. He is not a thief." Chinta went to bed crying. The adults stayed up talking about the event, saying they should have handed the bohurupee over to the police. I was petrified by the incident but fell asleep. I don't remember if we ate dinner or not.

Chinta was the first to arise the next morning. She awakened me and said, "Let's go for a walk near the farmer's canal." She was jolly, showing no trace of the distress of the night before. It was clear she had forgotten the bohurupee, but I hadn't. I was still sad. The sun was barely up, and the sky was blue with a layer of pink near the horizon. If the bracelet were not lost, I'd have enthusiastically jumped out of bed to run around with Chinta. Instead, I simply plodded behind her.

We passed the kitchen and saw the unwashed dishes from last night. A crow pecked at a few grains of rice on a plate. As we stepped down from the veranda, Chinta stopped, as if she remembered something, and looked toward the far corner on the courtyard. There was a little playhouse made of loose bricks and worn-out planks behind a tree. "I made that house yesterday," she said, and walked over to it. I followed her. There was a handkerchief on the ground, and on it a hairbrush, her pink ribbons, and the bracelet. She picked it up. "Good, I found it." She put it on and commanded, "Let's run to the canal."

I looked away from her to the empty courtyard, to the spot under the mango tree where I had stood last night. The look on the bohurupee's face, just before he was pushed out of our house, came to me. My stomach tightened and I felt like walking back inside the house.

***

DeeDee gasped when Shankar finished the story. "Oh! How awful!" Shankar looked away from the children and stared at the spot where the robin had been.

"Can a bohurupee come here from India?" Raja asked, resting his head on his grandfather's chest. "I want to see one, Grandpa."

"They exist only in villages in India," Shankar told him, still gazing toward the backyard. Then, a sound from the road drew his attention. A car full of children passed by, probably returning from a game. Everything is so organized here, so driven by schedules and activities. Where would there even be any space in this culture for a bohurupee to breeze in, entertain children, without causing a great upheaval?

Raja and DeeDee slipped away, leaving their grandfather to his memories.

Shankar's eyes returned to the TV screen, but the magic show was over. He continued thinking about the bohurupee. They were a mystery, a surprise. No one knew when one would appear. But they returned and always in the evening. He didn't know if it was the same man or different bohurupees came on different occasions. Perhaps they didn't exist anymore.

He recalled Chinta's jolly mood the morning after the upheaval. Uma was so glad that Chinta found her bracelet, but Shankar remembered, she asked mother, "What about the bohurupee?"

"What about?"

"He didn't steal the bracelet!"

There was no answer. None of the adults expressed remorse for their actions. The adults in the house never thought the bohurupee could be an honest man, who loved performing magic for the children. His father believed he could not be good since he was not a brahmin because no brahmin would do such a menial job of going from house to house to entertain people. Shankar felt once the society had assigned a class system and established a hierarchy, it was hard, almost impossible, to change it.

Memories of Uma brought Shankar's younger sister to mind. As he had sent Uma to a remote corner of his mind, had he also done something similarly unjust to his younger sister? He had judged her poorly for not supporting his marriage to Durga, but had he given any thought to why she did that?

Shankar froze for several minutes. Earlier memories of Parvati came to him—the fun they had together; all his soccer and cricket games that she came to watch, and she even shielded him from mother on several occasions. Especially when he fell from the date tree that mother asked him not to climb. And when she found his shirt spoiled by sparks from fireworks, the shirt that their mother told him not to wear that night. Then he remembered a time when he had been frightened by a *Yaksa* story ... a man on stilts with a green coconut in his hand stalking the city. How much he needed Parvati that night.

Chapter Forty

Halloween Night

Dee Dee and Raja were excited to go out trick or treating on Halloween. They had been antsy ever since they had come home from school and were running around, full of nervous energy. Samir had promised to come home early and take the children out. A half-moon rose above the walnut trees and quietness prevailed in the garden except for the rustling of autumn leaves. A few late season chrysanthemums bobbed their heads in the breeze.

The first time Shankar had taken his son out for Halloween, Samir was young and overly excited. But he and Durga had no idea how to make him a costume, so Shankar bought an astronaut's costume from a local store: a polyester jumpsuit with white gloves and orange boot tops that fitted over shoes. It had the NASA logo screen-printed on the front and an inflatable tank at the back. The costume was for a more grownup boy, but Samir was happy. Shankar took him to the houses in the neighborhood and felt embarrassed to push him forward to collect candies. He felt as if he was sending him to beg. He didn't like it, but Samir and the other children were all animated and happy. The only consolation was that the neighbors seemed to enjoy giving candies to the kids. One neighbor even offered Shankar a beer! Samir wanted to go to more and more houses, but Shankar only prayed for it to be over. When they returned home, Samir was exhausted. Still, he couldn't fall asleep for two hours. Now it was Samir's turn. A smile spread on Shankar's face.

The kitchen door banged, and Raja came out running. "Did you hear the noise from the basement?" he cried out in a worried voice. "Someone's there. Come and see, Grandpa." He shook all over—thin, pale legs knocking in fright.

His older sister came behind him, her face showing some concern.

"A man stared at me through the living room window," Raja said. "His face looked scary! Then I heard the sound from the basement."

"The wind must have rattled the basement door" Shankar told him. "Come, sit with me on the porch." He put his hand around Raja's waist and pulled him closer.

DeeDee looked at her brother coolly. "Were you playing computer games again?"

"Yes, but I'm not imagining this. The man's face was big, and he had hair all over it, even on his ears. You'd have fainted if you saw him."

"Ha!"

"Then, why don't you go to the basement?"

She made no gesture to move. "I'm not stupid," she mumbled and looked away from Raja to her grandfather. She greatly feared ghosts, Shankar knew, but the faint light of the evening did not reveal any fear on her round, olive face. She twisted a strand of black hair with her fingers.

Shankar patted Raja. "Your father will come soon. I'll visit the basement after he gets home."

Raja sidled onto Shankar's lap. "Grandpa, were you ever scared?"

"Sometimes." Shankar massaged Raja's shoulders without saying any more.

DeeDee raised her head and gave her grandfather a penetrating look. "You had such a wonderful life in India, how could it be scary? Except for snakes, maybe, but really, you had nothing to be afraid of."

"It was about waking up at night and hearing someone calling my name."

"What was scary about that?" Raja asked. "I'll get up if you call my name."

Shankar turned Raja toward him. "My fear was, if I answered the call, I'd be under the spell of a very wicked man. I'd follow him and never be seen again. He'd force me to guard his things forever."

"Really?" exclaimed DeeDee.

"I'll tell you more after you return from 'trick or treat.' I don't want to scare you now with Indian stories. You go and put on your costumes. Daddy will come very soon."

When the children and Samir left the house, the scary story returned to Shankar, prompting thoughts of tender moments when Parvati was so good and comforted him after the soccer game.

***

Man on Stilts

One summer after a soccer game, I was chatting with my friends on the field, something we usually did until it was dark and time to go home. That day, an older boy played with us, a relative of one of the players. He came from a distant place. Thin and tall, he seemed to know a lot of things and fascinated us with captivating stories. We didn't want to leave him even after darkness fell.

"If someone calls your name on a full moon night while you are in bed," he said, "never answer or you will be a goner." His expression was grim. He silently stared at the far end of the field.

"What will happen?" Soumen quizzed him.

"Haven't you heard of the Yaksas?"

We had to admit we didn't know anything about the Yaksas.

"Let me tell you," he started. "They are one kind of evil spirit. They protect treasures in the world. You know, valuable stuff like gold, gems, and jewelry. Kuber is the king of the Yaksas. He is the richest being in the universe. In ancient times when someone acquired a lot of gold, precious stones, and diamonds, he prayed to King Kuber for protection, and Kuber would send a Yaksa to guard his wealth. They were good spirits then. But soon, evil men learned about the Yaksas. And they found a way to protect their hoards. What they did was villainous."

He didn't wish to tell us anymore, but all the boys wanted to know what the evil people did and why the Yaksas were dreadful. We clamored to hear more.

"Are you sure you guys want to hear this?" he said. "It's a deep ancient secret, and it's frightening. Let me tell you though, it's true. Don't believe anyone who tells you it's a myth." Then, in a low, spooky voice he said, "Never answer if anyone calls you late at night." His eyes seemed to glitter in the dark. He paused for a moment and again looked away toward the far end of the field. His voice seemed to become deeper. "It started a long time back with the *dacoits* in Bengal, the dreadful robbers who worshipped Goddess Kali before going out to prey on innocent people. They were ferocious. No one could stop them. They collected an inordinate amount of riches. Now what did they do with all the wealth they gathered? They hid it in a secret underground room or in a cave. They trusted no one. Often the leader of the gang slept on the gold they had acquired."

He then looked at me and asked, "Have you ever seen a lot of gold in one place?"

I hadn't.

"Gold and precious stones have a power of their own," he said somberly. "Many have gone mad because of it. What happened is, the robbers fell in love with their possessions. Soon they could think of nothing but the gold, the jewels, and the valuable stones they had. They spent all their time guarding them. They couldn't leave the place. They lived in constant fear someone would steal their treasure; even murder them. Incredibly deplorable! Many died in the secret places where they kept their caches. Their spirits hung around the treasure like ghosts. Some have seen such spirits in obscure places. Oh, it's such a dreadful sight. Most of those who have seen those spirits have died right there. Of heart failure, I guess, but no blood was left in them. Only a few were able to run away."

The face of our visitor shrunk as he described the sad state of the robbers, and he moved his head back and forth in dismay. An owl flew through the darkening sky over our heads in search of unsuspecting mice in the field, and a chill ran down our spines, but we stayed glued to his words.

"The evil guys studied the ancient Tantric rituals," he continued, "and found a way to protect their treasures; they learned how to create a Yaksa who would listen to them and guard their wealth. The way to do it is to transform a young boy into a Yaksa."

"I've never heard of this," one of my friends told him. "This is an old folks' tale."

"Haven't you heard of boys getting lost and never returning home?" the big boy replied, annoyed. "Where do you think they go?"

They admitted their parents often warned them about boys being abducted by strangers, and they didn't know what happened to them. "Some of them became Yaksas, I'm sure," he told us confidently.

"What does it have to do with answering my name at night?" I asked him.

"Aah," he said, "that's the important part. First, the guy who wants to create a Yaksa performs a worship service. He purifies himself by eating only vegetarian food for a whole month. Then he initiates a *yagnya* ceremony three days before the full moon. He starts a little fire with sacred wood from a bel tree. He lights incense and offers fruits to the gods. He smears his forehead with red vermilion and puts sandalwood paste on his arms. Sitting cross-legged in front of the consecrated fire, he then prays to King Kuber. He stays there and doesn't eat anything during the ceremony. Then he takes a fresh green coconut and offers it to King Kuber. This is the essential part of the ceremony and must be done correctly. He puts auspicious marks on the green coconut with red vermilion.

"When the full moon rises in the sky, he holds the green coconut in one hand and with the other hand slices its top with a very sharp knife. It must be done in one stroke. He does it in a way that not a single drop of water falls out, and he immediately closes the coconut with the top he cut out. From outside it looks like an uncut green coconut. Then he gets on stilts and goes out with the green coconut in his hand. If you see him now, you will be extremely frightened. His eyes become sharp and penetrating, burning red with deep intent; his hair looks matted like he has not washed it for years, and his body looks thin and strong like steel. He moves on the stilts amazingly fast—like a strong wind. No one can catch him."

"Have you seen one of them on stilts?" a boy asked—so meekly that his voice was barely audible.

"No. Never!" he bellowed. "If you see him on stilts, you will become unconscious and may never awake. He is deadly. No boy can look at him." He became silent for a moment.

We were frozen as he continued, "He goes to a neighborhood far away from his secret cave and looks for a young boy. Because he is on stilts, he can see far and inside each window. When he finds a suitable boy sleeping, he goes next to his window. He opens the top of the green coconut and calls the boy's name. He calls in a very soothing voice. If the boy wakes up and answers his call, he immediately closes the coconut. Then he has captured the boy's spirit. It is trapped in the green coconut. The boy will now obey him and do whatever he tells him to do. He calls the boy's name again. The boy gets up from his bed, opens the door of his room and the house, and follows the stilt-walker as if sleepwalking. The boy has no power of his own. The man brings him to the cave and completes his worship service with the boy sitting next to him. He puts red holy marks of vermilion and ash from the fire on the boy's forehead. Then he extinguishes the fire with the coconut water and asks the boy to kneel and pray with his head low near the floor. While the boy does that, the man closes the door from outside."

The older boy stopped telling us the story and stared away to the goal posts. We sat there silently. Our throats were dry, and no one could ask him what happened next. Soon he continued in a low voice. "No food or water will be given. The boy will cry and cry, and scream, 'Ma, Baba, Ma, Baba,' but no one will hear him. Frantically he will move around in the dark to find a way out. But he will never find it. He can only feel the gold all around him. Tired and exhausted, he falls asleep. When he wakes up, he does the same thing; he cries for help and searches for an exit in the dark, but he only stumbles on the gold and jewelry. Eventually he dies and becomes a Yaksa. He will guard the stilt-walker's wealth forever."

Shivers ran down our spines. It had become quite dark by then. The older boy started to walk back home; the rest of us simply followed him. I was so scared; I knew I could not sleep near a window that night.

When bedtime came, I asked Parvati to sleep in my room. She stared at my face for a few seconds. I did not know what she saw there, but she brought her pillow with her to my room. When she was scared, it was I who had told her stories until she fell asleep. This time she comforted me by talking to me endlessly. Her chatter was incoherent but that distracted me and, being tired from a soccer game, I soon fell asleep.

Chapter Forty-One

Ancient Customs

A snowstorm came after Thanksgiving, but the winter in Bellport was milder than in Ann Arbor. Shankar and Durga took a break from evening walks. Life became more home centered when the schools closed for the holidays. Their major outdoor activities were taking DeeDee and Raja to the skating rink and hot chocolates afterward, which Durga and Shankar cherished. Shankar helped the children build a snowman, but admitted defeat to them when it came to snowball fights. Life was cozy around the fireplace with chats, snacks, and his stories. Shankar and Durga found the winter more pleasant surrounded by family than the winters in Ann Arbor.

"We're going to see the show *Holiday Spectacular on Ice* the Sunday before Christmas," Samir declared during breakfast.

"All of us going to Manhattan?" Durga asked.

"No. It will come to our own Gateway Playhouse program at the Patchogue Theatre. That's an old theater restored to its former glory—proscenium pillars and 1920s decorations and all."

"I saw it when I was at Columbia. It'll be fun for all of us." Julie got up and went to inform the children who squealed in delight.

Bellport became extra-charming with Christmas decorations on the streets and in the store windows on South Country Road. Shankar and Durga strolled with the children and helped them buy gifts. The small village felt intimate and more enjoyable to them compared to the college town of Ann Arbor.

On the Monday after Christmas, only Shankar and Julie were at the breakfast table, reading the paper and sipping tea. Julie put the paper down and told Shankar about a recent homework assignment she had given her students: *How India might reduce its population growth.* "You know," she said with a wry smile, "they think they can do it easily. I'm curious to see what they write."

"Indira Gandhi lost her Prime Minister position trying to force birth control," Shankar said.

Julie nodded and went upstairs to read her students' submissions.

Shankar stayed at the table and admired how beautiful the snow was outside. The evergreens looked magical with fresh snow sparkling from their branches in the bright, cold sunshine. Such a sight had always brought back his first experience of snow in Philadelphia, which had fallen while he slept completely unaware. What a surprise and joy it had been in the morning to see everything white. He couldn't get enough of the view.

Shankar moved to the living room and slumped on his favorite blue armchair, eyes half closed and hands together on his lap as if meditating. Somehow, he felt, the winter's cold made him tire easily.

DeeDee came to him. "Grandpa, do you know why the priests wouldn't let Mommy inside a temple when she first went to India?"

"Why do you ask such a question?"

"Mommy gave me the photo album of her trip to India. I found the picture of a temple and she wrote, 'I couldn't get in.' She's busy, so I thought I'd ask you."

"This is the Durga Temple in Benares," Shankar said, examining the photo. He pulled DeeDee closer. "Durga is the Mother Goddess. She watches over us. Do you know grandma's name?'

DeeDee gently nodded. "She is our Mother Goddess!"

"Right. So always be nice to her."

Just then Durga came down with the *Economic and Political Weekly* in her hand. She read that magazine regularly to keep abreast of developments in India from many sides—society, academic, and politics. She went to her usual corner near the bookshelf.

Shankar saw Durga. "Your Grandma is here. Ask her, she will tell you."

When DeeDee asked, Durga said, "Your mother wore a skirt—western dress. That's why they wouldn't let her in."

"Weird!" DeeDee replied and sat down with the album, flipping through the pages.

Durga glanced at her husband. "You look like an Indian guru this morning," she told Shankar with a quiet chuckle.

"I take that as a compliment, my dear." Shankar knew he had changed in the last decade. When he looked at his face in the mirror, his hair was almost all white. His skin was still smooth, but some wrinkles showed around his eyes. At seventy, he was happy that except for the white hair, the mirror didn't show his age, that he didn't look too haggard.

"Grandpa, what does religion have to do with what you wear?" DeeDee persisted. Her face was serious, eyes steady on her grandfather.

Shankar looked at DeeDee's inquisitive face. "The Hindu religion is very old," he told her, "so it has many archaic customs." He loved that his granddaughter was raising an intelligent question. These questions hadn't occurred to him at her age. He was carried by the current of his family and the society that surrounded them, and by the religious festivities. He didn't question why they did what they did. For example, he happily took his mother to the Ganges River for a dip because Hindus believed a bath in the sacred river earned blessings from the River Goddess, and he dutifully carried a pot of the sacred water home. Until he grew older, he never asked why.

DeeDee gazed at him, her head tilted to the side, eyebrows raised.

"You know, most of the time the priests fabricated these rules," he told DeeDee. "Some of these customs are not important to the religion." He scratched his head. The dark face of a priest at a temple gate in South India came to him. "I also faced a similar situation in South India."

"But you're Indian!"

Shankar remembered the priest's stern, disapproving stare.

"What happened?"

Shankar patted her fluffy hair. "Did you know most Indians put oil on their hair before they take a bath?"

"Oil on your hair?"

"Yes. It makes their hair dark and shiny. In Calcutta, we massaged our bodies with mustard oil before showering, but used coconut oil for our hair. I never asked why. Same with religious customs."

"That's crazy, Grandpa. And gross. And what does that have to do with anything?"

"I guess I will have to tell you what happened at the temple."

"Yes, please."

***

Temple Dress Code

When I was a graduate student in Calcutta, I came to know a senior research scholar from South India, Balakrishnan. I called him Baal for short. Once he was going on a trip to South India with a visiting Swedish scientist who was working with him on a research project. He invited me to join them. I was elated and immediately agreed.

My father was not happy when I told him about my desire to go on the trip. He pressed his lips tight and frowned. He slowly shook his head. "Do you understand why crossing the ocean is forbidden in our religion?"

I shook my head.

"It has nothing to do with the oceans. It's because you can't carry out the daily required practices. You encounter *mlechchas*, the non-believers. And who knows what you'd eat and drink? You will destroy the high standing that God has given you. Do you want to lose that?"

"Baba, we are going to visit wonderful South Indian temples."

My father became quiet and walked back and forth, finally saying, "You must eat only vegetarian food and say the *Gayatri* mantra in the mornings and evenings every day."

I agreed to do that. I didn't tell my father that a foreigner, a mlechcha, was going with us.

Baal rented a car in Bangalore and we traveled to the coastal region of Kerala. Coconut trees were everywhere, lining the inlets and backwaters. Baal told our visitor no other state in India has such a verdant countryside. The value of property was measured there by the number of coconut trees one had. We stopped in a village and observed that every bit of the coconut tree was used: the soft meat inside the coconut for food and oil; the husks for coir brushes, mats, fishnets, and rope; the dry leaves for roofs; and the trunks for the outside walls of houses and for small boats. It was amazing.

We were traveling in late August and our car didn't have air-conditioning. The Swedish scientist truly suffered in the heat. His shirt was drenched with sweat. He opened the window, but the hot air didn't help much. In late afternoon, when we stopped at a beach in Varkala, he jumped out of the car and waded into the water. The pink, sandy beach was small but charming. White waves crashed in a gentle rhythm toward the few huts and sheds—interspersed among coconut trees and protected by a line of randomly packed rocks. A cloudless sky met the blue water at the horizon. Not far away, the low red cliffs guarded the sparkling water like sentinels. On top of the cliffs, coconut trees watched over the scene. Locals sat on large rocks, relaxing and chatting. No one seemed to be in any hurry. The pristine landscape delighted us, and we remained there in the cool breeze. No one came to sell souvenirs and disturb the peace. I was absorbed and could have stayed there for a long time. All too soon Baal tapped on my shoulder. "We should be going if we want to see the temple."

How could he want to leave this beautiful place so soon? I stared at him without a word. He was a short, slim, muscular man with a larger than ordinary head. His hair was nicely oiled and combed straight from one side to the other—the classic 'comb-over' that fools no one except the bald man looking in the mirror. There was no visible movement of any muscle on his face, but his round eyes had a steady radiance—neither commanding nor pleading.

"How far away is the city?" the Swedish fellow asked.

"About an hour's drive," Baal replied.

"Couldn't I stay here and meet you later?" the fellow appealed in a low voice. He smiled wistfully. He was a middle-aged man, a respected scientist, who had traveled extensively in Europe and America, but he was helpless in the hands of Baal, his very officious Indian 'guide.'

Surprised at his train of thought, I blurted out, "No, no. You haven't seen a South Indian temple. They are beautiful. You must come with us. They are certainly something to see. You must not miss it."

Baal enthusiastically described the famous Vishnu temple. "The eighteen-foot stone idol, wrapped in gold and precious stones, lies in a reclining position over a coiled snake. Vishnu's head is shielded under the snake's five heads—like an umbrella. It's something to see."

The Swedish fellow reluctantly came out of the water, and we drove on. The car was hot. He remained silent, fully lowered the car window, and read his travel guide; I watched the scenery.

The sun was almost down when we arrived in Trivandrum, the capital of Kerala—an ancient city with a three-thousand-year-old trading tradition. The town is perched on undulating terrain formed by seven low coastal hills. As soon as we checked into our hotel, Baal changed to a South Indian style dhuti and I put on clean pants and a shirt. Our Swedish friend didn't change. He kept his shorts on, and the light short-sleeve shirt he had bought in Bombay. He said the weather was too hot for him to put on good clothes.

When we reached the gate, we were stunned by the majestic beauty of the temple standing tall above its surroundings. The temple could be seen from afar. We hadn't noticed it because the traffic concerned us more; cars seemed to come at us from all sides. Baal knew Indians drive much more slowly than people do in the West, but the Swedish fellow and I, who had never driven a car, were not used to seeing cars drive directly at us. We both held on to our seats as Baal maneuvered through the city.

The temple looked exactly like the pictures in books. Magnificent arrays of gods, goddesses, nymphs, and demons adorned the seven-story tower. Several long steps led to the gate. Like any other pilgrimage site in India, souvenir shops lined the street. But the place was not crowded.

"It must be gorgeous inside," the Swedish fellow said, and plodded up the steps, eager to see. His pale face, now red with sunburn, stood out among the dark South Indians.

We were about to enter the temple compound when an aged priest, about my height, stopped us by raising his hand. He was wearing a cotton shirt and a white dhuti wrapped around his legs, in the same style Baal wore his. We could see a sacred thread hung down from his left shoulder under his thin, white shirt. His face didn't reflect the happy smile of welcome that we, his visitors, had expected. He talked with Baal in the local dialect. I saw Baal's face dim and shrink. The priest stood before us stiff and rigid. Baal took us aside and told us the temple didn't allow foreigners inside. 'It is only for the Hindus.'

Our foreign visitor said, "I understand." He turned without any hesitation. "I'll see you at dinner time." There was no anger or resentment in his voice. He went down the steps and walked into the warren of streets opposite the temple.

We stood there, dumbstruck, watching him go; there was nothing we could do for him. I wondered: Was this why he hadn't put on good clothes? Had he read about this happening in some temples in the guidebook, but not told us?

The priest then looked me over. I was obviously an Indian from a different area. He said, "You can't come inside with these heathen western clothes."

I was eagerly looking forward to seeing the inside of the temple. And I also wanted to impress my father. That was the only reason he had let me go. "My clothes are clean and fresh," I pleaded.

"It does not matter," he told me grimly. "Don't you have a dhuti?" He stared without blinking, as if asking me, 'What kind of an Indian are you?'

I glanced at the priest's dark brown face. This was the most famous temple in Kerala and, after driving so far, it would be sad not to see the interior and the deity. And how would I tell this to my father?

Baal understood my situation and drove me back to the hotel.

I had a dhuti I had worn the day before. It was not clean and certainly not ironed, but I put it on, wrapping it around my legs like a skirt. That's the way they wear dhuti in South India, and I thought they would like the visitors dressed that way too. I didn't want to create more problems by wearing it in the style of my home city, Calcutta. I wore the wrinkled Indian shirt I had worn during the journey, and we rushed back to the temple.

The priest looked at me and nodded in satisfaction.

***

"So, they liked you in dirty clothes better?" DeeDee shook her head. "That's crazy. They should change the rules."

"The Travancore kings built the Vishnu temple 700 years ago," Shankar told her. "The priests have followed these rules since that time. They are now holy rules. No one is going to change them."

Shankar looked outside, wondering how these rules had developed. He reflected on how the most renowned interpreter of the Hindu religion, Adi Shankara, had been born in Kerala where the temple was. This man had emphasized the Vedic essence of the religion—God is everywhere and within everybody. But sadly, in the region of his own birth, a foreigner could not enter a Hindu temple.

"Did Mommy ever get inside the Durga temple?" DeeDee nudged him.

"On another trip to India, your grandma took her inside. Your mother wore a sari, held on to Grandma's hand and kept her head down. That's all."

"Good that Grandma knew what to do." But DeeDee seemed unimpressed.

"You see another photo in the album? Your mother took that picture from inside the temple of other Westerners on the balcony who couldn't get in."

DeeDee went away but the priest at the temple was still on Shankar's mind and reminded him of his father. Physically they had no similarity, but both followed religious customs literally. Shankar was sure the priest was controlling to his family, like his father, to their ruin. His father's scowling face came to him, shouting, "You decided to marry a non-brahmin girl?" He closed his eyes. Despite Jacco's sincere advice to forgive and be at peace, Shankar could not conjure forgiveness for his father's deeds. The fireplace was blazing, but he felt a shiver and put another log on the flames. Since Vedic time, Agni, fire, has been considered a medium of communication, between man and the gods—a link between man's consciousness and the cosmic consciousness. Pure and sacred, Agni does not distinguish between brahmins and non-brahmins or locals and foreigners.

As he gazed at the fire, Shankar wondered why he did not protest or at least say anything to Baal against the silly dress rule. Baal was from the south where people followed conservative religious dictums, such as not allowing a non-believer to enter temples to keep them 'pure,' but discriminating against him because of his clothes? The priest in Kerala reminded Shankar of the temple gatekeeper in Orissa; he had quietly but fervently fought against his outdated rules but didn't succeed. Was that why he had quietly obeyed the priest in Kerala?

Chapter Forty-Two

An Evening with Rakhal-da

Winter seemed to be coming to its end. Snow on the streets was gone, but a cold wave had come down from Canada making the week frigidly cold. Children could not go out to play. They were all home on Saturday. Shankar read a book he had recently purchased, *Cosmology: A Very Short Introduction* by Peter Coles. This was a non-technical book but had received good reviews on introducing the development of the universe, what is believed and what is speculative and a summary of the latest ongoing research in cosmology.

"Grandpa, I'm bored." Raja walked in and grumbled. "Mommy told me to find something to do, but I can't find anything."

"Nothing to do?" Shankar asked. Raja nodded despondently.

"Come, sit with me. We'll figure out what to do."

But before he could talk with Raja, DeeDee showed up. "Mommy doesn't want me to go out with my friend. Grandpa, can you tell us a story?"

Shankar knew the temperature had dropped last night—too chilly to play outside. They were both bored. "Sit with me," he told DeeDee, "we will figure out something."

"I also want to hear a story," Raja chimed in.

"We can do many things together," Shankar said. "Tell me first, do you have a favorite teacher in the school?"

"I don't want to talk about school," Raja quickly said.

"I can read you a detective story."

"Do you remember Grandpa," DeeDee said, "you told us how you played with your cousins, throwing stones at night? About your cousin Chinta? You tell us about them."

"Hmm. About my cousins? You know I have lost touch with them. They are all old like me."

"Who was your favorite cousin?" DeeDee pressed on, suddenly perked up.

"Well, I have not told you about my most favorite cousin. He was always fun." His lifelike figure came to Shankar. He had not thought about him since he left Calcutta. A regret panged him. He felt sorry that he didn't know what had happened to Rakhal-da—the most wonderful cousin in the world—always jolly, always full of enthusiasm, and there was nothing he couldn't do. He was much older. Where could Rakhal-da be now? Was he still alive?

"Grandpa," Raja said, "Tell us about him. How come he was your most favorite cousin?"

DeeDee pulled Grandpa. "Please tell us about him."

"I can do that."

***

Cousin Rakhal-da

Once I was almost asleep when someone shouted: 'Rakhal-da!' and I jumped out of bed and ran to him. There was Rakhal-da all wet and no umbrella with him. Uma gave him two towels, asking him to dry up, but he said, "This is nothing compared to the place I just come from." Rakhal-da looked the same as always: tall, thin, and dark, with shiny, short curly hair. He wore a dhuti and a long white shirt with a chain of dusty-gold buttons—the top two unbuttoned. Always the same style.

"Where do you come from this time?" My mother came over from the kitchen.

"From the northeast, the land of rains," Rakhal-da said, and bent over and touched her feet as they do in Bengal when meeting older relatives. "It's a long story. I was there for the last eight months."

"What?" My mother's eyes became bigger. "Did you go to Cherrapunji? The place of the Khasis?"

"Yes, I was there exploring a mining opportunity, looking into mining precious metals."

"I see, another adventure," my mother said, and looked at him for a few moments. "If my sister were alive, she'd not allow you to wander around like this. I'm glad you remember us once in a while. You talk with the children while I go and make some dinner. Would you like some fried *ilish maachh*?"

"That would be wonderful; we don't get shad fish on the frontier."

Rakhal-da gave three of us a warm, group hug; then we dragged him to
the largest bedroom and gathered around him.

"What's new here?" he asked.

"Nothing," we answered in a chorus.

"Tell us about the northeast," my younger sister said. "Is it a
dangerous place?"

"Very!" His face turned stiff, "Very! Wild animals are there; you name
it ... tigers, leopards, cobras, rhinos, striped hyenas, and noxious insects
you've never heard of. In some areas, it rains every day, and the forest is so
dense, no one can enter. Then there are the savage tribes."

"But you can go there, right?" I asked.

Rakhal-da told us a little about his adventure in the northeast forests.
He then became silent, staring at the window.

"Did you really eat pig meat cooked by tribal people?" My oldest sister
asked him. "Unclean, unwashed, and just broiled. No curry?"

"I'm only telling you what I saw and ate. That's all."

"How you can eat meat only burned over fire I don't know," my oldest
sister said in disgust.

That put a little damper in our exuberance, but I wanted to hear more.
I was fascinated with the strange world he had encountered and didn't
care if it was safe or not to eat pig meat. I begged him to tell us about
Cherrapunji.

Rakhal-da looked at us quietly for a few moments, as if we had
reminded him of something. Then he said, "Never trust a man you don't
know, especially in the rain."

That certainly drew our attention! What did the man do to Rakhal-da?
We inched closer to him. Finally, when he had dried his head and began to
drink the tea mother had brought him, he said, "Well, I guess I have to tell
you what happened in Cherrapunji. I was there for over two months and it
was raining every day. One day it was drizzling lightly; a light drizzle is a
good day in Cherrapunji, so I went out to explore."

He hesitated for a few seconds to decide where to start. Then he said,
"First I must tell you about the land around Cherrapunji so you will
understand where I was. A long time back there was an old market known
as Chera in the mountains 30 miles south of Shillong. The Khasi tribal
people have lived there for hundreds of years. An exceptionally beautiful
place. When the British ruled India, they were interested in this area for
military reasons and that helped it grow into a nice little town.

"There is a beautiful waterfall, The Mawsmai Falls, four miles from the
market. It is one of the world's highest falls. A nearby cave, the Mawsmai
cave, is another wonder. It has several limestone pillars at the entrance.
People are fascinated by these pillars, but they don't venture far into the

cave. The rain and darkness hold them back. I was having breakfast near Mawsmai Falls, when this Khasi man introduced himself and sat down at my table.

"'From Calcutta?' he asked me.

"'Yes, just vacationing,' I told him. I didn't want to tell him why I was in Cherrapunji.

"'That's nice.' But he looked at me for a while and then said, 'You don't look like someone who would come here just for vacation. Anyway, that's your business. You seem to be a sturdy, capable man. Are you interested in an adventure?'

"I looked at him intently, trying to gauge what he was up to, but a Khasi face is hard to read. Like the stoic face of an old Chinese man. I couldn't figure out whether he had something serious to tell me, or he was a nut. 'What adventure?' I asked him somewhat rudely.

"'It's about the Mawsmai cave,' he whispered. 'Very few locals will share this with you. It's my family secret.'

"'What do you want from me?' I asked him in a slightly irritated tone, but I was also intrigued, eager to find out what he knew about the cave.

"Rakhal-da then leaned toward us children, and said in almost a whisper, 'You know, I was really there to explore the area on my own, for gems.'

"'Gems are hidden in the cave,' the Khasi man said as he winked and gave a little smile. 'If you will agree to help me, I have a proposition for you.'

"I was stunned. How did he know of my interest? His heavy round face, typical of a Khasi man, was like a stone sculpture. I couldn't read his mind. But what could I lose? 'Tell me more,' I said.

"'Only a few old tribal people know about it,' the Khasi man looked at me without blinking. 'My father stumbled upon an area inside the cave where light was glowing. Before he could figure out what it was, he slipped on a rock, twisted his ankle, and had to retreat. Unfortunately, he died soon thereafter. But he had told me where it is. I have tried to find it before but got lost several times. I don't want to work with any native man because they would tell others. And you know what would happen? All the Khasis would be inside the cave. So, I want to work with a partner who isn't from this area.'

"The man then told me how far he had progressed in his exploration and that the British knew about the place. They were keeping it a secret and planning to get the gems for themselves. They had even sent their army's Frontier Division to explore, but then WWII began, and the Indian Liberation army, backed by the Japanese, shelled near this area. That stopped the British. After India gained her independence, the Indian army found out about the British plan to explore the cave and get the gems. They haven't organized a search team yet; now would be the time for us to get there first and get the gems.

"The man stopped and continued to hold me in his unblinking gaze. I was astonished. I had heard something like this from my sources in the Indian army, so I was impressed with the man. He seemed to know what he was talking about. My friends in Calcutta Fort couldn't tell me where the secret place was; they only knew that there was something in a cave in the Khasi Hills, and that it was very much hushed up.

"I decided to go with him. We planned together; we went to the bazaar and picked up some items we might need, such as good flashlights and some ropes, and went on our expedition. We were deep inside the cave in an hour. I followed him, but I was careful to note the passage, particularly the rock formations, so I could come back alone if necessary. The cave tunnels went in several directions. Some of the tunnels were so small we could not go into them, but four tunnels were big enough for us to walk in. He told me two of the paths met again and came out in the open. He had explored the third tunnel and found it to be a dead end, so we followed the fourth branch. It went deep into the mountain, and the path became narrower and colder. It was humid and musty. Rainwater had leaked in through cracks in the rocky ceiling, and moss grew on the walls and floor, making them slippery. We proceeded carefully. It was so quiet we could hear our footsteps.

"We saw columns of stalagmites pointing up from the floor of the cavern. When we turned the flashlight on the walls, some portions glowed distinctly like gems. I wanted to break off a few of these stones and take them with me, but we moved on. The Khasi man wanted first to get to the place that his father had told him about before exploring anything else.

"After walking for another hour or so, we saw a faint streak of light in the distance. I thought it came from the outside, but the Khasi man became breathless with excitement. 'Ah huh,' he said in a hushed voice as if someone were going to listen to his secret, 'My father told me about this light.'

"We stopped and explored the area. We could see the walls better because of the faint light. It was all rough rock; there was no trace of gems. I smelled a slight rotten odor in the air. Perhaps it was not the place we were looking for. Then the man, in his hurry, stumbled on something and almost fell. I focused my light on him and saw he had tripped over a skeleton. The skeleton was in a kneeling position, head bent forward, as if praying. It was intact as if the man had died in that position and no one had moved his body. Perhaps no one had come here before us—except for this poor dead soul. The smallness of the skeleton told me it could be a Khasi man because they were short people. Then I wondered if the Japanese had sent a spy this far during WWII. The Japanese had recruited Indian prisoners of war into the Indian National Army during WWII and had attacked from the Burmese border to liberate India from the British. So, the skeleton could be a Japanese soldier. That thought intrigued me very much. We searched the area and found an old, dark dirty-green bag a military man might carry. It bore the insignia of the rising sun! There were no gems or rocks in it. The Khasi man gave the bag to me and went on ahead. I found a small bag inside one of the side pockets with small Japanese letters on it and took it out. I found no other artifacts in the area.

"We moved on and the light became stronger. Soon it took on a reddish-yellow tinge and we continued with eager anticipation because we thought we might be near something interesting. We saw a small side cavern, which was illuminated by the light. I was examining the wall, when suddenly the man pulled out a knife and lunged for my chest! But I had been careful, constantly watching him out of the corner of my eye. I simply sprang to one side, like a matador teasing a bull, and he lost his balance.

"'What are you doing?' I shouted at him.

"'This is our land, and the gems belong to us,' he said. He planted his legs firmly on the floor and raised his arms to fight me. Light reflected off his sharp knife.

"'Stop this,' I commanded.

"'No one but a native may have these gems.' His face became stern. I saw he was serious and determined to kill me. Then I calmly took out my gun and pointed it at him.

"'Drop your knife,' I commanded.

"He was surprised that I had a revolver. 'I shouldn't have brought you here,' he lamented, but obeyed me. I picked up his knife and told him to go forward."

We were listening to his story, spellbound, and we felt so proud of our cousin. My oldest sister asked, "You had a gun?"

"You have to be prepared for these situations," Rakhal-da told us, "I would not be here today if I hadn't been alert. I would be lying there like the Japanese fellow."

"Tell us, what happened then?" we clamored together. We wanted to know whether he had found any gems.

"We both entered the small cavern," Rakhal-da continued. "It glowed yellow in the faint light.

"'Gold,' the Khasi man muttered.

"I looked at the walls. No gems, but the walls looked rough and were the color of dirty gold, like large nuggets of pyrite I had seen. Fool's gold. 'Don't be fooled,' I told him, 'these are not worth anything.'

"The Khasi man kept on touching the walls and muttering, 'Gold, gold.'

"'You can take some if you like,' I told him, 'but it would be waste of time. Real gold doesn't look like that.'

"He took out a hammer and broke off several pieces. I took a piece as a souvenir. He took as much as he could carry. Then we moved deeper into the cave; I always let him walk in front of me.

"As we kept going, the light became brighter, and I was still hoping to discover the gems his father had claimed to have found. After some time, we came to a place where we could see the source of the light. It came from the outside through an opening in the rocks.

"I suddenly realized, why no Khasi man had told others about the "gold"—it was all pyrite. They didn't want to appear to be fools.

"We examined the rocks on this wall carefully. There was no trace of any gems. We followed the path out of the cave and soon found ourselves on the other side of the Mawsmai Falls. I told the Khasi man to get lost.

"I returned to Cherrapunji late at night. It had been an adventure indeed, I thought, as I was undressing to go to bed. Then I felt the small bag I had taken from the dead Japanese soldier and opened it. A small piece of paper with Japanese writing fell out and fell apart in my hand. The few other little things in the bag had been ruined by moisture and age, except for a little ivory figure of a fat, smiling man, the size of my thumb, with inlayed coral work on it. Then it dawned on me it was a netsuke. The Japanese soldier must have carried it with him as a token of good luck. Perhaps his fiancée gave it to him.

"But what had he been doing in the cave? I wondered if he had become lost when the British started their counter offensive. I knew the Indian National Army and the Japanese had captured Kohima, a nearby town, in April 1944, but soon the British troops had overrun the place with their superior airpower. Then the monsoon had started. Hiking through the jungle would have been almost impossible for a foreign soldier. He must have hidden in the cave and died there."

Rakhal-da finished his account, but my oldest sister asked him what he had done with the gold nugget piece.

His face shrank. "You don't want to know." He stared at the drizzling rain for a moment and then sighed. "Well, you are my pals. I'll tell you. I didn't care for the nugget, but last year when I returned to Calcutta, I took it to a jewelry store in Bou-bazaar. The storeowner took it inside to examine it. Pretty soon he came out hurriedly. He took me inside the store and told me, 'It's pure gold. Where did you find it?'

"'Real gold?' I asked flabbergasted.

"'Certainly. I know gold when I see it, and I tested it.'

"How much will you give me?

"'5000 rupees because I don't know its history.' The storeowner winked at me. 'It could be stolen material. How do I know?'

"'10,000,' I demanded.

"'That's too high.'

"We settled on a price, and I left."

Rakhal-da looked at us and said, "The Khasi man must have chiseled out the walls of the cavern by now."

Mother called us for dinner, and Rakhal-da got up. "Don't tell this to your mother," he commanded us. We giggled, in awe of our brave and adventurous cousin.

***

Shankar leaned back, his hands behind his head, and turned to DeeDee and Raja. "To me, the most exciting part of Rakhal-da's adventure was when he discovered the dead Japanese soldier in the cave."

"Why were the Japanese in India?" DeeDee was back to her usual self again—inquisitive.

"Ah!" Grandpa said. "It is old history. During World War II, the Japanese conquered Singapore and most of Southeast Asia. They even drove the British out of Burma. An Indian leader, known as Netaji, formed the Indian National Army in Southeast Asia using Indian soldiers who had been captured by the Japanese. His objective was to free India from British rule. He and his army entered India from Burma to fight against the British. They had some initial success, but the British defeated them with superior airpower.

"This attack created a lot of enthusiasm among the Indians. The British felt they could not trust the Indians in the army, and they felt insecure. This was partly responsible for India's quick freedom from the British after World War II."

"What is a netsuke, Grandpa?" Raja inquired in an unsure voice.

Such an obscure item! Shankar wondered how to explain this to them. Their history dates to Samurai times. "A long time back, Japanese men used them as personal ornaments," Shankar told Raja and squeezed him closer. "They are valuable antiques now."

"So, what did your Rakhal-da do with his?"

"We didn't care so much about the netsuke when Rakhal-da told us the story. But years later, when I realized it was an unbelievably valuable object, I asked him about it; he pretended he didn't remember. 'What netsuke?' Rakhal-da asked me.

"I reminded him of his trip to the Mawsmai Falls. Then he said, 'Oh that? I gave it to a Khasi friend of mine.'

"He gave it away?" DeeDee raised her eyebrows.

"There is no point in lamenting past activities," Rakhal-da had said.

Chapter Forty-Three

A Year Passed

Life progressed for Shankar and Durga without any discernible problems, and rather sneakily, a year passed in Bellport. Slowly their social circle expanded because of Durga's efforts to reach out, and some connections came unexpectedly. One day, Shankar saw a man in the Gristedes supermarket who looked familiar, and while he was gazing at him, the tall, slim man came over.

"Weren't you in my physics class at Penn?" he asked.

Then, it came to Shankar. This was the student who sat next to him in his quantum mechanics class and told him his mark of 69 on his first test barely qualified for a C grade! How could he forget that lanky boy who came to Penn from Cornell?

"Aah, Peter! I recognize you. After so many years!"

"Remember, Dr. Cohen? We used to do his crazy electro-magnetism problems together in my apartment?" He laughed loudly.

"Yes! Yes!" Peter Hakim was the first person who befriended him in Philadelphia. Peter gave him a ride from the supermarket. He was the one who offered him an apple after taking a bite while they were struggling with homework in Peter's apartment. Shankar, being new to American ways, couldn't imagine offering an apple to someone already moistened with saliva. Only later he realized it was an intimate gesture.

"What a coincidence." They said at the same time and looked at each other, examining how they had changed physically.

"Let's get together for coffee and catch up." Peter gave him a business card from his wallet.

Then, Shankar met another fellow from Ann Arbor who, like them, came to Bellport because of his grandchildren. They discovered several other couples who made this area their retirement place because of their sons or daughters, or because they grew up on Long Island. Durga was even better at expanding their circle through various women's groups—the American Association of University Women and a book club. It took them about a year to feel comfortably settled.

During their evening walk, Shankar told Durga that he was wrong in his initial skepticism of the move.

"We have succeeded," she said, "in achieving your goal to move to America. Haven't we?"

Shankar nodded. He had seen how much Julie appreciated and loved everything Durga brought to the family, from new recipes to engaging activities for the children. Indeed, Durga had taken charge of the kitchen as a mother does in an Indian family, cooking special Bengali dishes she rarely cooked in Ann Arbor and emulating the many celebrations of her youth. Those simply boiled down to having a good time with the family. Durga had grown on Julie steadily like butter melting in warm sunshine.

A wistful thought flashed through Shankar's mind. How wonderful it could have been if his mother accepted Durga into their family. Their acceptance of Julie, and her acceptance of them, made life so much easier, and so different from what Durga had gone through.

The other thing that had shattered his cynical fear was their grandchildren's spontaneous acceptance of them. Shankar had recently wondered why he had not thought of moving closer to his son, rather than his son practically forcing him to move. Telling stories to his grandchildren came naturally to Shankar. Depending on the context of what the children were doing or clamored to hear about, they flew into his mind with ease. They weren't simply *stories*. They were his own childhood, his past life, some of which he had worked hard to forget. But it was hard to take Calcutta out of him. He relived the time of his youth. Most of the time, however, they reminded him of the many things he'd done as adventures, most of which his family wouldn't have liked him to do. Sometimes a chuckle came to him, sometimes a melancholy feeling, sometimes regrets, and more often discontent and anger.

Shankar and Durga wished to do something different on Saturday, the anniversary of their arrival—something lively. The day turned out bright and warm, a perfect day for an outing. They decided to do what they had enjoyed very much in Michigan—going out for a leisurely drive. They took the grandchildren with them for a venture out to the end of Long Island, Montauk Point. "We'll see the first lighthouse constructed in New York state," Shankar told DeeDee and Raja, "Built even before I was born."

DeeDee raised her eyebrows. "How long ago?"

"Over two hundred years," Shankar said and laughed.

***

Shankar took Route 27, the Sunrise Highway, which goes all the way to Montauk Point. At the beginning there was nothing interesting to see as they drove by less dense, and apparently poorer, communities of Moriches. They passed by trailer houses and some tracts of farmland where the fields had only started to show signs of green. After Eastport, DeeDee spotted a sign for Speonk and said, "Look there, Raja, a funny name!" They both started to repeat, "Sponk, sponk, sponk," and laughed with each other. "It's a Native American Indian word meaning 'high place,'" Shankar told them.

"I read there were huge duck farms in Long Island," Durga said. "These are the areas where that business started and thrived. Now there are almost no duck farms on the island."

Soon signs for Hampton Bay and a County Park appeared and they saw a sign directing them to a 'big duck' with arrows on Route twenty-four. Shankar followed the sign and came to The Big Duck. A building, the size of a small cottage, in the shape of a duck, was nestled on the edge of the park. It was shiny white and quite startling to see—sitting there quietly. Shankar half expected it to quack! Originally built in 1931 four miles away in Flanders, it used to be a shop to sell ducks and duck eggs. It was now a gift shop with a plethora of whimsical duck-related items. DeeDee and Raja ran and went inside the duck, followed slowly by Shankar and Durga. Durga bought a toy duck for Raja and a duck magnet for DeeDee.

After the break, they drove over the Shinnecock canal that connects Peconic Bay in the north with Shinnecock Bay in the south. When they reached the Hamptons, they took a detour to see the white beaches and quaint villages. They peeked at nice homes interspersed with working farms and visited posh shops. Durga said she would like to show DeeDee and Raja a windmill in Water Mill on their way home. The mill was used to grind grain in colonial times and was over 200 years old.

They passed by East Hampton and entered a smooth and straight section of the road that ran through pine barrens and sand dunes. Soon a short road on a traffic stop took them to the lighthouse on a bluff overlooking the ocean. Waves crashed on rocks at the bottom of the bluff; the stout, octagonal lighthouse stood tall above them. The middle was painted red, with the top and bottom painted white.

Shankar raised his grandson up so he could see further. "I see a boat, Grandpa." Raja stretched his arm forward and started to wiggle with excitement.

"At night," Shankar told him. "the light from the lighthouse tells sailors they are near land and must be careful."

DeeDee and Durga strolled near the gate of the lighthouse. They decided to climb up the steps to the metal deck above and called Raja. Shankar stayed on the ground. When they came down from the lighthouse, Durga said, "It's good that you didn't go up. There are 137 steps, narrow and steep. I am exhausted. But the view was breathtaking."

The children held Shankar's hands and strolled around the lighthouse. Durga found a grassy place with a view of the ocean and spread a blanket. "The climb has made me hungry." She brought food and drinks from the trunk of the car. The blanket and food drew them together.

"I've read a ghost story about a lighthouse, Grandpa," DeeDee said. "A boat crashed on a rock in Maine because the sailors didn't see it. Only a little bit of the rock was sticking out. Two men from the boat swam to the rock, but they didn't have food or water, so they died there."

Shankar nodded. "Those kinds of accidents happened many times before lighthouses were built."

"Then other sailors started seeing shadowy images of two people on the rock," DeeDee continued. "They looked like ghosts, waving as if they were calling the sailors to them. Sailors thought the place was haunted, so nobody went closer, and no one died. Later, a lighthouse was built there, and no one saw the ghosts anymore."

"Sounds like a good story," Durga said. "Some claim they have seen ghosts at this light house also."

"Really?" DeeDee gaped.

"Indeed, many sailors have died here—often because of bad tides, storms, and bad luck," Durga said. "A young lady, Abigail, a passenger of a shipwreck during the Christmas of 1811 managed to survive and land on the beach below the lighthouse. She was rescued and brought up the cliff and inside the lighthouse. But she was so exhausted from fighting the waves that she died. Since then, many claimed to have heard her voice echoing inside the lighthouse. Some have seen her strolling the grounds or climbing the steps. Some have felt their shirt pulled and framed pictures rattling inside the lighthouse while there was no one else inside. Abigail's story has become a legend."

"Grandma, I don't want to be here at night," DeeDee said.

"We read lots of ghost stories when we were young like you."

"Were they scary, Grandma?"

"Very scary." Durga leaned toward her. "Ghosts coming out at night in cremation sites near the river!"

DeeDee turned to Shankar. "Do you believe in ghosts, Grandpa?"

Shankar looked at his watch. "Ghosts? I don't know." He remembered scaring his younger sister Parvati when she was little, but when she became older, she lost her fear of ghosts. Once he took her to the backyard at night and showed a white cloth fluttering on a pole behind a tree, hoping she would get scared, scream, and run back home, but she had gone to the pole and pulled down the cloth—mother's petticoat left to dry.

After Durga gave them sandwiches and drinks, Raja said, "Grandpa, DeeDee said there's a ghost in the tree at the end of our backyard."

"Jimmy has seen it twice," DeeDee asserted, referring to the boy next door. "I won't go out there at night."

"You know, children, Grandpa knows many ghost stories." Durga threw a mischievous smile at Shankar. "He used to scare me when we were first married."

"Grandpa tell us a real ghost story," Raja pleaded.

DeeDee nodded energetically but with raised eyebrows.

Shankar looked at the eager faces of the children. "Eat your sandwich. I'll tell you what happened to me once."

"*You saw a ghost?*"

"I don't know if I saw a ghost. When I was young, I imagined so many things, but later, I wasn't sure if I actually saw anything."

Shankar looked out toward the waves crashing on the boulders at the base of the lighthouse cliff. The waves' rhythmic pattern had continued for millions of years and would continue even when he was no longer around. Change is a fact of life; the children would also move from ghost stories to the realities of life. But for now, he had their undivided attention. "I'll tell you what I saw, and you decide," he told the children.

***

Decaying Palace

I was about twelve or thirteen at that time. I didn't believe in ghosts, but my friends did. They read many ghost stories—of good ghosts and nasty ghosts. I argued with them. I told them, "Ghosts are all imagination—stories made up to scare others."

Ramu was a friend who played with us, but he had another group of friends who were from wealthier families. His family owned a large bicycle store in the city and often rode the latest model bicycles. One day he told me, "If you don't believe in ghosts, can you go to the *Purano Praasaad* at night?"

The Purano Praasaad was an old palace, about a mile and half from our house. A long time back, it belonged to a great Bengali General—a hundred years back, perhaps. Once it had beautiful buildings, open pools, gardens, fountains, and statues, but now the walls surrounding the palace were broken, with gaping holes, and old uneven bricks exposed everywhere.

We boys went there sometimes during the day. The columns in the front were still intact and the rooms were large with high ceilings, but everything was dusty and full of cobwebs. People thought the ghost of the General's grandson lived there. He fought against the British and didn't want any British to enter his palace. But he lost the battle and shot himself in his favorite garden. I was told no one performed a cremation ceremony for him because the British soldiers took his body away as proof of their victory. Those who had seen the body were aghast; there was a peculiar smile on his face. They thought a *Pret*, a nasty spirit, had taken over his body because he committed suicide and died unhappy. He could neither go to heaven nor to hell; his spirit was forced to live in that between state forever. The villagers believed he roamed the Purano Praasaad at night and guarded it so no British could ever live in his palace. Some tried, but they all left after one or two nights.

What my friends proposed was scary, but I said, "Why not? What will you give me if I do?"

Ramu said he'd let me ride his new bike. That was something. No one could touch his bike. So, I agreed. Then another boy said, "You have to go on a full moon night, when ghosts dance in the garden."

They argued for some time about which night would be best. Any night was fine with me. Ramu said, "We can't wait too long, you'll get cold feet and not do it. Let's do it tomorrow. There will be enough moonlight for ghosts to come out."

I didn't care. I told them, "I'll go at midnight and plant a stake in the garden. You can check it in the morning."

"I'll give you a special stake," Ramu told me, "so we know you did it."

For a second, I thought some form of a spirit might protect the palace and I shouldn't be going there, but I kept silent.

When I came home, my father was near the kitchen, and I asked him if he believed in ghosts. I remember he looked at me for a few seconds. "Are you scared of ghosts?" he asked me.

I shook my head.

"Then don't worry. Ghosts exist, but they are not as bad as you read in stories. When a man dies and proper funeral rites are not done, his soul cannot move on to the next phase. It remains perturbed and restless and roams around as a spirit. People call these spirits ghosts. They like dilapidated buildings, abandoned places, riverbanks—dark places to hide. They stay in desolate areas because they want to be left alone. As soon as proper funeral services are carried out, the spirit is released and moves on to take another body—reborn into a new life."

"Can they harm us?"

"No. Unless the man dies very unsatisfied or in a very bad state of mind."

"I don't believe in ghosts," I told my father with trepidation. He was fine with that.

"The stories you read in books," he told me, "are all bogus stories to scare young children. Adults don't read them." After a pause, he said in his usual commanding voice, "Stay away from old, deserted places anyway."

I went to my room, thinking I was grown up and could handle anything. Soon a question came to me: *'When is a funeral not proper?'* I didn't want to go to my father again. I went to my mother in the kitchen and asked her.

"Why do you ask?" she stopped stirring the vegetables she was cooking. Her face was serious. I got a little nervous that she suspected I was up to something.

"Father said that is how a soul becomes a ghost."

"I see. An improper funeral is when a son doesn't offer rice and water to the deceased soul." Her face relaxed. "We're glad we have a son. Remember to do our last rites."

"Sure, I'll do that." I left her, relieved. I didn't want my parents' souls to become ghosts—I would do the funeral rites when they died someday.

The next day it rained, but it cleared in the afternoon. In late evening, Ramu brought me a stake with a cat carved on top. I was to push it into the soil in the garden. He asked if I wanted to back out, but I said no.

I snuck out of the house at about 10 o'clock. My friends followed me for some time and then held back, saying, "We will wait for you near your house."

I understood they didn't want to be anywhere near the palace in case a ghost followed me. I was determined to accomplish the job and come back victorious. I would go in, plant the stake, and come out. It shouldn't take more than half an hour. A few clouds lingered in the sky and there was no breeze. A half-moon rose and the sky looked beautiful. I was proud, fearless, and impatient to show my friends there was nothing like ghosts in the palace garden. Soon, I faced the walls of the Purano Praasaad.

As I came closer, everything around me felt calm. No sound anywhere, of any kind. A few clouds floated in the sky, but the moon shone brighter than before, and I could see the palace clearly. It was eerie. I went in through the broken wall. The ground was wet, a little soggy even. I looked around. Everything was as I had expected, except it was so silent and so bright in the blue light of the moon.

The white marble fountain in the garden looked exquisite, as if it were brand new. The palace looked striking in the faint moonlight. How beautiful the palace must have been when the General lived there! I decided to set the stake in front of the fountain. Then a breeze started to blow—a sweet spring breeze. I heard some noises and thought little animals were scurrying around . . . but I couldn't see any. I wanted to finish my job and leave. I bent down to plant the stake; then I felt a mist on my face, as if the fountain were working. I raised my head and saw a large tree with green leaves next to the fountain. There had been no tree a few minutes before, I was sure of it.

I felt as if some-one was behind me, watching me intently. My heart started to pound, but I couldn't look back. I couldn't even lift my face for fear of seeing someone or something in that lonely place. I held the carved wooden cat on the stake to press it down. Then I heard a horse trotting, and I raised my head. A big lightning bolt struck from the sky, and for a moment I saw a muscular man in military uniform under the tree. I screamed and tried to run away but fell on the wet grass. I felt some one pulling me by my shirt. I cried and slipped on the grass again. Somehow, I got up and started to run. I was sure someone was chasing me. I don't remember how long I ran. Finally, I saw my friends in the distance, waiting near my house. But as I went closer, they ran away. I called them but my voice was choked.

The next thing I remember, it was morning, and I was in my bed. My mother was sitting next to me. "I told you not to go out at night," she said, "but you wouldn't listen." I asked her what happened. She said I came home with muddy clothes, and I was shivering and saying things she didn't understand. She had changed my clothes and put me to bed.

Later, my friends came and told me they had run away from me because I looked like a ghost. I walked strangely, like a drugged man. I looked dark to them. How could I have dark clothes on when I went into the palace with clean white clothes?

Then Ramu asked me, "Did you go near the fountain?"

I said, "Yes." I was going to tell them I didn't plant the stake. I couldn't even remember where I left it. But they didn't wait for my answer. They immediately started to walk toward the Purano Praasaad, talking among themselves.

When we reached the palace wall, they ran ahead of me; they weren't afraid in the daylight. Soon I heard Ramu saying, "Here's the stake with the cat; it's so strongly planted. Help me! I can't pull it out."

As I entered, I saw marks on the grass where I had fallen. I also saw my footprints. The boys circled around Ramu near the fountain, trying to pull the stake out. Then I remembered I had dropped the stake at the bottom of the steps when I was running away.

Before I could say anything, my friends lifted me up on their shoulders and proclaimed I was the bravest boy in the group. Ramu said, "You can ride my bike any time you want."

***

"I knew ghosts exist!" DeeDee exclaimed.

"Did you really see a ghost?" Raja asked, his face tense and eyes wide open.

"No, stupid!" DeeDee told her brother. "The ghost attacked him from behind."

"So, who planted the stake?" Raja challenged her.

DeeDee walked away. "Ghosts act strange. You'll understand when you're older."

"I'm glad the ghost didn't catch me," Shankar said. "You two couldn't be here then, you see."

"Even I like the story," said Durga, giving him a playful hug. "No wonder the children want to be with you all the time. Our English literature discussions in college have finally come in handy, isn't it so?"

"If you think about it, really, those English discussions are the cause of everything that happened to us. Sometimes I wondered if you wanted to teach me English or that was only an excuse to see me. You can tell me now."

"You'll never know." Her eyes twinkled.

"I knew it!"

Shankar sat there and stared at the ocean. His mother's voice rang in his heart. "Remember to do our last rites."

LIFE IN BELLPORT 3

JULY - SEPTEMBER 2005

Chapter Forty-Four

Fourth of July

G randpa, look!" DeeDee called her grandfather to the living room window. "Mr. Gordon is coming to our house with Raja." It was early evening; the summer sun had not gone down yet. Mr. Gordon's house was at the end of their block. DeeDee and Shankar went to the front door to meet them.

"I'm sorry to have to come over," Mr. Gordon said. "Raja and another older boy were lighting Roman candles in the field behind our backyard. I thought you should know. One almost went straight to our roof. He could have burned the house down. I don't know what goes on in children's heads."

Raja stood there with a brown bag from which a few Roman candles and a large bottle stuck out.

"Where did you get those?" DeeDee asked in a rather adult-sounding tone, tilting her head to the side.

Raja shifted his weight and looked at the front lawn without answering her.

"Thank you for telling us," Shankar said to Mr. Gordon. "We'll have a talk with Raja and let his father know."

"If he wants to light these fireworks, he should go to the beach," Mr. Gordon said as he left.

After Mr. Gordon left, Shankar put his hand on Raja's shoulder. "Where did you get these fireworks?"

"From a store on the street. They go really high in the air." His eyes flashed.

"But you know they're unsafe?"

"I was very careful, Grandpa. Daddy will not let me light them from our backyard." Raja raised his voice a little to register his complaint.

"You are not old enough to play with this kind of fireworks." Shankar's scolding was mild. "Your father will be very disturbed when he hears about it."

"You don't understand, Grandpa," he grumbled.

But Shankar understood very well. He glanced at the driveway and saw a small, slightly burnt, pale green cardboard army tank lying on its side— one of the fireworks Raja had enjoyed lighting the evening before. Burnt packets of fountains, ash-colored marks of 'snakes,' and a few sparkler wires lay on the edge of the driveway. He remembered the sulfuric smell of the fireworks and sighed. He had not been able to sleep well because of the fireworks exploding late into the night. He could not, however, blame anyone. He knew what fun it was for young boys. Right then, a rocket shot into the sky with a loud squeal. Shankar wished the Fourth of July celebration was over.

"This year's fireworks are very good, aren't they, Grandpa?" DeeDee said.

"I wish we had good fireworks," Raja griped. "What Daddy bought aren't the good ones that go high into the sky."

"Flower ran away last year because of the loud firecrackers," DeeDee reminded Raja, glancing at her brother with an annoyed look. "She is such a good doggy, but we had a lot of trouble finding her."

Shankar was quiet for a moment. "You know," he said, "In Calcutta, I also had fun with fireworks." A smile creased his face.

"See? You played with fireworks too!" Raja exclaimed, seeking an alliance with his grandfather.

"I'm sure he didn't play with unsafe fireworks," DeeDee told Raja.

"Did you know," Shankar turned to DeeDee, "we made our own fireworks when I was young?"

She looked at him, as if digesting what her grandfather had just revealed. "You made fireworks?" She spoke in a soft, halting voice.

"Really, Grandpa?" Raja perked up. "Can we make our own fireworks?" His thin face beamed with excitement. He pulled Shankar's shirt. "Can we, can we, Grandpa?"

Shankar looked at him. Sure, Raja had his bloodline, no doubt there.

"Did Daddy also make fireworks with you?" DeeDee asked.

"No. We didn't. It's illegal here," Shankar said calmly. "Your father was an exceptionally good boy. He listened to what we told him. We made fireworks in India, but we can't do it here."

DeeDee's face glowed with admiration for Shankar. "Do girls make fireworks there, Grandpa?" Her eyes were wide and shimmering.

"In my time, they didn't. You know, making fireworks is a little risky; only boys take those risks, not girls. Girls are smarter. They decorated the house with earthen lamps and joined in lighting the fireworks."

"That's not fair, Grandpa." DeeDee pushed Shankar with her right hand. "If boys made fireworks, I'd make them too."

"Here it's different," Shankar told her.

"What kind of fireworks did you make?"

"Yes! Tell us what kind!" Raja chimed in.

Shankar saw the concern that had been there a few minutes ago was gone from their minds. Such is the case with children. He hesitated for a second and looked sideways at the neighbors' house. The lawn was cut, bushes trimmed, and the garden made picture perfect for the Fourth of July celebration. The old shingles on the roof startled him; sparks from falling fireworks could start a fire. He had not thought about this when he was young. Houses in Indian cities were made of bricks and concrete!

"I mostly made fountains. We made them in small earthen pots. Oh, how brilliantly the bright blue sparks come out in the middle of the yellow-orange shower of sparkles. I was not keen on making risky fireworks. The ones I made were relatively safe." Shankar remembered the excitement; there would be talks among boys and boasting of how good their fireworks would be. "Once, I made little fireworks that looked like mini-cigarettes, thin but conical. They went zigzag in the air, but for only three or four seconds. One time, I lit one that landed inside the clothes of a man. You know, the long, white cloth men wear in India. I ran away in fear." Shankar smiled broadly. "Sometimes it chases the boy who lit it! I never made them again."

"I want to know how to make the fountains," Raja said and pulled Grandpa's hand. "Please, Grandpa?"

"You can't get the ingredients for fireworks here," Grandpa told DeeDee and Raja.

"Tell us anyway," DeeDee said.

"Fountains are made with finely ground charcoal, sulfur, saltpeter, iron filings and a few aluminum flakes. They are safe. We lit those on fireworks night."

"You had a night set aside for fireworks?" DeeDee asked.

"Yes. Like the Fourth of July here. In Calcutta it is the new moon night for Goddess Kali, usually near the end of October. People decorate their houses with earthen lamps on the roofs, balconies, doors, and windows. Silhouettes of houses glow in the dark and look so beautiful. Then, the sparkles and sounds of fireworks come from everywhere. A marvelous night." The memory of fireworks night cheered Shankar. Oh, what fun it was to make the fireworks and light them. He remembered the cheerful, enthusiastic face of his cousin Suresh who made flying fountains and Shankar had himself participated in that endeavor. Looking at Raja's eager face, he could not tell him how nasty fireworks could be. Youngsters never grasp danger. That's the way boys are and will always be.

"Let's make fireworks next year, Grandpa," Raja said, nudging him. "I'm eight. You can teach me now." His eyes were beaming with curiosity and excitement.

Shankar stared at the empty, black road. The trees shimmered in the last light of the day—their shadows almost indistinct. Shankar did not want to encourage Raja by telling him his involvement in making fireworks. "Let's go inside," he said. But he vividly remembered the night he made flying fountains with Suresh.

***

Fireworks Night

Suresh wanted to make *uranta tubri*, flying fountains. "It will be lots of fun," he told me. He came to spend the puja vacation with us; we all tried to make his stay fun and accommodated his wishes. I had never made flying fountains, so I was curious. I took him to a store near the railway station that sold fireworks materials. Suresh pointed out little half-round, clay pots, about an inch wide. "We'll use these," he stated. They were light and had little holes on one end for the sparks to come out. The opening at the other end was larger to stuff the fireworks mixture in, like the heavier, palm-size, clay pots I used for fountains. "It works like a rocket," Suresh explained, "when sparks come out through the little hole, that thrusts the pot upward."

When we came home, Suresh said, "We must now find the right kind of wood to make the charcoal powder."

"I use dried eggplant stems for my fountains," I told him, but he said, "No, those aren't light enough. We must find dry branches of *kul* trees; they are the best."

Kul trees produce a sweet and sour berry with a special fragrance. They are like crab apple trees, and they have thorns. We hunted all over the neighborhood and collected a bunch of dead kul tree branches. We knew how to make charcoal. We lit a bonfire and when the wood was burned, we extinguished the fire with soil. The next day, we sorted out the charcoal pieces.

We had already bought clay pots, clear white potassium nitrate crystals, and bright yellow sulfur. "We must have a very accurate scale," Suresh said.

Together, we went to the local pharmacy. "Could we borrow your scale for a few hours?" I asked the owner who knew our family.

"Making fireworks, eh?" he asked, pushing his glasses back onto the top of his head. "What're you making?"

"This is my cousin from South Calcutta," I introduced Suresh. "He will make uranta tubri."

The old man's face brightened. He pushed a lock of white hair from his forehead. "I made those once," he told us, confidingly. "A lot of fun! You borrow the scale when you need it, but be extra careful. Flying fountains are rough." He gave us a wink and went away to help customers.

We dried the ingredients in the sun for several days to remove all moisture. Then we ground them into fine powder with a mortar and pestle. That was hard work. We dried them separately in the sun again. We dried the clay pots too.

The final moment came two days before Kali puja, the fireworks night. Suresh unfolded a worn-out page and gave a wry smile. "It is my formula. Do not reveal this to anyone."

Fireworks formulas are big secrets for boys. If someone revealed his formula, you could never be sure he was telling it accurately. I felt immensely proud to know his formula. Suresh measured out each powder and mixed them well in a bowl. "We must now be very careful," Suresh said. "Make sure there are no matches or any flammable material around." He put a little of the mixture into one of the little clay pots and pressed the mixture with his thumb to make it stick there. He added a little more at a time and kept on pressing with his thumb until the mixture would not fall out when he turned it upside down. He let me help some.

We were absorbed in putting the mixture into the pots, when Shibu came running to us. "Did you hear what Naren-da is making this year?"

"We are busy making our own! How would we know?" I retorted.

"He wants to surprise everyone," Shibu said animatedly. "They are making bombs on the grounds of the elementary school."

"Big bombs?" I asked.

"Yeah," Shibu said. "He has prepared a special mixture of gun powder and collected stone chips from railway tracks. He thinks his bombs will be the loudest."

"In the school compound . . . *really?*" I asked.

"Yes," Shibu said. "Naren-da thinks no one will find him there. You know Naren-da is always doing unusual things. This time he wants to make the loudest bomb this neighborhood has ever experienced; he will explode it at midnight."

"We will have an even bigger surprise this year," Suresh told him.

"Really?" Shibu was intrigued.

"It's a secret," Suresh said and turned to me, whispering, "I do not want to tell anyone what we are making. I am afraid word will get around and someone will stop us."

"I won't tell anyone," Shibu promised.

"It'll be the biggest show in the sky," Suresh told him, "better than Naren-da's. Ours is safer than his." He then added, coldly gazing at Shibu, "Naren-da will be lucky not to blow his hands off."

"No fireworks are safe," Shibu commented.

"Come to our house on Kali puja night," I told him. "We will show you our new fireworks. After that we can all go out together."

"Great. I will do that," Shibu said, and walked away.

"Bring your fireworks with you," Suresh shouted behind him. "We will burn fireworks all night. And show our fireworks to your Naren-da. We will see whose is better."

My hand froze in the clay pot I was stuffing. I did not want to have this kind of a competition. Fireworks for me were only for fun.

Looking at my face, Suresh said, "Don't worry. What we are doing is safe." He kept on stuffing a clay pot. His nonchalant response surprised me.

We finally closed the end of clay pots with soil from the garden and let them dry in the sun. When the night of the fireworks came, we forgot about Naren-da; we were excited to try out our own fireworks. I was ready with my fountains that I made each year. I put on a new shirt to dress up.

"Shankar, don't wear that tonight," my mother said, "one little spark will ruin it."

"Okay," I replied but I put it on anyway after she left. I wanted everything to be perfect for our celebration.

Suresh also put on his best shirt. When it became dusk, we went out to the soccer field to test our creations. I lit one of my fountains and it was excellent, as in the past. The sparks went high up and spread wide. Suresh took out one flying fountain, held it between his mid and forefinger, and lit it. As the sparks came out, he held it a little distance away from his body and rotated his hand in a round circle. Sparks fell on the ground in a jet. Then, when he felt a good force had built up to push it up, he let go of the pot. It hovered for a moment in the air and then lifted in the sky like a rocket. We cheered and hugged; it was a success. We burned another and returned home elated.

The new moon night is always very dark. We saw the whole neighborhood had changed as if by magic. Little lamps, uniformly lined up on the roofs and windows, made beautiful silhouettes of the houses.

All were waiting for us to start the fireworks. I quickly lit one of mine and everyone cheered. My sisters brought out sparklers and lit them. Then

Suresh came out and lit one of his. He rotated the uranta tubri in a circle, as he had done in the field, and then let go of it. It went up smoothly like a comet and vanished high up in the air. 'Another, another!' my sisters shouted. Suresh lit a second one. It went up again beautifully. Everyone watched it with admiration.

My uncle lit ground bloomers, my sisters held sparklers in their hands, and I lit another fountain. My parents stood near the wall, watching. The scene became lively and colorful with different fireworks smells. My older sister came with a lit sparkler and rotated it around Suresh as if worshipping him. Suresh enjoyed the attention and told her, "Watch this one, it will go even further with a siren."

My sister moved back and shouted, "Look, another going up." Everyone turned to Suresh, but before he could release it, the flying fountain burst out in his hand. Sparks came out all around and he screamed, "My hand . . . my face!" He fell on the ground and cried in pain. His shirt was also on fire.

The adults rushed to him. My father fetched a bucket of water and threw it on Suresh. My uncle picked him up and took him inside. Suresh screamed all the way. His hand was severely burned, and sparks had fallen on his face.

"My eyes are burning," Suresh cried.

"Can you open your eyes?" My uncle asked him.

"It's all dark," he shrieked.

Everyone became quiet. My father said, "We must take him to a doctor immediately."

My uncle and father rushed out, carrying him to the doctor.

As soon as they left, silence fell in the house, which had been so vibrant a few moments before. Fireworks sounds floated in from the neighborhood, but my family was smothered in sadness. A few minutes later, my mother started to wail. "What will I tell his mother," she lamented as tears ran down her face.

My mother and sisters started to blame me. "You have encouraged him. He came to visit for fun, and now look what happened to him. Why didn't you stop him?"

Father returned after an hour. He looked devastated. He only said, "Suresh cannot see anything. Half of one finger may be gone." He went to his room, and my mother cried louder.

I went out to the backyard. *Indeed, why didn't I try to stop him?*

I did not observe that Shibu had quietly snuck up behind me. "Did you hear about the explosion in the school ground where Naren-da was secretly making bombs?"

222

"At the school compound?"

"Yes," Shibu confirmed, but his voice was sober. "He was making a big bomb for tonight. In his zeal, he pulled the string too tight and the bomb exploded in his hand."

"Oh, no!"

"Blood was seeping out of his hands. Several people have taken him to St. Michael's Medical Hospital," Shibu went on. "They think two of his fingers are blown off."

"Terrible," I said.

"Where's your cousin?"

I told him what had happened.

Shibu left, murmuring, "We should stop making fireworks."

Sad and disheartened, I took all our fireworks to the farmer's pond and dumped them into the water. As I walked home, I saw sparks of fireworks in the sky and heard elated shouts of boys in the distance, but I found no interest. In the faint light of the streetlamp, I then noticed that several sparks had fallen on my shirt and burned a couple of holes after all.

***

Shankar knew Suresh's fireworks were risky, but he did not act on his good sense. He could not bring himself to talk about flying fountains with the kids and sent them to play on the back porch until their dad came home. He quietly sat on his chair, thinking.

Chapter Forty-Five

Reflections of the Past

There is an article in today's paper about recovered memories of child abuse," said Samir, lowering the paper so he could see his father's face. "I wonder how much a child remembers."

"I only remember glimpses of early childhood, but not much." Shankar took a sip from his cup. "Perhaps young children remember deep, hurtful emotions, but how can one be sure how much of their memory is influenced by events of later life? Or even imprinted by anecdotes told by adults based on their likes and dislikes of the events?"

"Baba, how far back do you remember?"

"I vaguely remember the birth of my sister when I was four years old. It is an unpleasant memory—vague, but oppressive. For two weeks, maybe a month, my mother was confined in a special room. No one would tell me anything about what was going on. I remember how unfamiliar it felt to me. I wanted to go in to see my mother, but I was not allowed. I banged on the door, but my father would take me away. I thought Mother was dying; I was scared. Then one day, everything changed. Someone, I don't remember now who, brought a small baby from the room to show me, and said, 'You have a new sister.' After a few more days, Mother came out of the room with the baby. I do not remember how the baby looked or what else happened during that time."

"You remember it," Samir said, "because you faced something contrary to your expectations, even as a child. This article explains that ordinary events get drowned in the sea of memories. When we face situations conflicting with our expectations, morals, or ethics, they tend to go deep into the memory bank. It sometimes takes only a little effort to bring them to the surface."

Julie came down the stairs and joined them. She poured herself a cup of tea and stood at the window looking out at the Ostrich Plume Asters she had planted for their large feathery flowers. Their dark purple, pink, and white flowers had bloomed profusely and made her smile with pleasure. They had bloomed just when she wanted them—early fall. She took a sip and sat down at the table. "I have a good group of graduate students in my class this year," she told her father-in-law.

"What are you teaching?" Shankar asked.

"Effects of colonization on Indian civilization."

"Such a broad topic."

"It's a two-semester course. But quite basic. I plan to introduce them to Indian society before Colonial rule, and then to social changes that occurred during the 20th century."

Shankar's interest peaked. "I'd like to read the textbook you will use."

"There is no one textbook; we'll do readings from six books. I'll bring them home for you. I'll have to decide what to teach. This is the first time I'm teaching this class; I'll learn as we go along."

"It'll keep you busy."

She looked around and asked, "Where's Ma?"

"She had tea earlier," Shankar replied. "She's playing with the children in the living room." It then occurred to him, like an epiphany, that she had always excused herself from the Sunday breakfast table, leaving him and Samir alone. She must have deliberately done that to allow them some father-son time together, an opportunity to build a relationship, one that Shankar's father had never built with him.

Julie took a sip of her tea and looked at her father-in-law. "I'm going to make Bengali *Halwa* for breakfast. Would you like that?"

"Do you have sliced almonds and raisins? My mother would add those when she had them." Mother's kitchen in Calcutta came to his mind; how she cooked sitting on a low wooden stool in front of a tiny 'bucket' coal stove. He had never seen his father in the kitchen. That was her territory; what she cooked and how she managed the kitchen was her business.

"Yes," Julie told Shankar, "Ma taught me."

She squeezed her husband's shoulder and went to the kitchen.

Shankar noticed that Julie did not acknowledge her husband in her usual way and Samir didn't pour a cup of tea for her. Had some tension developed between them? Then, he remembered a Bengali phrase: about bickering between husband and wife, never pay any attention, as they end up in nothing—like two male goats charging at each other, rise on their back legs and you feel they are going to smash each other, but they gently touch each other's horns. He chuckled internally as these two were like all other married couples.

Samir continued his discussion on the child abuse case. "You remember the feeling of happiness, but the details go away. Unhappy memories are stronger."

Shankar took a sip from his cup. "Yes, the memories that come back to me often are the memories of regrets, hurts, and disappointments. Deeds not done." He shifted his view to the outside.

"The brain treats positive and negative feelings differently."

Shankar nodded but was unable to add anything.

"Negative emotions require more processing and analysis than positive emotions. We ruminate more about unpleasant events. More activity by the brain. It makes the event stay in our memory."

Shankar silently concurred with Samir. The familiar aroma of cream of wheat frying in ghee floated in from the kitchen. He saw Julie slightly bent over the burner, stirring. He took a sip of tea and saw the sun's rays sweep over the lush green of the arborvitae hedge. Nature is so beautiful! He reflected that nature doesn't remember the last year or care about what had happened before. The past has no meaning, only the present counts. Soumen had told him that the Buddha had said this many times ... dwell in the present moment—not the past or the future. But the human brain doesn't stay in the present. The memories hover over us.

He turned to Samir. "You're right. Negative memories are hard to erase, as if deeply ingrained in our brain. I remember how my friends and I, and many others chased after a Muslim man. Some wanted to see him killed or at least beaten up severely."

"What do you remember?"

***

Chasing a Muslim

When I was a teenager, I spent most of my time studying—like all good students in Calcutta. Every day, I awoke before dawn and studied on my bed under a mosquito net. On Sundays, however, I didn't study long and went out in late morning to sit with my friends on the red cement steps in front of Bikash's house. We would have a great *adda*—a convivial chat—from our own lives to the happenings in the wide world. Cool and comfortable, the cement steps were also good for girl-watching; the black asphalt road next to the steps went to the train station and the market, and everyone used this road. When one of us noticed a girl at the bend by the coal store, his voice would trail off. The others would follow his eyes, and they would quiet down until the girl passed by with her eyes lowered demurely. We would often forget what we had been debating so passionately moments earlier.

This Sunday, Bikash announced, "No college tomorrow."

I was surprised. "Why not?"

"Haven't you heard? No buses are running."

"Last night there was a riot in Barabazar," Soumen said. "Didn't you know?"

"How would he know?" Bikash's tone was sarcastic. "He is only studying for the exam!"

"During the Muharram parade," said Soumen, "the Muslims got rowdy and looted some of the Hindu stores. That started the riot. Several people were killed—both Hindus and Muslims. Now the disturbance has spread all over the city."

"Yesterday," Ranjit added, "the Muslims pulled a bus driver over and beat him so badly he will probably die. Now the buses are on strike."

"If this continues, there will be a curfew tonight." Soumen nodded, knowingly. "I'm sure it is already on in Muslim areas."

I wasn't happy. I wanted a book from the library for the coming exam. I couldn't afford to lose time. My friends kept on chatting about the riot, but I couldn't work up any enthusiasm. I left them. Eight years had passed since India and Pakistan became independent. Why more riots now? I wondered on the way home. Would the killings continue? I had always thought killing in the name of religion was wrong; religion was an individual thing, a private matter. As I went up the stairs, I smelled the fragrance of goat curry. The meaty smell, rich with garam masala, filled the air. My family had meat only once every two or three weeks. The fragrance cheered me, and I forgot about the Hindu-Muslim problems.

My friends called me in the evening from outside the house in a hushed voice, "Come out quickly. There's no time."

I bounded down the stairs. "What is it?"

"They caught a Muslim man on Seven Tanks Lane," Ranjit told me. He could barely hold his excitement.

We immediately started to walk fast.

"A Muslim here?"

"Yes," Bikash emphasized. "You know how devious they are."

"How did it happen?" I asked.

"Well," Ranjit replied, "a man saw him loitering near Ganguly's house. He had pockmarks on his face and was wearing a checkered shirt like the ones Muslims wear. When the man asked what he was doing, the man didn't answer and started to leave. He acted secretive, so several men chased him. You never know what the Muslims will do. My brother saw the crowd running after the man."

As we walked, Bikash and Ranjit discussed the harm the Muslims could bring to the neighborhood, but I remained silent. I didn't know any Muslim family and was not sure if what we heard was true. At the same time, I was eager to see the Muslim man who came to the neighborhood and know why he had come. I was also scared of the possibility the Muslims were infiltrating our area, which was all Hindu. Would a riot erupt here?

Soon, we came to the Seven Tanks Lane and joined more people going in the same direction.

"We will tear his limbs off," one man shouted.

"How dare they come here?" another man responded.

Excited by the mood of the crowd, we hurried faster. We had never encountered this before. But we had heard stories of the massacres during the 1947 Partition riot; I had a distinct childhood memory of fires burning in the distance and the fear of what the Muslims could do during the riot.

The crowd at Seven Tanks Lane became thick as we pressed forward. Soon, we came to an area with two-story houses, which were newer and owned by well-to-do people. But we could not go any farther; the crowd had surrounded a house farther down the street. Muffled murmurs of many voices came from all sides.

"He is hiding in that house," a man proclaimed.

"He is finished," another man said. "No police car can enter here. We will drag him out. Salah, *Suarer baccha*, son of a pig!" he shouted.

"Has anyone seen him?" I asked.

"What is there to see?" a man shouted over the din of the crowd. "He came here to spy on us, to find ways to murder us! *Kill him.*"

All were agitated and expressed their opinions. I remembered a story I had read in the paper two days before. The body of an old Muslim man had been found near the train tracks. From the description, I realized I had walked there once to see a dead python. The man's throat had been slit and his shirt badly torn, though his *lungi* was still intact and tightly tied at the waist. Blood drenched his upper body, even his white beard. No one knew the identity of the man. He had been carrying a worn-out jute bag with a handful of rice and lentils and an empty can. His walking stick lay next to him. The police thought the man lived in a shed near the dirty pond across the train lines and surmised he was returning home after the day's work. Witnesses said they had seen him begging at the station, but no one would come forward with anything definite. They only said, "He was a Musalman." The police suspected the murder was not committed by one man but by a gang. I was horrified when I read the paper; that same feeling arose again in me as I recalled the senseless murder. The poor man's only crime was being a Muslim. What did it achieve?

A new commotion on the street brought me back from the newspaper story; people near the house started to shout, "Release the Musalman! We will take care of him!"

Many were raising their hands and pointing to the house. Their loud roar hurt my ears. But the windows and shutters remained closed, and the doors shut. The crowd waited, hoping to see something happen, but even after two hours, nothing took place, so the crowd started to thin out.

As he was leaving, a man said, "I don't want to see a man being killed. I came because everyone else did."

"What good is killing one Muslim?" another man said. "There are millions."

We moved closer to the unlit house. Then I recognized it. Surprised, I blurted out, "Hey, this is where Bhupen lives, Bhupen from our college."

"Ah, the new fellow," Soumen said. "There's something strange about him. He keeps to himself."

"They came from Nainital, where his father worked for a drug company," Bikash said.

"Nainital? That's far away in Uttar Pradesh," I told them.

We realized we didn't know much about Bhupen.

The night lengthened, the fervent shouting subsided to only a murmur, and most people wandered away.

I finally said, "Let's go home. We will find out from Bhupen tomorrow."

"I want to see the end. I will stay here," Bikash said. His eyes glowed; he was wide awake with excitement.

I went home alone.

My friends returned home later without seeing how it ended.

The next day, the papers reported no serious incidents. Due to strong police patrols and urgings from political leaders, the riots came under control, and the city returned to normalcy two days later. All the offices, schools, and colleges opened. By the end of the week, no one talked about the incident, and people went on with their daily routines as if nothing had happened. No one remembered the fervor with which they had all rushed to Seven Tanks Lane.

I saw Bhupen at college, but I felt shy and awkward and couldn't ask him about the Muslim man. It seemed such a distant matter; no one was interested anymore. On Sunday, however, when we met on the red cement steps, we saw Bhupen walking by. Soumen jumped out and caught up with him. "So, tell us what happened."

"About what?"

"About the Muslim man in your house," Soumen said.

"Were you in the crowd?" Bhupen asked. He straightened his shiny black hair with his hands while giving us a hard look.

"Yup. We were right there," Bikash said, "but you kept the doors and windows shut."

"Did you also yell to release the man?"

"Certainly," said Ranjit.

"Do you really want to know?" Bhupen said calmly. A glint came to his eyes. "My father was standing on the road when the man ran to our house. 'Please save me!' the man said. My father quickly let him in and closed the door. The exhausted man was ashen and panting. He only said, 'Can't trust the mob.' My father gave him water to drink and fanned him. Still, it was hard to get anything out of him. He kept on saying, 'Can't trust the mob.'

"My father asked me to close all the windows and doors and turn off the lights. Then he paced back and forth, wishing we had a phone. I had never seen my father so determined. He would not talk with the people outside. He said they were a mob now and wouldn't listen to anything. He stayed awake the whole night with the man. We heard occasional shouts from outside even in the early hours of the morning: 'Release the Musalman to us.' When we heard words like that, the pale man shivered in fear. We put warm blankets on him. Finally, when the sun rose, my father went to our next-door neighbor and brought him over.

"My father told him, 'This is Jagdish Sen, chased by the crowd last night.' The man, who was better then, said, 'Yes, sir. I work at the Calcutta Corporation. I came to look at the area, to see if I want to buy a house here.' Our neighbor and my father then took Mr. Sen to his home."

"A Hindu!" Soumen said with great surprise, and we exchanged uneasy glances.

Bhupen stared at our faces without saying anything. "And what if he wasn't a Hindu?" he murmured, as he walked away.

Speechless, I kept on gazing at Bhupen's receding back. "How embarrassing!" The words came out of me involuntarily. We stared away from each other. I simply walked away.

***

No wonder, Baba," Samir exclaimed. "You remember it so well."

"That's what I was telling you. Such experiences stay deep in the brain. You cannot forget."

Shankar didn't have the same mentality as the others who chased the 'Muslim' man; he had simply followed his friends and couldn't leave quickly enough. He had felt like an alien observer. Now, he thought this was probably his first sign that he didn't belong to the society he was raised in. His ideas were different; he might never have fit in. At the time he didn't know he was destined to leave his culture. No one knows what makes a person different, but he clearly was different. He glanced at his son. Samir, as far as he knew, had no such hurtful experiences. Events like chasing an innocent man on false supposition. Chanting for him to be killed? Never.

Julie brought two plates of Halwa, asking Shankar, "Tell me if it tastes like your mother's cooking."

She brought her own plate. After tasting a spoonful, she squeezed her husband's arm. "Does it taste like your mother's cooking?"

"I like it. It's better than what I remember from Ann Arbor."

Shankar ate quietly, debating in his mind why he hadn't pulled his friends out of the chase. He did not even raise the question of their supposition that the man was a Muslim spy. Or that killing a Muslim, like some had done along the train lines, would not have solved anything. He was complicit in the chase. When finally, he did quit, he had not made any attempt to convince his friends to leave with him. Another thought crossed his mind, *was their act different from his father's deeds based on unquestioned beliefs?* He got up abruptly from the breakfast table and went to the living room. He must find some happy memories to replace these thoughts.

Chapter Forty-Six

Happy Memories

The next Sunday, after Julie took the children out to the Greek Fest in Hicksville, Durga came to the breakfast table. "What were you two talking about today?" she asked.

"We've been healthy in this family," Samir said. "We're wondering if that has something to do with our past." He served a cup of tea to his mother.

"Isn't that obvious?" She took a sip from the cup. "It's all in the genes."

"I guess so, Ma. But we were discussing if a happy childhood leads to better health later."

"Oh, I was reading about that in a magazine," Durga said. "If you remember happy memories more than sad or bad memories you have less depression or chronic diseases."

"Exactly," confirmed Samir.

"I had a wonderful life in Calcutta," Durga said. "I have lots of nice memories. Our family is close, as you have seen when you visited them. We had fun together with our brother and sisters."

"Do you think of those days often, Ma?"

"Well, often enough."

"Good relationship with parents is certainly a factor," Shankar interjected.

"People don't know this consciously," Samir said, "but more affection from parents will lead to better physical health for children and fewer depressive symptoms later in life. I think this is good for parents also."

"You do pretty well with the children." Durga told her son. "In India, fathers are often remote and don't show much love, as if that was the mother's job; and later they often compel them to learn the family line of work."

"My father never played with us, children," Shankar uttered under his breath. "No embrace." His father would have perhaps loved him if he had followed in his footsteps eagerly. He gently shook his head and looked away.

"Playing with children and showing affection is common here," Samir said. "But I don't know what happens later as I often see relations become frosty."

"Spend more time with DeeDee and Raja," Durga told Samir. "Give them more hugs." She looked away for a moment. "What happy memories do you remember most, Samir, from your days in Ann Arbor?"

"I was most happy when you or Baba were pleased with me. For something I did well at school or camp or when we were together on the weekend—'hanging out.' I still remember how proud Baba was when I got admission to Columbia. Memories like that."

"Yes, all your accomplishments brought joy to us," Shankar said.

"What are the happy memories you have, Baba?"

"The best was in my early childhood when my younger sister and I sneaked out of the house and roamed around the neighborhood."

"And later?" Durga leaned toward Shankar, focusing on him.

"When I did things on my own like flying kites or playing outside with friends or reading novels." He stopped and lifted his cup and looked at Durga. "Then, when I saw you at college."

"Really? I didn't know that!"

"You never asked."

"These are certainly fond memories," Samir said. "The point is, the more you think of these memories the better your health will be."

Durga was still looking at Shankar. "If I knew this, I'd have seen you more often."

"That's where my theory of fate comes in." Shankar said, "You can't know these things in advance." He shifted his gaze out the window. What a deep green verdant backyard! Soon, another happy memory came to him: a memory of trying to hatch an egg with his older sister. Even though it did not produce a koel; he remembered the joy he had working together with Uma.

During the day, however, instead of happy memories, unpleasant memories of Dum Dum occupied Shankar's mind. How restrictive their style of living was! He drifted to the time of his early youth. How hesitantly he had eaten a little puffed rice in his non-brahmin classmate's house. His friend's mother was so nice and happy to have him visit them, but he could not feel at ease. After he tasted an omelet and told his mother, he remained fearful for days that his father might force him to eat cow dung for his purification. One event stirred him the most. How rudely his father had refused to perform the wedding of a man's son because of an inter-caste marriage. He had just walked away keeping the man standing in their courtyard. That was when he had stopped being open with anyone in his family.

He must cultivate happy memories. Shankar shifted his thoughts to his college days, always glad to be there whether it was in class, the lab, or the library. No one restricted him from doing any reasonable thing and there were no barriers among friends of caste, color, heredity, which high schools one came from, or whether they belong to families from East Bengal or West Bengal. All were looking forward to learning and enjoying their college days. He had thrived in that atmosphere. He couldn't sustain the halcyon moments, however, as he drifted to the thought that he hadn't made any effort to stand up, not even talking with his siblings or relatives.

Chapter Forty-Seven

A Realization

On Sunday while Shankar and Samir read the paper, Durga cooked Dhakai Paratha, a many layered, fried crispy paratha, and Chana dal with raisins—two special Bengali dishes. "Bright sunlight this morning has inspired me to make these today," she told Julie who was helping her. Spicy fragrance of food wafted in from the kitchen.

"Did I tell you," Shankar heard Durga saying in a cheerful voice, "about the toast we ate for breakfast in Calcutta? Sometimes you can make these for the children. They'll like it. You toast the bread until brown and crunchy, put butter all over it; then hold it over the sugar bowl and pour sugar on it and let the sugar slide off into the bowl."

"You ate that for breakfast?"

"Yes, and I rediscovered it one day in Ann Arbor. I forgot how good it tasted." Durga chuckled.

Julie told Durga that they had a version here in the States too. "It's called cinnamon toast, because here they put a mix of cinnamon sugar on it."

The breakfast turned out to be a feast. "I've not had this since I left Calcutta," Shankar said, beaming. "This is superb, Durga. Now-a-days you will have to go to Bangladesh to eat this."

Julie got up from the table earlier than usual, saying, "I'm taking Ma and the children shopping—before it gets too crowded. Macy's has a special Halloween sale."

Samir looked up from reading the paper. "It will be hot today. Come back early and we'll go to Fire Island."

"Sounds good." Julie smiled at Samir. "Don't forget to go to the supermarket," she reminded him as the four rose to get ready.

Soon, Durga, Julie and the children walked out the door jubilantly as if they were going on an excursion to Disneyland. Sometime after they left, Samir turned to his father. "I know Ma is clearly happy living with us, but I wonder about you." He stopped for a few heartbeats, as if not sure if it was the right time for the discussion. "We kind of forced you to leave your life in Ann Arbor and your friends."

Shankar put down the newspaper and gazed at his son. "It has worked out better than I thought it would." He spoke slowly, thoughtfully. "DeeDee and Raja are one reason. It's time for me to be a grandfather. Julie has accepted us wholeheartedly. And I am happy your mother has found a way to recreate some of her family's happy times here."

Samir's face relaxed. He let out a breath and looked out toward the garden. "I've never seen my grandfather," he said, turning back to his father, "and there were no relatives when I grew up. That's why we brought you and Ma here. I wanted DeeDee and Raja to feel they have a family, more than only parents."

"And you have carried out your wish!" Shankar said approvingly, looking tenderly at his son. "I do not remember my grandfather. My father didn't talk much about him, but on rare occasions when he mentioned him, he'd get choked up with emotion. He was so learned, so wise. My father felt he was nothing compared to my grandfather. He felt he hadn't lived up to his father's expectations." Shankar couldn't say any more and looked away.

Samir watched his father sniffle and take out a handkerchief to wipe his nose. He didn't ask any more questions about his grandfather and changed the subject. "A class friend of mine who is teaching in Michigan has asked me if I want to collaborate on a project. We've been talking about it for some time."

"Good idea." Shankar said. "You should strive for something more than earning money, something you care about. Later, these efforts may not appear so significant in your life, but now is your time."

"I think you're right." Samir nodded.

"I did all I could besides teaching," Shankar mused aloud. "I wrote and published papers on nuclear physics. I even got a travel grant from the National Science Foundation to go to Tokyo to present a paper. But now that research does not seem so momentous. ... Other things become more important with time." Shankar paused, then continued. "One good thing about being here is that I have lots of time to myself. If I were in Ann Arbor, I would have done the same routine activities. Here, I wonder and explore, and pretty much do what I want to do. I have time for meditation. I like it here."

"That's good." Samir looked at his watch and stood up. "I better change to do what Julie asked."

Shankar remained in the breakfast room. The house felt empty and silent. He thought about what would have happened if he had stayed in Ann Arbor. As time passed, life would have been harder for him. He used to attend seminars at the university, but he had already seen his colleagues stop attending. His circle of friends had started to shrink as one by one, people moved away. He gazed outside at the flowers in the garden.

Then, a new revelation dawned on him. What Samir had done for them was the best that could happen to a man and woman in their old age. He hadn't or couldn't do that for his parents. It was his proper duty, but circumstances had failed him. Shankar did not know what the last days of his father's life were like, but he found this to be a relatively happy time for himself. He had no complaints and no stress about moving up in the world, nor anxiety over losing status or not having enough to provide for his family. This was wonderful. He pondered his son's question of his happiness and concluded he was even happier here than Durga was, except for these troublesome memories of his family.

After Samir left the house, Shankar sat quietly in his favorite sofa-chair and looked at nothing, being in a kind of premeditative stage. Samir's query about his happiness triggered something in his mind. He had told him he was happy in their move, but he found a deep unhappiness that had no remedies. Samir was clearly following the good wisdom from ancient India; he himself had not followed the wisdom. The Upanishad said, 'Respect your parents like divine'. He remembered his mother's hunched sitting posture in the kitchen in front of the fire, cooking. Slowly, his eyes dimmed, and sadness came to him as he remembered he had not fulfilled the only thing she had asked him to do.

Between his father and mother, he had his reasons for grudges and anger against his father but there was no such intense feeling of hatred toward his mother although she had also rejected his plan to marry Durga. His mother was a victim of the deeply ingrained Hindu culture. And his mother had simply followed his father, as an Indian wife was supposed to. He should have given her some company and support after his father's death. He could have easily flown to India for a visit, but he had not. He didn't, and perhaps couldn't, think these things through as clearly then as he was doing now. Shankar closed his eyes and released a heavy sigh—how he had failed to act, to do something that was well within his power to relieve someone's suffering, especially his own mother's, with little inconvenience to himself! Rightly or wrongly, his inaction was deliberate. Then, another realization detonated in his mind, as a long-forgotten incident of a refugee woman came to him.

***

Refugee Woman

Shankar stood at the bus stop near the big market in Shyambazar. It was early afternoon. The smell of rotting vegetable trimmings on the sidewalk suffused the area, competing with the suffocating exhaust of buses and taxis that whizzed by. Hand-pulled rickshaws and carts loaded with goods crowded the street. He saw a sweet store nearby, displaying layers of decorated *sandesh, rasogollas,* and *samosas* inside a glass cabinet. A street-dog sat at the entrance of the store, looking at the sweets and occasionally wagging its tail.

He looked at the far end of the street; a tram was coming but no bus. His eyes shifted to a large billboard on top of the opposite building with a brightly colored poster advertising a Hindi film; the hero looked eagerly at a slim–waisted, heavy–bosomed dancer, one leg stretched forward with decorative silver bells on her ankle. In the background, a train was climbing a beautiful scenic hill with green pine trees and snowy mountains—a dreamland.

Then, his attention drifted to an older lady under the concrete bridge over the canal. Thin, dark, shriveled, she wore only a dirty rag that looked as if it had never been washed. A refugee. She squatted before a small open fire. She had cooked rice in a can over her fire. Steam was still rising. Shankar recognized the can, a Ganesh Oil can. She must have collected it from the garbage and was using it as her cooking pot. He kept on watching the lady. She had a little bundle next to her and a long stick. Her graying hair was long, dusty, and knotted. There was something unusual about her. He didn't know what it was, perhaps her wide, black eyes, and her quiet demeanor. Perhaps her aloneness.

He started to imagine her life and how she happened to come to this spot; perhaps she was the only survivor on a train, fleeing from east Bengal, dripping with blood—all other passengers killed by the swords of the Muslims.

A double-decker bus came. His bus? No. There must be something wrong; why was the bus so late today? He was annoyed and gazed again at the lady, who cleaned around the cooking place with her bare hand. The woman looked old, but she was probably in her mid-thirties—at most forty. She must have been forced to leave East Bengal in her prime, a decade and a half back. According to the custom Shankar knew, she must have been married off early, as most girls were at that time, perhaps to a landless laborer. But life wasn't so bad in East Bengal; there were fish in the rivers and ponds, and rain and warm weather allowed rice and vegetables to grow abundantly in the fertile delta.

Another bus came, obstructing his view. Some men got down, some got up, the bus rolled away belching dense, black diesel fumes. No sign of his bus. His view went back to the refugee woman. She was transferring the cooked rice into another can. The water from the boiled rice looked brown when she slopped it onto the ground; it wasn't the color he had seen in his mother's kitchen.

The sun's rays cast sharp shadows from the bridge. Watching those geometric patterns, Shankar drifted to daydreams, continuing to imagine the life of the refugee woman in East Bengal. He saw a village with lush green trees and rice fields. The woman was now young and standing in front of a hut with a *gamcha*—a thin, red cotton towel—in her hand. She wore a clean, white cotton sari with blue border, part of which she had pulled over her head, as married Hindu women do. She had a large red mark of sindur on her forehead. How young, how healthy, she looked. Then, he imagined her husband coming from a distance with sweaty body and dirty feet. He only said, "Give." She gave him the towel and he marched away to the tube well to wash. She went inside to prepare his supper.

The loud shout of the sweet shop owner distracted my reverie. "Hut, hut, go away." The sweetshop owner cursed the stray dog.

Still there was no sign of Shankar's bus. He looked at the woman again. She was taking a morsel from the can to her mouth. Only boiled rice. That's all she would have, perhaps, until the next day. The vision of an actual scene of a wedding feast Shankar had observed a month before came to his mind. A variety of wonderful food was cooked—meat, fish, and sweets. And more food was served than the guests could eat. It was part of the custom. The leftover food on the banana leaf plates were then rolled up quickly to clear the place for the next batch of eaters and thrown away into dustbins. Beggars waited outside the house and fought over the food—a piece of fish, meat, or sweet they had not tasted for so long they had forgotten it existed. They fought like dogs.

The shrill crying sound of the dog woke Shankar from daydreaming. The shop owner must have given it a good kick.

"Stupid dog, entering my store?" The voice came loudly to him.

The dog ran almost blindly, limping and crying.

"Oh, not there," Shankar cried out as he saw the dog run toward the lady and dash into her. The woman fell on her side, and the can dropped from her hand. A small amount of rice spilled out on the dusty concrete path of the bridge. He wished someone would lift her up, but no one came to her. It seemed no one had noticed the event.

The haggard woman pulled herself up and, dropping to her hands and knees on the hard cement, fumbled to collect the scattered rice. She then used a corner of her sari to wipe dirt from the rice and placed her handful back into the tin can.

That was inviting disease; she shouldn't be eating anything from the dirty ground. Shankar's heart sank and he sighed deeply, wishing for a miracle. But nothing happened. The woman bent down and collected a few more of the scattered rice grains. Then it occurred to him perhaps he could do something for the poor lady. Hadn't she suffered enough? He reached into his pocket and found he had two rupees and a few coins; he could buy her food. Perhaps today, once in many years, he could make her happy. He could buy something right here from the sweet store.

Right then, a double-decker bus arrived. It was his bus! He hesitated for a moment. The bus obstructed the view of the refugee woman, and somehow, he reverted to habit and boarded the bus in a sort of daze.

As he reached the top deck, he looked back and saw the lady still picking rice up from the wet ground. He looked back at the steps, which were jammed with new passengers. He couldn't get out of the bus even if he wanted to, he told himself.

"What are you looking back at the bridge for?" the man behind him asked. "It will be there tomorrow. Please move forward, so we can stand at ease."

The bus gave a jerk and moved on.

***

Shankar sat in the living room staring at the picture of the Himalayan range on the wall. The refugee woman was dead now. His mother was also dead. So many instances when he could have done something, but he hadn't. The realization shocked him. But only now did he see his failures clearly. Was there any way to redress his inactions?

Chapter Forty-Eight

Wildlife Refuge

Shankar's inner struggles grew all through the summer and fall. What disturbed him most was that he had neglected both his mother and his sisters, even rejected them. He was angry with Parvati, but he had nothing against his older sister. Since he told the grandchildren about the koel bird fiasco, Uma had haunted him. How he had forgotten her! If he had stayed in Calcutta, he surely would not have relegated her to a distant memory. This estrangement was not all their fault . . . but had happened because of father! These thoughts fueled his anger. His father had taken away his equilibrium. He would never forgive him. How could he? His life had been lived as a reaction to him.

He had carried on without an outward sign of his inner disorder. But now these long-suppressed cares had come crashing down on him. For several days he didn't turn on the TV and kept to himself. He read the book Samir had given him earlier, 'How to be Happy in Retirement.' It emphasized not brooding over the past. One should move forward as if starting a new life—to experience new things, to reach out and enjoy. The author suggested travel, joining various local groups, starting a new hobby, writing a memoir, even dancing. He had not tried any of those activities except for reviving his old interest in cosmology. Perhaps there was some truth in what the author said.

But he could not sleep well at night. He had been having strange dreams. Could he ever find peace? He thought he would find refuge in the outdoors. Being in natural surroundings had always calmed him.

"I'd like to spend some time in a nature preserve," he told his wife in the evening. "Let us go to the wildlife refuge in Shirley—a beautiful bird and animal sanctuary. It's so close, but we haven't gone there."

Durga willingly agreed.

They selected the White Oak Trail, about 2 miles long, which had a walking bridge over the Carman River, for a serene walk in the woods. They soon came across a few white egrets near the river marshland. The scenery was beautiful with patches of tranquil water surrounded by long green reeds. This lifted Shankar's heart. After some time, he confided to Durga that he had a strange dream at night.

"Strange?"

"I accidentally fell through a hole; I couldn't stop sliding down."

"Oh my! That's terrible," Durga spoke out before Shankar could describe the dream. "Dreams of falling into a hole usually refer to a difficult situation in life such as you are in trouble and don't know how to deal with it." She looked intently at him and murmured, "The hole could be a symbol that something is missing or incomplete in your life."

"It was a peculiar dream." Shankar nodded. "But I wasn't scared and didn't panic."

"I thought you are happy living here."

"In some ways, yes. But the stories I tell Raja and DeeDee have taken me back to my life in Dum Dum. Now I dwell in those memories."

They spotted two kayakers and stopped to watch how gracefully they were gliding on the water. Green branches of several trees bent over the banks of the river. On the marshy edges of the refuge, where the river opened out to form a pond, long green reeds formed a thick barrier. A serene scene.

"We cannot undo the past," Durga said. "What's done is done. ... Tell me the rest of the dream."

"It was a slow fall. I had no injury and no pain. I was conscious and I was thinking that when it stopped, I could climb out pushing my hands and legs against the wall, but the ride didn't stop and went on. As I slid down further, the hole got narrower. It wasn't dark. Pinkish light surrounded the hole. I felt I was inside a long, narrow stomach of a living creature. Soon the hole became so narrow I couldn't move my legs. Finally, my hands and legs were stuck by the sides of the hole and the slide stopped. The amazing thing was that I was calm and analyzed how I could get out. No one could hear me. I realized there was no way to escape and I'd die there. I was not fearful and accepted this as my fate. After some time, I woke up."

"Scary," Durga said. "Did you panic near the end?"

"This is the strange thing: no, I had a resigned calmness."

"Did you know yourself as Shankar?"

"I had no question about who I was, what was my past. I only wondered a little how the end would come."

Durga moved a few steps forward with her head down and murmured, "Something is bothering you deep inside."

"I think it has something to do with my banishment. I have never been able to come to terms with the past. It is always with me and I've not been able to move on. Remember, I mentioned this to you in the fall. The memories are haunting me more now. I am stuck in the hole, conscious and dying slowly."

"I prayed and believed that you had gone beyond the past." Her voice had a tinge of despair. "But no." She shook her head silently. This was unusual for ever-positive Durga.

"This wasn't a problem in Ann Arbor; I kept myself too busy. But now, my life—contented, retired—seems to be a façade. I'm hiding behind it, trying to avoid the trauma of my past life."

They came to the parking lot. "I think," Durga said, "We must face this problem together and discuss it more. You cannot live the rest of your life in gloom."

Shankar embraced her, whispering, "We will find a solution." However, his tremulous voice did not reflect the certainty of his words.

Chapter Forty-Nine

Seven Generations

Julie lifted her head and gazed at her father-in-law reading the paper. Today, Samir had left early. A slight smell of dry-fried cumin seeds Julie had put in the omelets hung in the air. She looked around. The voices of DeeDee and Raja playing with Durga floated into the room. She poured more tea into her cup and took a sip. "Baba, do you miss Calcutta?"

Quickly, Shankar lowered the paper, leaned forward, and looked at her with wide open eyes. He liked talking with Julie, but she had rarely asked him a personal question. After a long pause, he replied, "Many have asked me this question, and I tell everyone who asks, 'after so many years, it's not important anymore.' But you know me better." He was quiet for a moment while Julie's gaze remained fixed on him. "Yes, sometimes I miss Calcutta, especially when I tell stories to DeeDee and Raja and think back on my childhood."

"I know my Indian students miss home," Julie said, "but they are new. I wonder what happens to someone after staying away for such a long time. What does it feel like?"

Shankar remained silent.

"I ask this because, except for the stories you tell the children, you rarely mention your life in India. Most older people, my father for example, like to talk about their lives, but you seem to avoid it." Her eyes were full of sympathy, her voice soft, loving.

Shankar seemed to be engaged and attentive to her, yet he was distant, as if hypnotized.

"You came to study like my students, then stayed over, devoting your life to teaching. You've never gone back, not once. That's so different from these students. They want to go back for a visit in the summer."

He sipped the last drop from his cup and stared at the family portrait that hung in the dining room. Samir, Julie, DeeDee, Raja, Shankar, and Durga smiled back at him from the wall. Samir insisted on having this portrait done the year before when they first arrived in Bellport. After some time, he said, "Julie, you make me think." His body rocked gently, as if trying to comfort himself subconsciously. "Perhaps I want to forget my experiences in Calcutta." He tried to smile but the result was a grimace.

"But DeeDee and Raja want to go back to live the wonderful life you had in Dum Dum. What's the catch here?"

"You cannot change the past, why bother discussing it?" he deflected.

"That doesn't sound like you," she said, a bit taken aback.

Shankar remained silent.

"You know, there are many reasons to visit our memories," she continued. "We learn from past events and often they bring families together, by their common experience or by developing a common front. They bring subliminal answers to our questions."

"Maybe you are right."

"As men age," Julie continued, "they're eager to talk and give advice, but you appear reticent. Except when you are with the children."

"You know what they say in India, you are not grown up until you raise your own children. From that point of view, I never really lived as an adult in India. That's why perhaps I do not mention my adult life and talk about my childhood with DeeDee and Raja."

"I'd love to know about you and your experiences because social changes are happening in Calcutta and you were there at the beginning of it all when India became independent."

Shankar looked beyond Julie toward the garden. He didn't want to start a conversation about his experiences in Calcutta as one answer would lead to another question, and eventually he would have to reveal the things he didn't want to bring up about his family. "My life in Calcutta, appears remote, far away in the past."

"I have no specific questions in my mind, Baba, but it surprises me sometimes that Samir doesn't know much about his family history. He doesn't even know his relatives like aunts and uncles on your side of the family—their names or where they are."

Startled, Shankar thought it must be obvious to Julie he was hiding his past life or at least he was not open to his own family? Was it really that transparent?

"You know, Americans, when they grow older, they want to know their heredity. Who were their grandparents or great-grand parents? We aren't curious when we are young, as we put all our effort in advancing forward. But later, the past haunts us because we know so little."

Shankar nodded.

"You remind me of a story in Greek mythology. It is not relevant to our discussion, but I think you have a lot of knowledge that we are not learning from you."

"Greek mythology, huh!"

"The story is about Proteus, an assistant to Poseidon, who knew all things—the past, present and the future but he abhorred divulging what he knew. If anyone needed information, he would have to surprise Proteus during his noonday slumber and bind him as he changed his shape from one sea animal to another. If one held him long enough, he returned to his original form and answered questions. I admire how the Greeks had thought of characters that are compelling, even applicable today."

"Fascinating." Shankar laughed hard. "I reminded you of Proteus?"

"No, no. Not that way!" She blushed but recouped quickly. "You have a lot of knowledge of India. You should tell us."

"Samir wants to know more?"

"It is an American thing. Like I said, we get curious about our past when we get older. I know Indian families keep a record of their lineage for at least seven generations—for weddings and funerals. At least they know their names and their dates of birth and death."

"Yes, that's true," he replied with a nod. "Before they perform any solemn service, they honor their ancestors and give food and water to their souls."

"It's a normal thing in India but ask an American the name of their great-grandfather. They wouldn't know where to get it," Julie said with a tinge of regret. "In my family we know them for three or four generations because we have been in Connecticut for a long time. But I was surprised when I asked Samir."

Shankar nodded again but looked away from her gazing eyes—to the distant trees in the backyard, perhaps as far away as he could, to the space-time where no one could find him.

Chapter Fifty

Vegetable Garden

The next Sunday, breakfast did not last long because Samir wanted to work in the garden before the ground froze. Shankar went to the living room to watch *The Week in Review* on TV. But DeeDee left Durga and came near the fireplace, facing him, tilting her face to the side. "Grandpa, what did children do in India on Sundays?"

Shankar stared at her for some time, wondering what led to this question and how these questions popped up in her mind. Was she bored or simply inquisitive? "In my time, young boys played outside with marbles or played soccer with rubber balls. They played with whatever they could make with materials they found."

"And girls?"

"Girls stayed indoors and played on the roofs, which had walls around them so no one would fall off, or on verandas and courtyards—skipping and hop-scotching—and they played with dolls. They also played house with friends."

"Barbie dolls?"

Shankar had a soft spot for her—she always wanted to know more. "No," he told her with delight. "They had homemade dolls."

DeeDee's mouth fell open. "Grandpa, how did they make dolls at home?"

"They weren't the kind of dolls you have. They were ordinary dolls. Mother and aunts made them out of worn-out clothes. My mother hand-stitched eyes, noses, and mouths using colorful threads pulled from the borders of old saris. But the dolls' hands and legs were stiff; you couldn't move them or bend them."

"I'd like to have one of those dolls," she murmured. "Can we get one, Grandpa?" Her eyes brightened. "Can we, really, Grandpa?"

"They aren't very nice." He shook his head. "In my time, girls adored the pink, plastic dolls because they were new and different. If you ask your grandma, maybe she could make one for you."

DeeDee shuffled away with a dreamy look. Shankar knew she was scheming about how to approach grandma to make her a doll. He got up to visit Samir in the garden and watched him turn over the soil in the vegetable patch with a spade. He was making three rows, about a foot apart and each only a little deep.

"This will make enough for us," Samir said and took out large garlic bulbs from a brown bag and broke them apart keeping the papery husks on the individual cloves. He poked each clove two inches into the soil with the tips up keeping them about three inches apart. "They'll grow through the fall and winter and be ready for harvest in June or July."

"We didn't have much of a backyard in Calcutta for gardening," Shankar said. And even if people had space, Shankar knew they did not do garden work. They would hire someone. It would be their garden, built and maintained with someone else's labor. Toiling with one's hands was not appreciated among the middle and upper classes, especially not in his family—lower class people did that kind of manual labor. This fitted with the Indian tradition that the Munis and Rishis, the learned people in ancient times, studied and meditated. They were the educated class, the highest class, admired and revered by all. Shankar's father considered his family descendants of those sages and aspired to live up to their standards. Manual labor was low in this tradition. Shankar was happy and a little astonished that his son had taken his mother's interest in gardening to the next level and was digging in the soil and growing vegetables.

"I like to see plants grow," Samir told him. "I feel joy when little vegetables emerge and when I see fruits. Gardening has become a good diversion for me."

His father nodded. Not that he had any experience himself to know, but he could see how it brought his son enjoyment.

"DeeDee and Raja also love gardening. If Long Island gets cut off in some disaster, we could grow our own food and survive," Samir said.

"This is what I appreciate most in American culture," Shankar acknowledged. "Working with your own hands and being proud of what you have done or made, even if it's not the best or the most beautiful product. You didn't get that spirit from me, but it's good you got it from somewhere." Shankar shook his head and chuckled.

Samir put the spade against the vegetable garden fence. "I wanted to turn the soil over for the next season, but this is enough for today." He picked up his can of Miller beer from the ground. The two stood there enjoying the warm afternoon. The leaves on the tall walnut trees, were already starting to turn red and threatening to fall. Julie's flower garden was a riot of warm autumn colors—yellow, purple, and maroon mums in the border behind the house, pansies perking up after the hot summer, and the pink and purple asters on the side of the house by the dining room, all seemed to sing an end-of-season chorus.

"I've had a question on my mind for some time." Samir turned to his father. "As you know, before we brought you here, we went on a tour of India. We did that on an impulse—for our 15th wedding anniversary. We didn't take the children with us."

Shankar remembered how miffed Durga had been when the children stayed with Julie's friend in Stony Brook. Durga would have loved to have them.

"We had only four days in Calcutta," Samir continued, "but we had a wonderful time. I remember how surprised we were when Ma's brother, both sisters, and many of their children came to receive us at the airport and took us to their home. They wouldn't let us stay in a hotel."

Julie had told them about their visit, but he hadn't heard the details from Samir. "Same house in Shalkia?" he asked.

"Yes, but they must have enlarged it. Our room was quite large. Grandpa and grandma were not alive. But Julie did *pranam*, properly bending down to touch the feet of the aunts and uncles, and that melted everyone's heart. There was so much affection for us. I understood why Indians think of visiting home all the time."

"I know."

"Ma's family kept us very busy, visiting Victoria Memorial, the Botanical Garden, Belur Math, and meeting other family members." Samir looked at his father. He rubbed the back of his neck and said, "That puzzled me while in Shalkia. No one mentioned anything about your family. On the last day, the aunties and nieces took Julie out to buy saris and jewelry, and they surely didn't want me to tag along. I ventured out to Dum Dum alone. I had an idea of the location of Grandfather's house from Ma. When I found the house, I stood there taking it in and trying to imagine you there. A man came out of the house and asked, 'Who are you looking for?'

"'The Lahiri Family, the owners of this house.'

"'The Lahiris?'

"'Their son was Shankar Lahiri,' I told him. 'He went to America.'

"'Ah! I recognize the name. He was a well-known student, a long time back. But they left this place long ago. No Lahiris live here now.' The man stared at me, as I obviously looked a little out of place. I explained who I was and then asked, 'Could I see the inside?'

"He let me in. I saw the central courtyard and a veranda around it—exactly like you described to me once. I didn't linger long inside the house; I thanked him and left."

Shankar listened to Samir in total surprise like an animal caught in the headlights. He couldn't nod his head or say anything; he simply stared at his son.

"I wanted to talk to you about this. I didn't mention it until now, because when we visited you in Ann Arbor, we were in a rush. Bringing you to Bellport was more important to me at the time. I decided there would be plenty of time to talk about Dum Dum later. I didn't want to disturb that move." He glanced at his father. "I thought there must be a reason why you never told me our family had left Dum Dum, or why they did." Samir's forehead betrayed a worry wrinkle, his anxiety almost palpable, and he held onto the nearly finished beer can as if to drink, but without taking a sip.

Shankar kept looking at Samir as if expecting him to say more, but Samir didn't say any more. A look of dismay crossed Shankar's face. What led him to go to see their house in Dum Dum? Was he looking for his roots? Samir must have turned this over in his mind many times since he had gone to India. Another thought flew through his mind. Despite Shankar's determination to lead a new type of life in America, he could see their relationship had almost replicated the Indian father-son relationship. That relationship was more formal. Children did not ask their Indian fathers any question that popped into their heads; fathers play a different role there. They take care of their children's future—that meant making sure they got a good education and guiding them through life. Another reason must be that Shankar had kept himself remarkably busy and spent little time discussing his family with Samir.

He looked tenderly at his son and said, "I should have told you earlier." He shifted his gaze to the walnut tree for a moment. "My older sister was married off to a Sanskrit teacher in Allahabad, in a different state and far away from Calcutta. My father arranged the marriage when I was a senior at high school, but we lost touch with her after her marriage. Then, as soon as I left Calcutta, and before I arrived in Philadelphia, my father arranged my younger sister's marriage to someone in Bhatpara, not as far as Allahabad, but still a distance away from Calcutta. Bhatpara is a small and unique community. The brahmins there have no interest in the modern world. I guess that suited my father."

"Your younger sister was married off quite young then?"

"Yes." Shankar sighed. "She was a teenager in college. As soon as I left to come here, her marriage was arranged in a hurry, as if something bad about our family had been discovered and they wanted to get her married off before anyone could find out."

"Like a mental illness?"

"Yes, that is a good example." Shankar sat down on the garden bench and motioned for his son to sit beside him. "Then my father took early retirement, sold the house, and they moved to Benares."

"All the way to Benares?"

"The holiest city in India. Bengalis like to spend their last days there." Shankar paused, struggling with his thoughts. "At the time, I was busy with my studies in Philadelphia. I wasn't told any of this. That's the way my father was. He did everything his way. I had good relations with my uncle; I got to know this from him. But he also moved, to Nagpur outside of Bengal, and died there—so no more family news came my way."

"Ah. Now I understand why we didn't meet anyone from your family." They sat silently on the bench for a while. "Our family really fell apart," Samir said.

Shankar nodded, but he didn't say a word about what his father had done to him. "You are the main descendant of the Lahiri family now," he told Samir after some time. "You, and then Raja, will carry our name."

"That trip was a big reason why I went to Ann Arbor and got you and Ma to live with us." Samir was quiet for a few seconds, and then whispered, "I didn't want to lose you."

They sat there silently for a little while without looking at each other. Shankar looked at his son and told him something that perhaps, he didn't want to tell him ever, but the words came out spontaneously. "I have a regret I might as well tell you. I wished I visited my mother before she died."

Samir cocked his head, with a puzzled expression on his face. "You could have easily flown to India for a visit."

"By the time I was ready, she was already dead." Shankar looked away, toward the garden; he didn't want to face his son, didn't want to know what his son thought of him.

Samir watched his father's distant stare and waited for some time. Then he quietly went inside. He closed the back door gently without disturbing his father.

Durga was busy, but Shankar was eager to get out of the house and think through what Samir had told him. He went out alone for a walk along Beaver Dam Road and came to Great South Bay. Shankar was relieved he was finally able to mollify Samir's unease about what had happened to their family in Calcutta after he left for the U.S. But he had only told him what was on the surface of the story. Samir didn't inquire further, and Shankar couldn't bring himself to tell Samir what led his father to get Parvati married off so quickly. Samir might not have fully grasped that his grandfather was at the root of the destruction of his own family!

Yes, Samir's grandfather was the cause. Shankar's quiet revolt was only the instrument that triggered the family's disintegration. His resentment toward his father surged back; his face flushed, and the muscles in his neck and back stiffened. Because of their father, the family was forced into an ancient and sclerotic path that should have been abandoned. Because of their father, his older sister was sent to live far away, and Parvati was hurriedly married off. Because of their father, everyone lost touch with one another. Shankar was no more than a bystander, watching the tragedy play out. It was heartbreaking, but Shankar had not done anything to change it. He knew he could not. Instead, he had fled to the U.S.

When Shankar reached the marina, a beautiful scene opened before him—many boats skimming across the water under a clear evening sky. Sailboats made a spangled collage of yellow, white, and orange against the deep blue expanse of the bay. A small boat caught his attention. An elderly man was sailing alone in a small sloop. Its two sails were striking: one thin triangular royal blue, and the other a large cranberry sail, fat and swollen by the wind. The cranberry sail glowed in the waning tendrils of sunlight. It appeared to Shankar the man was navigating toward the horizon. Staring at the lone sailor, the peanut seller from his neighborhood in Dum Dum floated into his mind. It had been years since he had thought of the vendor.

***

The Peanut Seller

The peanut seller was a unique man, like the cranberry boatman. The vendor sat with his basket under the lamppost at the corner of the small park near our house where we played soccer and sat with friends to eat peanuts bought from him. His face was round to match his stout body, smooth and tanned, shiny dark brown from the sun. He had a crew cut and his tiki always stood out.

The peanut seller's name was Jawaharlal, the same name as the first Prime Minister of India, but everyone called him Jahore, which meant diamond. The peanut seller had the best peanuts in town and the chutney he gave with the peanuts was wonderful. It was green, salty, sour, and hot and went very well with the peanuts. The green color came from green tamarind, the long, sour fruit that looked like fat green beans. I remembered the taste as if I ate it yesterday.

One time I asked the peanut seller how he prepared the chutney, but he had simply laughed. "You don't need to learn this," he said with a twinkle in his eyes. "When you finish college, you'll have a good job; you can always buy it from me."

Every evening when my friends and I bought peanuts, we lingered for a few minutes to chat with him. That was a part of the ritual of buying peanuts. The conversations were often teasing and bantering, but they were always jovial. Sometimes we briefly discussed local incidents and the news. Then we sat on the grass in the park and shared the peanuts. There, we talked about everything, from sports to our aspirations in life. But we did not discuss anything about Jahore. He was a peanut seller, and he registered on our minds only for a thin slice of time.

When we went home in late evening, Jahore still sat quietly at his place, the evening light from the lamppost illuminating him and his basket.

The peanut seller once asked us why anyone would want to study politics, history, and such subjects. "The good jobs are in science and engineering, aren't they?" He turned a father-like gaze upon his teenage customers.

"It's true," Ranjit said in a serious tone. "India needs engineers. We must develop and build industries of all kinds if we expect to prosper. We can't keep on buying finished products from other countries."

"Wouldn't it be fun to sell goods back to England?" Soumen posed with a sparkle in his eyes.

"Yeah," Bikash supported him. "Someday we ought to get back all they took from us."

Then we walked away with our peanuts, forgetting what Jahore had asked. We had a cordial relationship with him, but I never wondered why Jahore asked such questions and what difference the answers made to him.

Sometimes, Jahore asked us what we studied at school and we told him a little. It was to make conversation. The vendor could not read or write, but he was intelligent and knew what to say to keep the conversation lively. One time we had an unexpected conversation with him. We had been talking about how hard it was to choose the right profession and how distressing the quest was.

"What are you complaining about?" Jahore had interrupted our discussion. "You go to school and will have good jobs someday. I never had an option. I'm too poor to do anything but sell peanuts. And I've been here for more than 30 years!"

We didn't know how to respond to Jahore's lamentation. I simply stared at his dark body covered by a bluish half-shirt and short dhuti raised up to his knees. Jahore had worn the same clothes, so it seemed, every day. I kept on looking at him, noticing Jahore had no watch. His hands were bare except for a single, copper ring on one finger.

"What do you want?" Bikash asked him haughtily. Jahore raised his head without saying a word, and Bikash went on, "True, you earn less, but your needs are also less. Your children start earning as soon as they become ten, and you live fine."

Jahore looked down at his basket. "I guess," he mumbled, "it's our fate. Born poor and die poor."

"Look," Soumen told him calmly, "you don't know our problems, the pressures and the stress we have. You're happy with a simple life."

"Let's go," Ranjit said to end the bickering conversation.

"He has no idea of our lives," Bikash said and walked toward the park.

I had followed them, but the condescending tone and words of the conversation did not leave me for some time.

One day, we sat on the grass after the high school's final exam, discussing which college to go to, what to study, and what salary one needed for a good life. Ranjit abruptly asked, "Any of you have any idea what Jahore makes?"

Each, in turn, shrugged. But we agreed with certainty he barely made enough to live. Jahore had to buy peanuts, roast them, and buy other ingredients for chutney and spices. Even if he were lucky with many customers, he might barely make five rupees a day, the equivalent of a dollar.

"Who roasts the peanuts for you?" Ranjit asked him the next day.

"Why? I must do it myself," he told the boys.

"And the chutney?"

"I buy the ingredients and make that, too. I work late into the night, readying for the next day. A good night is four hours sleep for me."

One day he was not at the lamppost. The spot looked empty without him. We thought about him seriously for the first time, realizing how little we knew of him. Almost nothing! We didn't know his last name, where he lived, and if his family lived with him. He was a peanut seller and we bought peanuts from him; that was all. There was a class barrier; we lived in our world and he in his. Despite all the friendly conversations, our relationship ended as soon as we walked away with our peanuts.

"I wonder, does he think of sending his children to school?" Ranjit asked as they waited under the lamppost.

"He probably lives in a palm thatch bustee with a dirt floor," Soumen said. "They don't go to school."

"His son will probably follow his profession," Bikash said confidently.

"I would like to know how he lives," I murmured.

We decided we would follow him one night and see where he lived. We knew if we asked him directly, Jahore would simply say, "I live beyond the train station," and not say much more. Then, we couldn't ask him more.

When one knew someone lived in a bustee, in the lowest possible living condition, one didn't ask for an address.

Jahore walked to his corner hurriedly, saying, "Sorry, I got delayed at the post office." He quickly arranged his wares and gave us our regular peanuts. We didn't ask him anything. But, the next few days, sitting in the park and munching roasted peanuts with green chutney, we planned our strategy, thrilling at the prospect of uncovering his secret. When we went to Jahore to buy peanuts, we furtively glanced at him with surreptitious glee. Our excitement grew as the day of the planned sleuthing expedition approached.

We knew we had to follow him from a distance because by the time Jahore went home, the crowds would be thin, and he could spot us easily!

We followed him to an area beyond the train station, about a mile from our neighborhood. Then, Jahore turned off the main road into a narrow lane, between two shacks with thatched roofs. The path was winding; people had built hovels of various sizes made of woven palm fronds or whatever material they could find. Some of the better ones had tin roofs. The huts were set against each other haphazardly, wherever they found space. It was a ghetto. We soon lost him. Not many people were there, and the one or two who went by looked thin with calloused hands and feet, people low on the socioeconomic ladder. I grew uneasy. We couldn't bring ourselves to ask anyone where the peanut seller lived. How would we describe him? We didn't know his last name or his address. Then, we became concerned. No one wore clothes like ours. We didn't belong there. Someone might ask what we were doing in the neighborhood. We quickly left the place. The enormity of the difference of our status in life dawned on us. We hurried home silently, as if there was nothing to talk about.

The year we went to college was the turning point in our lives. We didn't have free time anymore. Our evening walks became rare, except on the weekends. We still bought peanuts from the same peanut seller but talking about our new experiences affected all other concerns. We didn't have time to chat with Jahore. We discussed our classes and our teachers while buying peanuts. Jahore listened to us silently.

During that time, Jahore took longer to give us peanuts and the green chutney. But we didn't notice his slow delivery because we were so busy in our new world. Our manner was not new to Jahore. For many years, he had seen boys going to colleges, and like their older brothers before them, they got busy in their own world. Jahore's destiny was to fade from their lives slowly and surely.

One day Jahore said, surprising us, "I wish I had the chance to go to school."

"Really?" Bikash exclaimed with disbelief.

"What would you have studied?" Ranjit quickly followed.

"Engineering."

"What kind of engineering?" I asked.

"Engineering," he repeated, shrugging his shoulders. "What's the difference?"

"But you haven't even gone to high school!" Soumen said.

"How could I?" he lamented. "I have worked from the time I was ten." His voice faded to silence.

No one continued the discussion with Jahore. "Did you read about the construction of the new stadium in today's paper?" Bikash asked Ranjit.

"Oh, yes," Soumen answered. "It'll be the biggest soccer field in India. Once it is finished, we can see world matches in Calcutta."

We walked away to the park. I heard something and turned back and saw Jahore watching us as we vanished into the park.

How the years had passed by. Thoughts of Jahore and our conversations were only distant memories. I recalled my last encounter with him. How could I have forgotten it? One night I heard a knock at the front door. I opened the door and was startled to find Jahore standing there with his basket balanced on his head, the way he walked from place to place.

"If you have a minute," Jahore mumbled and then hesitated. "I don't know whom to ask this, so I came to you." He looked at the floor for a second and finally blurted out, "I want my son to go to college and have a job, not become a peanut seller like me." His voice was firm.

"Your son?"

"Yes. I want him to have a college education. What does he have to do to become an engineer?"

"It will take a lot of money," I said, staring in astonishment at the ragged figure before me.

Jahore nodded, saying nothing. His eyes pleaded with me.

"First, he'll have to complete elementary school. If he does well enough, you need to send him to high school. Then ask him to get a job at a factory. He could then become a technician. That will be a lot like being an engineer."

"If he excels in high school, can he go to college?" Jahore asked.

"Yes, yes," I said to pacify him. "But, as I said, it will take a lot money. More, I'm afraid, than you earn."

"Thank you." Jahore turned and walked away. There was enthusiasm in his steps I had never noticed before.

Who will sell peanuts to us then? I thought after Jahore left and laughed at my own humor.

When I was nearing retirement, Ranjit came to the U.S. for a year and visited us in Ann Arbor. Durga and I were delighted. It was such a pleasure to see a childhood friend in America—after so many years. He told me with some elation how proud our friends and the neighborhood were of my success in America. I listened to him, but I couldn't feel his excitement. "You know," I told him, "I ended up teaching in an ordinary university."

Ranjit looked at me for a second. "We are older now and have gone through plenty of upheavals. After all, what do you want in life? If you had published a few more scientific papers or given a few more talks at conferences, you would have felt better, but in the end, they do not mean much. Being able to come here from Calcutta as a student with financial support from a university was, itself, a success. Then, you received the highest degree in physics from an Ivy League University. You had a respectable job as a professor of physics, and everyone had high regards for your teaching. What more can we expect?"

He had a point. I nodded in agreement.

Durga brought tea and left us alone.

We talked about all the things we had done together and how our lives had evolved. I was telling him about our daily routines in the U.S., when Ranjit asked, "Do you remember Jahore?"

"Our peanut seller?"

"Yeah," Ranjit answered. His eyes dimmed and his face drooped as if in remorse.

"What happened?" I asked him.

"He was doing good business because many more people had moved into our neighborhood, but he grew old and thin," Ranjit said. "I felt sad to see him looking so bad."

"Sorry to hear it," I replied, as I nibbled on a biscuit. But I wasn't upset. The affairs of the peanut seller were not high on my list of priorities.

"Remember the time when we tried to follow him and find out where he lived?" Ranjit asked me.

"Yes, I remember."

"I have seen his house."

That perked me up. "You followed him?"

"Yes and no," Ranjit said. "A few years after we graduated from college and you had already gone to America, one evening when no one was around, Jahore asked me earnestly if I could help him. I thought he wanted money. Then it occurred to me for all the years we had known him, he had never asked us for anything. He looked so old; his tiki had turned all white. I told him I would try to help him.

"He told me he wanted help in filling out a form. It was for his son. 'Let me see,' I said. But Jahore did not have the form with him. He kept it locked in a trunk in his hut. He asked me if I could please go home with him.

"I thought," Ranjit told me, "I would have to come back at night when Jahore finished his sales, but he started to pack his basket and then stood up. 'We will go now,' he said.

'What about your sales today?' I asked him.

'This is more important,' he said."

"Completing a form for his son?" I asked Ranjit. I thought about the shy, thin boy Jahore sometimes brought with him. I remembered the boy fidgeted nervously around us. I also remembered we did not bother to inquire who the boy was.

"Yes. Let me tell you what happened," Ranjit told me. "We went back to the same area where we followed him once—those narrow lanes beyond the train station. His hut was small, but clean and well kept. I saw a big round oven in the small courtyard in front of his room, where I guessed he roasted peanuts. He brought out the paper his son had sent him. It was a financial assistance form from an engineering school.

"'Your son is in engineering school?' I asked Jahore, flabbergasted. I stared at him in disbelief.

'He is a good boy,' Jahore said bashfully, 'I didn't want him to sit under a lamppost like me and see the world pass by.'

"I looked at Jahore and realized why he had become so thin. He had been starving himself to save money for his son.

"I filled out the form and told him where to sign. I told him to go to the post office in the morning to imprint his thumb for the signature.

"'I am sure your son will get the money,' I told Jahore. How could he not? Jahore earned the equivalent of only forty dollars a month, but I wrote twenty-five dollars to make the application look even better."

Ranjit paused for a moment and looked out the window. He turned to me and said, "As I was leaving, Jahore asked me to wait for a minute. He brought a bag from his room and handed it to me. 'These are the best quality peanuts; I roasted them yesterday.' I didn't want to take the peanuts from a poor man for simply helping him fill out a form, but Jahore insisted. 'Please take this little gift from me. It'll make me happy.' I saw his face was glowing with joy. I knew it came from his heart. I accepted the peanuts and left. There was a large portion of the green chutney in the bag too, which I discovered later."

Then, Ranjit took out a newspaper clipping from his pocket and handed it to me. The fold mark was almost torn through the old paper and the print had faded. I was barely able to make out what it said:

A peanut seller, named Jawaharlal, died yesterday at the Medical College Hospital. He was alone, hallucinating, with an advanced case of pneumonia. His family lives in a village 100 miles away from Calcutta and was not aware of his condition. He gave an envelope containing money, Rs. 531, to the doctor, pleading, 'Please send this to my son in Patna Engineering College, money for his last semester.' At first the doctor did not believe his words, but when the peanut seller was dying, the doctor contacted the college and found his story to be true. The son arrived at the hospital, but by then the peanut seller had died.

It dawned on me I had never understood the depth of the peanut seller's queries. I felt deeply sorry, but it was too late; I stared at Ranjit, speechless. I could tell Ranjit shared my sense of wretchedness; that was why he must have carried the paper with him all the way from India.

***

The sun went below the horizon on Great South Bay and crimson rays spread over the evening sky. At this hour, Jahore would still be sitting under the lamppost, and the electric light would come on and shine on him and his basket of peanuts. Shankar visualized him—a large forehead, crew cut hair, and the tiki. The image became so clear it seemed real. He had never cared for the little guy in the past, but how noble the neglected peanut seller turned out to be. A melancholy feeling and shame came over him. It was compounded by the revelation that Samir was struggling to figure out his roots, which he was still hiding from him.

The vast bay stretching before him made him philosophical. For a long time, Indian society had denigrated poor people like the peanut seller, assigning them to a lower class and mentally confining them to a different style of living, presuming they didn't have the same feelings or aspirations as the well-off—as if the poor were simply a different species. It reminded Shankar of boundary value problems in physics—the way each problem is defined in terms of its unique boundary conditions. The lower class was set with different boundary values than the higher class. Most significant was the realization that his own attitude reflected the class he belonged to. He had grown up absorbing the convictions of his family: the people of lower castes were different from them and not relevant to their lives. The class system was no different than the caste system and just as destructive. He sighed.

Then, out of the blue, the face of the long-lost bohurupee came to his mind; he felt deep regret for the man. How the adults in his family had treated him! He was too little then and scared of what was happening. It turned out to be a gross injustice, but when the truth was discovered, no one thought of the poor bohurupee.

It occurred to him that perhaps the peanut seller's son understood his father's sacrifice; after all, he had seen him at work. They both had realized their situation and were trying to rectify it. How different that was from Shankar's situation. Samir was trying to follow the good examples of the Indian lifestyle, while he was running away from it. And he hadn't been able to be open with him. Samir probably thought his father was like other Indians who came here to study and stayed on. Then another thought that had troubled him recently surfaced in his mind: the peanut seller was an example, but had he always thought only about himself? Forgetting the hopes and aspirations of all others? It was a disturbing thought, but he couldn't get rid of it. He kept on gazing at the expanse of the bay as light dimmed all around him.

MORE CONSTERNATION

OCTOBER - NOVEMBER 2005

Chapter Fifty-One

Walk in Town with Durga

Samir worked on the vegetable garden for two more weekends, turning over the soil and mixing some mulch and organic compost for the next year. Shankar had watched and admired his diligent labor. He was a little anxious about what more his son might ask about his family, but Samir never brought up the subject. Shankar was quite unsettled for the last few days. He had never been able to let go of the past with equanimity, accepting that what had happened could not be altered. He carried considerable guilt because he had not performed funeral services for his parents, which, as their only son, was his paramount duty. The intentional secrecy of his past life ate him alive, especially now, when he realized Samir wanted to know more about his heredity. Julie had told him this plainly, unrealizing the devastating weight of its meaning.

When he left Calcutta, Shankar was certain of his decision, but Samir had not yet been born. Now he saw that he had not fully thought everything through. Julie had probably suspected that there was a reason her father-in-law never talked about his family. Samir's questions regarding their family must have percolated in his mind for some time, but Shankar had no prior inkling of that. Why else would Samir go to Dum Dum? He was glad his son understood what had become of their family, but he had not told him about the deeper reasons why their family in Dum Dum fell apart. That would have violated his original reason for coming to the U.S.—not to bring any trace of his past life with him. He felt stuck.

When Shankar began this journey, he had only thought of himself. His family had been so hurtful that he had abandoned them and left his home country behind. And Durga was a willing participant in his decision. But now Samir . . . the past dissolution of his family was no longer Shankar's only concern. If Samir knew his paternal family had rejected his mother, he would probably understand Shankar's reaction. But the possibility of disappointing his son seized the breath in Shankar's lungs. He could picture Samir's face when he would find out how his beloved father had rejected his own blood and never looked back–Samir would feign understanding, but confusion would be held behind his kind eyes. Shankar couldn't bear it.

Today was Halloween. Heavy rains had poured down for the last few days, and Shankar had felt compelled to regale his moping grandchildren with stories from his childhood, presenting a picture of his wonderful youth. Certainly, Grandfather hiding a one-eyed frog in his room was hilarious. A smile spread on Shankar's face. But that was how his double life had continued.

That morning as he thought about these things, silently sitting in his comfortable chair, a most unexpected thing had happened. DeeDee brought Parvati's letter. Shankar had deflected DeeDee's desire to read the letter immediately, but when he had read it, the letter threw him into deep turmoil. He fretted the rest of the day, waiting to talk with Durga. She was the only one with whom he could deliberate about his predicament. A cloudless blue sky emerged, but his heart had turned pitch dark.

Durga agreed they should go out early on their walk because of Halloween, and suggested that they walk in town. They wore light colored jackets for safety because the sun set early, around five. They passed by the Bellport-Brookhaven Historical Society, a well-maintained white colonial two-story building with dark green shutters, which reflected the community's firm belief in their stability and continuity. Shankar wished his life were similar. When they came to South Country Road, they turned right, away from the golf course.

Although Parvati's letter dominated his mind, Shankar hesitated to broach the subject. He felt shame for his family and a complex mixture of shame and guilt for himself. "Are you still in communication with your Wayne State colleagues?" he asked Durga. He wasn't interested in her answer, but it kept thoughts of the letter at bay.

"I talk with some; many are still teaching." She pulled the end of her sari around her neck like a muffler. "I get the faculty news. Women keep in touch you know," she said with an amused look on her face.

"Maybe. I am losing touch with my friends. At the beginning some called; now they rarely do."

Durga glanced at him. "Don't worry. Of course, we lose touch with time and distance, but that would have happened anyway. We've made this place our home and we have our family around us. We will be fine." She said confidently. "I like being here with our family." She stepped sideways to avoid another couple coming from the Methodist Church. The man looked curiously at her sari. That was one thing she had not changed. She even taught classes wearing a sari.

Shankar walked on silently. Durga had been a stable pillar for him in each place they had lived. She had made his life in America pleasant. He remembered the days when he'd first arrived in the City of Brotherly Love. He'd known truly little of American life or culture. Then Durga had arrived and they survived. When he had a hard time finding a research position, it was her insistence not to return to India that led them from Philadelphia to a teaching position at Michigan State University. Their lives had moved on from Calcutta to Philadelphia, to Ann Arbor and now to Bellport. His shoulders hunched and he frowned at the thought of Parvati's letter. He ached to tell Durga—but should he? Revulsion and sadness rose in his heart. After much hesitation, he decided not to; he must first understand his own feelings. Durga did not know his sister, and Parvati had not attended their wedding. He hadn't told Durga about the first letter; it had arrived long before she came to America. They built a new life in the U.S., deliberately not looking back and not lamenting the life they could have had in India. Why drag up something from the past now? Especially when he had tried so hard to forget. It was for the best not to tell her.

People walked busily in and out of the stores along South Country Road. The sidewalk was not conducive to a relaxing stroll at this time of day. They turned right onto Brewster Lane—an older street with well-kept homes and nice lawns—and walked in silence for a while.

"I'm spending more time with the University Women's Club ladies here," Durga said after some time.

"That's great. I like that you're involved with projects like the ones you had in Ann Arbor."

She nodded but didn't say any more.

Shankar's thoughts went back to Parvati. She was merely a teenager when he had last spoken with her. She was not raised to have her own opinions, to mold her own life. He had expected her to be more mature than was possible in their family, under their father. He had learned and adjusted to American culture from the time of his arrival in Philadelphia. He had matured. Perhaps Parvati had matured too.

Chapter Fifty-Two

Parvati's Letter

B y the time Shankar and Durga returned home from their walk, Parvati's letter dominated Shankar's thoughts completely. Each cell of his body and mind felt the rustle of the letter in his shirt pocket, as if a large thorn had pricked his conscience. He went out on the porch where he could be alone and, switching on the porch light, took the letter out. He read it again.

September 30, 2005
Dear Dada,
I know I was not strong enough to stand up for you. Even as a teenager, I was the only one in the family who could have understood you. You have every reason to be angry with me. We are old now, and I have no one else to write to.
Perhaps you don't know what happened. Father took me out of college as soon as you left and married me off to a priest in Bhatpara. I had no say in the matter. My husband was fifteen years older than me. He had never gone to college and had no interests except reading the scriptures. The family lived jointly with four brothers; their only income came from performing worship services in the community. They were poor, barely living on the charity of a few well-off families. I could not continue studying, not even read books or magazines. My role was to be a Brahmin priest's dutiful

*wife—a friendless, lonely life. No one from our family ever
visited me or wrote to me.*

*My husband passed away six years ago. Since then, because I
am childless, the women in the house treat me like a maid. I
have no one to talk to and no place to go; I prayed for death,
but the gods were not kind to me.*

*Now I am sick and feeble. Finally, I think my relief is near. I
have always loved you and pray that you forgive me.*

Your sister,
Parvati

The first time Shankar read the letter, he felt miserable for Parvati—
how sad her life had turned out to be. Now he wished he had read her first
letter. What could she have written? That she was sorry about how she
had reacted to him during their last encounter. That she had realized her
imprudence when their father was forcing her into a horrible marriage?
Had she even had time to discuss her marriage with their parents? Often in
conservative families, a girl comes home from school and is told she will be
married next week. Did Parvati feel utterly helpless and perhaps thought
of her older brother when she was being led to the chopping block, as they
had done with goats during Kali puja? At least the goat protests at the top
of its lungs, but she could not. Both were sacrificed in the name of pure
conservative religion.

Shankar could not stop thinking that whatever she had written so
many years ago might have changed how his own life had evolved. Surely,
he would have felt sympathy . . . perhaps even responded and tried to help
her. Perhaps ... perhaps it could have saved him too, from a lifetime of
hateful denial and unbearable anger. Had they both suffered alone because
of his own indifference?

Their father's archaic view of religion led him to direct his children's
lives in such a cruel and horrible manner. Appalling! So backward! He had
sacrificed his daughter and married her off early to protect their family's
and his own religious reputation. And to someone unsuitable in this
modern world. Her life was utterly ruined. The anger in his heart against
his father's action exploded in his mind and could barely be contained.

"Grandpa," Raja pulled him from behind. "How do you like my
Halloween outfit?"

Shankar turned and saw him with a Harry Potter costume: ankle-
length black coat, bright red muffler with yellow stripes hanging from his
neck and a wand in hand. He also had round glasses. He pushed Parvati to
the back of his mind and exclaimed, "Wow! Raja, this is perfect."

"Baba got it for me." He looked up and said, "But you know, I had to promise to memorize the multiplication table and write a whole page on my costume."

"It's worth it!" Shankar chuckled. "Yours will be the best in the neighborhood."

"What do you think of mine, Grandpa?" DeeDee was suddenly transformed into Dorothy, red shoes, and all.

"You look just like her. Who did your braids?"

"Grandma! Mother watched and laughed when Grandma made my braids."

"You two will have the best Halloween this year. Is Baba home already?"

"He is on his way," DeeDee said.

"Raja, use your wizardry on bad guys only," Shankar said.

Chapter Fifty-Three

By the Copper Beech Tree

The morning heralded a beautiful autumn day. But Shankar had not had a peaceful moment. He was unsure of what he could do about Parvati. He slept fretfully at night and remained quiet during the day. The day before, he hadn't been able to tell Durga about the letter. He also hadn't told her about his conversations with Julie or with Samir. In the past, when he was conflicted or needed someone to bounce ideas around with, he talked with her effortlessly; now he was ashamed by his lack of empathy and action for others. He avoided sharing his anguish with her. What was stuck in his heart found no way out. How could it? His parents were already dead, and now Parvati was likely dying. His tortured soul found no escape.

In the afternoon when Julie came home, she casually mentioned, "Last night DeeDee told me about your sister's letter. Anything important from home?"

Shankar was taken aback. Blood drained from his face. He stared at her as if not understanding what she had asked. "We're going out for our walk now," he babbled . . . Sundown comes so early now-a-days. I'll talk with you later."

He ran upstairs to Durga immediately. "Shall we go to the copper beech tree today?"

"Oh, it's time for our walk. Let's go." As they came out of the house, she said, "Tuesdays we often walk by Bernard Baruch's house and the golf course? Why not also today."

Durga was talkative and informed Shankar that the Bellport Historical Society ladies had invited her to give a talk at their lunch. "They liked that I was a professor of economics in Michigan. Exotic, you know," she giggled.

"You're special, that's why." Shankar gave a wry smile and squeezed her hand. "How did you break into their circle?"

"Julie has spread the news about us; eventually it gets to all corners. The Society wants me to talk about the education of women in India."

"You are our social connection to high society," he said drily.

Durga's mind was already elsewhere. "After we go home today, you keep Raja busy. I have to show DeeDee how to make Indian dolls."

"Indian dolls?"

"She got the idea from what you told her."

"I see."

When they came to the copper beech tree, they stopped for a minute. Shankar loved the dark copper color of its leaves in spring and its late fall color—a beautiful reddish purple. He was thankful that the current owner had not cut down the majestic tree. The Baruch house must have been a gorgeous place in its day but had lost its old glory—wisteria vines, allowed to run wild, were trying to rip the porch off the front of the house. They walked quietly for a little while. Shankar was absent-minded, gazing into the distance most of the time. Almost abruptly, Durga pulled his hand and slowed his pace. "The other day, Samir told me you wished you had visited your mother." She leaned forward and looked into his eyes. "This is new. With the rage you harbored in your heart, I couldn't have guessed this."

Shankar was silent for a few moments. "She was also a victim," he said and paused, trying to gauge Durga's reaction. "She was trained to obey her husband ... blindly. All in the name of religion! Think of the *Sati-Daha* idea. In the old days, a few women might have willingly jumped onto the funeral pyre, but most were dragged and burned alive. She probably would have been forced to do that if the practice had not been abolished."

Durga nodded, but it was a hesitant nod as if uncertain of what to make of this new revelation or how to respond to her husband.

"I feel sorry for my mother." Shankar soldiered on, staring at the distance.

Durga tugged his hand, looking into his eyes. "They have both been dead for some time. Can you—"

"I don't know. I wish I could lift the stone sitting on my chest."

"I know. Isn't it time you let it go?"

Shankar did not reply and resumed his walk. After some time, he turned to Durga. "Yesterday I got a letter from my younger sister, Parvati. She was ruined by my father."

"Ruined?"

"As soon as we married, my father got Parvati married off to an old priest. I suppose he was afraid no serious brahmin family would marry into ours. She had a horrible life."

"Oh, my. I didn't know this. This happened as a reaction to our marriage? How awful!"

"I also got a letter from Parvati earlier in Philadelphia, I think just before her marriage. I was so irritated with her I didn't read it. I tore it to pieces and threw it out. … I had a good relationship with her and went to her college to talk with her before our marriage, hoping she would meet with you and welcome you." He bent forward to Durga and said, "I thought at least she would understand me and support us, but no." His voice was bitter. "She aligned herself with my father and asked me how I could marry someone against our family traditions?"

"I wish I'd known this before. I feel so sorry." After a pause, she asked, "So, you don't know what she wanted to tell you in her letter."

"Right." Shankar knew it was a terrible mistake on his part and looked away from his wife.

"Perhaps she realized her mistake and was sorry."

Shankar took out Parvati's letter from his pocket and handed it to her. He stood next to her while she read it, looking quietly toward the bay.

After she read the letter, she pulled Shankar to her and held him in an embrace without saying anything. Relieved a little that he had shared Parvati's news with her, he rested his cheek against hers.

"Are you thinking of doing something for your sister?" Durga asked him.

"It's beyond anything I can do. Parvati has no children, and it seems she may soon be dead." Shankar looked away from her.

A chilly wind blew off the water and they unconsciously pulled their jackets more tightly around. The sailboats that had dotted the bay a few weeks before were already tucked up in their winter shelters; a few motorboats were still cruising. Occasional shrills of the seagulls did not bother Shankar, but the motorboat sounds disturbed him. Shankar stared at the horizon. The waves glistened in the setting sun, which was dipping near the horizon. He appeared mesmerized and did not turn or look back at his wife.

Durga tugged his arm and saw tears on his cheeks. He was trying hard to control his emotions. Again, she pulled him toward her without a word and held him.

"So many lives wasted," he murmured and clung to her, his pillar of support.

She pulled out the end of her sari and used it to wipe his face, as Indian mothers do with their children.

"I want to do something, but I'm not sure what to do." Shankar lamented.

"You talk about fate all the time. This was indeed fate, beyond your control."

He straightened and put his hands on her shoulders. "Like Karna?"

"Perhaps ... Karna tried hard, but he couldn't alter his fate."

They stood there gazing at the bay as the line between sea and sky blended into inky darkness. Finally, Durga said, "Let's go home."

On their walk back, Shankar's entire life seemed to be laid out in front of him: how he had wrestled with the conservative ideas of his family, faced the challenges of his unconventional marriage, and adapted to a foreign culture with no extended family support. But for the last three decades, he had been coasting. Where had Shankar's spirit of accepting challenges and fighting for the right thing gone? Had he given up in life? Was he gradually withering away? The image of the long-lost water carrying man came to him—dark and shiny from long hours in the sun. "The water carrying man gave up his fight and accepted what came to him," he mumbled to Durga.

"What made you remember this man now?"

"I was wondering," Shankar murmured, "if I've truly become like the water carrying man."

"Accepted defeat in life? You are not like that. We had a different goal. And we succeeded."

"I'm thinking about what to do about Parvati. I feel I have lost my courage. I have no spirit left."

"No, no. That is not you. You are now overwhelmed with sadness and guilt, but you will rise to the occasion. You have always done that. And you don't have to face this alone. We will face it together."

After walking silently for a minute, Durga asked, "Is there a way to find out Parvati's condition?"

"I'm sure they don't have a phone, and I don't know anyone who could find this for us. A letter will take too long."

When they came near their home, Durga held his hand and said, "What you should do will come from within you."

RECOGNITION AND ACCEPTANCE

NOVEMBER 2005

Chapter Fifty-Four

Visit by a Classmate

As soon as Shankar and Durga entered the house, Julie told Shankar that his friend from Dum Dum had called. She paused, grinning, and looking at her father-in-law's inquisitive face, but not revealing who called. Finally, she said, "Soumen."

"Soumen called from India?"

"No. He is in Manhattan visiting his daughter and grandchildren." She gave Shankar a telephone number to call.

Shankar had last seen Soumen at the airport when he left Calcutta, over forty years before. They were best friends in school and college days, but they had not kept up with each other for the last several years. Life had carried them into different worlds. But the old days came back to Shankar, and he perked up. He called his friend right away and urged him to come by train to Patchogue at once. "I am so excited . . . after so many years! If you don't, I'm coming to your place tonight."

Soumen had no choice and agreed to come the next morning.

"Last time, Ranjit visited us in Ann Arbor. Now Soumen!" he told his wife animatedly. "The world has changed. Now they come from Dum Dum to visit us!" Memories of Soumen kept Shankar's thoughts about Parvati at bay.

Durga had not seen Shankar so jubilant since their college days. "You know," Shankar said, "We had many adventures together in our younger days. Almost everything we did outside our homes, we did together.

He was also the one who took me to visit his uncle where I ate my first omelet." Shankar guffawed.

She nodded. "Yes, I know."

"Another thing that stood out to me was that he studied Buddhism seriously—when we were young, all on his own."

Shankar remained cheerful and vibrant, forgetting Julie's inquiry about Parvati's letter. Wednesday turned out to be a wonderful day with temperatures in the mid-thirties and a clear sky. After warm hugs at the train station, Soumen said, "You know, we are still the same, and look almost the same. Aged a little. That's all."

The two talked and talked and caught up with their lives. When DeeDee and Raja returned from playing with friends, Shankar introduced Soumen to them. "This is my friend from Dum Dum. Remember the stories I told you? He was *in* the stories."

"You went with Grandpa to get dates from a date tree?" DeeDee asked him.

Soumen nodded. "We did many things together."

Shankar looked at Soumen. "We had lots of fun, didn't we?"

"Will you tell Grandpa to take us to Dum Dum?" Raja said. "I want to go to the date tree and get dates."

Soumen looked at Shankar. "The date trees in Raja Bagan near the pond?" he asked. Shankar nodded. "You told him about our childhood adventures?"

Soumen turned to Raja and told him, "I will take you there and to large mango trees also."

Durga took the children to the kitchen for afternoon snacks, leaving the two friends in the living room. It was a crisp cool day, but bright, warm sunshine poured through the window, while chilly autumn winds stayed outside—perfect for reminiscing about the good old days. After a cup of tea, Soumen said, "You remember our Jr. High English teacher?"

"He is the one who caned us," Shankar said with a chuckle as he now felt free to mention it. "I had an encounter with him the day our school final exam results came out."

"I mention him," Soumen said, "because he turned out to be a remarkable man. Most of us don't do much after retirement, but he established a free tutoring class for students. Anyone could come to the class. Can you imagine that?"

They both knew that teachers had private tutoring classes in their homes to supplement their meagre income, so not charging anything was unheard of.

Soumen continued, "A few would bring him something or offer a few rupees, but he did not ask for anything. You would not know this, but he helped many to stand on their feet. The day he died, the whole town came over to pay him respect. A big procession carried his body to the Ganges River for cremation."

"Really!"

"Now, there are several scholarships in his name." Soumen looked at Shankar. "You and I got more degrees and better jobs, but I feel small when I compare myself with him." Soumen's voice choked and he could not speak any more. He got up and walked toward the end of the room and ambled out toward the tall walnut trees.

Shankar remembered their school days. How wonderful it was every morning to walk to school together with Soumen and the other boys, bantering with each other. The junior high teacher was long dead. Even now Shankar could see his thin face with small, round glasses, a wide forehead and sparse black hair. He was the best teacher of English. His method was different; he did not simply read a piece and explain it. He stopped at many words explaining different uses of the words. How he emphasized the importance of prepositions! He used to say, 'See how different the language is from Bengali. The word "look" means seeing with your eyes, also turning your attention to something. Now, add a preposition, it changes the meaning completely: look for, look out, etc.' Then Shankar had to copy the meanings of the verbs with different prepositions and memorize them. The English he had learned was all from that teacher.

One day, he remembered, they went to school a little early, but that day the English teacher was late. They stayed at their benches because he could show up any moment, but they talked and laughed loudly. Ravi from another bench said, "Yesterday there was an eating contest in Bally: whoever can eat the maximum number of chapattis during lunch wins. Last year's winner ate 98 chapattis, but the same guy ate only 50 this year. He couldn't eat a single piece more. When people asked him, what had happened to him, he said, 'I can't figure it out. I had a practice run in the morning, and I ate 73 chapattis.'"

The entire class laughed at his gestures and imitation of the man. But that innocent joke led into something that no one could foresee. But today, Soumen brought memories of the event back and they were suddenly sharp and prominent in his thoughts.

***

The English Teacher

A boy from behind said, "What are you guys laughing about? That's an old joke, Salah!"

"How dare you call me Salah?" Ravi retorted.

"Never mind, you don't even have a sister," the boy replied.

"You know what salah means?" Bikash whispered to Shankar with a grin on his face.

"Salah?" Shankar said. "That is a bad word."

"Only laborers use that word in our house," Ravi added.

"It is not a dirty word," a boy behind them said. "It means wife's brother."

Another boy jumped in, "Yeah if I call you salah, your sister is married to me. Ha ha ha."

Ravi then called the first boy, "Salah, come here." And they all laughed. "Salah, salah, salah." The word sounded so naughty. They reveled in it, calling each other salah and laughing loudly.

Just then the teacher, a tall, thin man, entered the room. They quieted down immediately and sat up straight on their benches. The teacher put the roll-call book on his table with a thud. "The whole school can hear the boisterous noise from this class." His brown face had turned purple. Exasperated, he looked at the entire class and asked, "What were you all laughing about?"

No one answered him and remained silent. That made the teacher more annoyed. He looked around the classroom. Then a boy from behind pointed to those sitting in the first bench, and said, "They were saying a bad word, sir, and laughing."

The teacher turned to Shankar and his friends more inquisitively. "You, the best students in my class?" He took a step toward them. "Bad word, eh? What was that?"

It was a word they felt they were not supposed to know, and they couldn't tell him. They remained silent. The teacher strolled back and forth in front of the class. He then asked one boy at a time in Shankar's bench what was so fascinating about the word, but no one said anything. It was as if the five of them—Soumen, Bikash, Ranjit, Debjit and he—had made a pact not to tell him. The teacher then was incensed and commanded them, "Stand up on the bench!"

They had to get up on the bench. That was a punishment. Standing did not cause any pain, but Shankar felt very wounded. The simplest punishment was to stand in one's place. Standing up on the bench was more grievous than that. It was an insult, and each boy felt embarrassed. There were other punishments like kneeling outside the door, where anyone passing by would see you. The worst was if you had to hold your ears with your hands while standing or kneeling. Teachers sometimes rendered physical punishments. Pulling an ear, pinching tummies, or hitting with a ruler were common; being hit with a cane was reserved for the worst offenders.

The teacher said, "You can sit down when you tell me what you were saying."

That day the teacher behaved so differently; he was fuming, and his mind was not on teaching. He had never been late before. Shankar thought something bad must have happened in his home that morning.

"Made the classroom a bazaar, eh," he said, "because I was a little late?" He pointed at Shankar and said, "You sit in the first bench. You should behave like model students and answer when I ask, but no. Probably because you have not been punished before."

The whole class stared at them. This had never happened to the good students.

The teacher walked back and forth and asked them again, "Well, are you going to tell me or simply stand there?"

The five students avoided his eyes and blankly looked at the wall.

"You don't give me a choice," he said, and stormed out of the room.

One boy from the back bench shouted, "Tell him what you were giggling about. Otherwise, you will get it." But it all happened so fast, so unexpectedly, the boys were stunned. Shankar did not know what to do. How could he tell the teacher what they were heehawing about? Especially about a word they thought was dirty.

The teacher came back with a cane. "You deserve a proper punishment." His eyes were burning. His white dhuti and long shirt seemed loose and haphazard, not like his regular crisply ironed clothes. He kept the long cane on his table and paced back and forth. The shiny, dirty-yellow cane was about the thickness of a middle finger. A shiver went down Shankar's spine.

He glanced at the five boys and smoothed his hair with his hands. He then lifted the cane. He bent it with his hands to test its flexibility and went to the first boy at the end of the bench.

"Stretch out your hand."

Bikash stretched his right hand forward with the palm up.

"You won't tell me, right?" The teacher waited a few seconds; then the cane fell sharply.

"Uh, uh," Bikash cried.

The teacher then went to the second boy and repeated the punishment. Finally, he came to Shankar; he was petrified by then. Besides being physically punished, he was horrified with the idea of being caned in school! The worst physical punishment one could have in school. How could this happen to him?

"So, you'll also follow your friends, right?" the teacher asked Shankar.

Shankar remained silent. How could he betray his friends and tell him anything? Besides, he could not say that bad word in front of his teacher. The teacher stared at him for a few seconds, and Shankar meekly stretched out his hand. His body stiffened and his heart stopped; then the cane came down. It burned his palm, like a thin line of fire.

It did hurt, but not as bad as Shankar had imagined. However, his heart swelled with the disheartening thought that now he had been caned in school. Soon his vision blurred, and tears started to wet his cheeks. Then the bell rang.

Shankar heard the teacher saying, "You can sit down now." He stormed out of the classroom.

The five were so embarrassed they could not even look at each other. They simply gazed at their books or stared out through the window the rest of the day. One boy from the back of the room remarked, "You were stupid. You could've made up a word for him."

When the school was over, they walked home silently. This was usually the most fun time for them, chatting and kidding with each other. But not that day. They couldn't discuss it later either. Somehow, they all avoided the subject. The school continued and they behaved as if the event were over, but Shankar could not purge it from his memory. It seemed to affect him deeply. Finally, the summer came, the school closed and Shankar along with other students got involved with various activities—playing games with friends like soccer and hide and seek or reading story books. The incident did not occupy Shankar's mind anymore.

The first day after the summer they returned to the classroom, and the caning incident came to Shankar's memory in a flash. He thought he had forgotten it, but no, he had not. He did not talk about it and behaved as if the incident had not happened, but it remained in his heart. He overcame his feelings about it only after the puja vacation, about three months after summer. During the puja season, all were happy and jolly for a whole month; there were gifts, feasts and treats, stage performances, and Shankar seemed to completely forget the event. The school opened and he carried on with his studies as usual. The English teacher also treated them with extra care. Then they moved on to eighth grade in January.

Three years passed by quickly, and they became senior students. They would go to college the next year. They were preoccupied, even obsessed with what they'd study, what they wished to become. The junior high teacher vanished from their minds.

Finally, the state-wide high school graduation exam day appeared, and they all took the exam. The day the results came out, Shankar was incredibly happy because he had won a national scholarship based on his performance in the exam and his name was in the city newspaper. He was walking to the bazaar to buy cardamom for his mother—she wanted to make his favorite desert, rice pudding. He met the junior high school teacher on the road.

The teacher greeted him warmly. Shankar had not seen him for some time and noticed he had aged in the last three years. Shankar bent down and touched his feet. The teacher lifted him up, eyes twinkling, saying, "I am proud of you. You have enhanced the name of our school. Keep it up; you will have a great future."

"Thank you. It is because I had good teachers like you."

The teacher's expression was a little shy. He put his hand on Shankar's shoulder. "I must admit one thing to you." He looked straight into his eyes, and Shankar had no idea what he was referring to. "Remember the day I caned you?" he asked.

Shankar was startled. That event had gone far down in his memory, and he had no contrite or sad feelings anymore. But the old scene came back to him. It was such an innocuous event, he wondered why they had giggled so much about a silly word and felt it so distasteful they could not utter it to anyone. Shankar simply stared at him.

"I do not remember what put me in such a bad mood that day," he said in a tender voice. "I should not have caned you. I was late and it was not your fault. You boys did the right thing by not telling me what you were cackling about." His voice cracked a little. He patted Shankar's shoulder and walked away.

Shankar was blown away that the teacher had remembered the event for so long. He felt a pang. The teacher had boldly admitted his mistake. He did not have to mention that minor incident after so many years; there was no reason to bring it up again. He stood there and watched the teacher vanish in the crowd.

***

This was the only time Shankar had been caned in school; he was so humiliated he could not ever tell anyone about it and bore the sadness silently in his heart. He had wished to forget the incident and the teacher, but it remained stuck in the deepest reaches of his memory. Now the incident came roaring back, this time with an unmistakable lesson. The vulnerability and bravery of the teacher struck him in a newer light.

Soumen had said it right—the junior high school teacher was a better man. He had even proved his inner goodness by serving disadvantaged students in his retirement. Shankar had thought that his own ideas and actions were right, and he expected everyone to side with him while he had no tolerance for their views. Now he felt he might not be as good as he had thought of himself.

His father was also a teacher. Maybe he had a side that Shankar couldn't see. His father was well respected and obeyed in school. His father's method was old—severe, with strict discipline. That was perhaps the method of some rishis in their ashrams to mold their students to their ways. Those students went to them willingly. But Shankar wanted to be a physicist, not an eminent religious scholar. Perhaps the partition of India had disrupted his father's life, ruining his personal goals, and he had been trying to achieve those through his son. His son was his only vehicle and hope. Shankar wished his parents had another son who could have fulfilled his father's dreams.

He ambled over to Soumen and put his arm around his shoulders as they had done in their youth. "You don't know what good you have done to me by coming here." Shankar's voice caught in his throat as he choked back tears.

Two days passed by quickly. Friday morning, when Shankar and Durga drove him to the Patchogue train station, Soumen expressed a wish that they would visit him in Calcutta. "Certainly," Durga said, glancing at Shankar, knowing that she—but not Shankar—would do that.

"Not even in my dreams could I have imagined seeing him here," Shankar told Durga on their way home, slowly shaking his head. "The world is changing so fast ... Soumen's visit has made me think of many things."

"Always wonderful to see a childhood friend, isn't it?"

He nodded.

"Soumen said we are not the first to reach old age!" Shankar told Durga and laughed. "Maybe when you retire in India, you start to think in terms of bigger perspectives." He glanced at his wife. "Somehow they become wiser. He also said all of us have problems, arising from our hopes and desires not being fulfilled."

"Yes." Durga nodded.

After they reached home, Shankar sat quietly in his chair in the living room. It was so good to see Soumen. *How the days have passed by!* Durga brought a hot cup of tea and left him alone. "The Buddha truly found something interesting," Soumen's words from the night before came to him. "He said our life, like a flowing river, is never the same. The older water has flown downstream and gone. The past is gone." Shankar stared at the tall trees in the far end of the backyard and recollected the story that led to the Buddha's words.

***

Everything Changes

Buddha was teaching his disciples under a tree when a man from the nearby village rushed up to him with glaring eyes and said, "You come to our village, say some nice things that people like to hear, so they give you what they can. You make a living that way. That is disgusting. Some of our boys even leave home to follow you. Leave this place. Get out of here." The man spat on the ground close to the Buddha.

This was an unimaginable insult. A murmur of protest rose among the disciples. The Buddha's head turned toward the man, and he asked him in a calm voice, "Suppose a man brings a gift to someone and he doesn't take it, then what happens to the gift?"

The man was expecting an angry reply and was perplexed by the Buddha's response. "The gift," he babbled, "then stays with the man."

"I do not accept your gift and so it stays with you." The Buddha turned toward his disciples and continued teaching.

The man stood there without knowing what to do and quietly walked away from the gathering. He was rude to the Buddha, but his nasty words fell off the Buddha like water drops off a lotus leaf. The man couldn't sleep that night. He went back to the Buddha the next day and apologized for his behavior. "I am sorry for my actions yesterday."

To the gasp of his disciples, the Buddha said, "I do not accept your apology."

The man stood there, helpless and lost. Then the Buddha explained to him, "When you look at a river, you see the same river, but the water in the stream is not the same that was there a moment before; that water flowed downstream. Our lives are like the river. You are not the same man as you were yesterday. I am not the same person either. You insulted someone yesterday who is not me you see in front of you. How can I accept your apology for what you did to someone else?"

***

Shankar sat still but he was awake. *We cannot hold on to our old self or our old grudges.*

Chapter Fifty-Five

Fire Island

S hankar had been lively the morning he and Soumen had gone to the door to send the children off to school, but now after Soumen had left, he did not feel like talking with anyone. The Jr. High teacher loomed prominently in his mind, and the idea that he was not as good as he had thought of himself tormented him. He dragged himself around the house. He gazed at the TV for a few minutes but did not listen to anything. He took a quick trip to the library hoping to see Jacco, but he was not there. Finally, he told Durga he wanted to go to Fire Island for a change.

"A little melancholy after Soumen left?" She looked at him tenderly. "I'll be happy to go for a wintery walk on the beach. Julie is taking the children from school to the Mall. She is also buying some things for me." She said with a concealing smile as if there was something she didn't wish to reveal to her husband. "Let's go. I have the time now; tomorrow will be hard. I have a lot of things to do."

Durga combed her hair and put on a thick brown sari and a white blouse before layering on a heavy sweater, coat, muffler, and hat. Similarly bundled up, Shankar drove. As they headed over Robert Moses Bridge, a short distance from Bellport, they saw very few cars going towards the beach. Still, Shankar looked forward to clearing his mind in the salty air of the Atlantic Ocean.

What a quiet, different scene from the summer. Too early for a blanket of snow, the scenery was barren and stark without the beachgoers. Only some wild grass and dry branches on the dunes made an impression. A few men and women were walking, and some were jogging on the beach. A man was searching around with a metal detector. It was chilly but the sun provided enough warmth for a stroll. Shankar and Durga headed eastward along the beach.

"I like to walk near the edge of the water," she said. A moderate breeze pushed the waves up on the shore. The bottom of her sari got a little wet occasionally, but she didn't seem to care.

Shankar walked along the dry sand, hunched forward but relaxed. He enjoyed watching the rhythmic pattern of the crashing waves. He paced parallel to Durga and liked seeing her behaving like the college student he had known in Calcutta. As a college professor, mother, and grandmother, she seldom exhibited this ebullient side. He felt good that he chose to come here. The lonesomeness that occupied him earlier receded to the back of his mind. The beach reminded Shankar of his fond memories from Puri, the sea town near Calcutta. He had visited the town only once, but not with his family. His family never went away on vacation.

He mentioned that to Durga while they strolled; Durga said she had gone to Puri several times with her family and those were joyous times for her.

"Have you visited Bhubaneswar, near Puri?" Shankar asked.

"Bhubaneswar?" She said as she paced carefully to test the wet sand. "No." She shook her head. "We only saw the station in early morning—the last stop before Puri for the express train. There we bought hot tea in tiny earthen cups from a *chaiwalah*. When we finished, we had fun throwing the cups out of the train and shattering them."

"I still get a laugh thinking of the journey I made with Soumen to Bhubaneswar," Shankar told her as he watched her lifting the edge of her sari when waves approached. "We were two boys on a silly adventure."

"I have never gone out on an excursion on my own," Durga said, stepping back from the edge of the water. "What made you think of it now?"

"I don't know. Perhaps Soumen. Perhaps seeing you amuse yourself, I thought of the few times I was away from my family and felt free. Perhaps because I remembered a temple gate keeper there, an old *panda*, who hassled us."

"He figured out you two were trouble?"

"No. Not that. It was his rules we didn't like."

"The rules!" Durga exclaimed. "The priests in Puri didn't allow Mrs. Indira Gandhi, the Prime Minister of India, and a Hindu, to enter the temple because she married a Parsi, a Zoroastrian."

He nodded and gave a wry smile.

"I know you have a rebellious spirit. Surely, you won't like old rules." She had a playful grin that went all the way to her eyes.

"It's nothing really." Shankar said and absently gazed at the long white waves crashing on the beach, in the repeating symphony of the sea.

A sudden wave rolled up the sand and Durga tried to move away, but her sari got wet. She looked at him and laughed her lovely crystal laugh. "Now I'd like to know what you two did in Bhubaneswar. Tell me."

***

Temple Panda

Once during the summer break in college, Soumen and I went on a tour of Bhubaneswar, the capital of the state of Odisha and the "Temple City of India." This would be our adventure—only the two of us. We took an overnight train and arrived in the morning. Cheerfully we walked under a cloudy sky along a road from the railway station to the temple area. The buildings on the road were incredibly old with beautiful architectural motifs on the facades, windows and roof borders, and pictures of gods and goddesses. Narrow lanes led off this road where smaller houses, some with tiled roofs, clustered together. There was a feeling of old India in those lanes.

Our first goal was to find an inexpensive hotel. We found a place near the temple, a *Dharamsala*, and inquired if they had a room available for us. To our delight, they did.

"How much?" Soumen asked the man sitting at the desk.

"This is a Dharamsala. It is free," he assured us. "Most people give us a donation when they leave."

We stared at him, flabbergasted.

"You can stay for only three nights," he stated matter-of-factly.

Sacred temples are usually in faraway places and most people can't afford the expense of a long journey plus lodging. Dharamsalas are there to help pilgrims, built and maintained by donations from wealthy devotees. For the last few centuries these free accommodations have made it possible for ordinary people to go on pilgrimages.

The desk clerk gave us a tour of the old two-story building, a solid concrete structure on the main road to the temple, which was only five minutes away. The dharamasala had many rooms built around a square courtyard and was exceptionally clean. Soumen and I looked at each other, signaling our happiness in finding the place.

The clerk handed us a heavy wrought iron key and told us the room was upstairs. As we turned to go, he added, "One more thing. Make sure you lock your room when you go out."

We went to the second floor and found our room, which was large with two wooden platform beds. Two large windows opened to a pleasant backyard with several mature trees. We had a view of houses in the distance and the top of the Lingaraja temple under an overcast sky. We happily put down our bedrolls and went out to see the town.

As we came to a nearby bazaar, we realized that Bhubaneswar was a small city. We saw fruits of various kinds—mangos, guavas and lichees—and they were quite inexpensive compared to the prices in Calcutta. Soumen pointed to a basket of mangos, saying, "There's an idea for a healthy, cheap breakfast for tomorrow."

I agreed.

We bought four large mangos and took them to our room. A traditional storage place in India is under the bed where mothers kept trunks of winter clothing. We kept the mangos under one of the beds. We weren't sure if we could keep food in the room, so that seemed to be a good place to hide them.

We went out again and decided while there was no rain, we would explore the nearby Udaygiri and Khandagiri hills. These hills have ancient Jain and Buddhist monasteries in caves and rocky hillsides that date back to the second century B.C.

Many of the caves have beautiful carvings on the outside. Unknown to me, Soumen had studied Buddhism quite seriously and was able to explain the meaning of a lot of the art and the significance of the Maha Stupa, which had remained essentially unaltered by time. "But the brahmins," he looked at me for a second and said, "sidelined the Buddha, turning him into a Hindu Avatar, and thus preserving their beliefs in the Vedas and ideas of caste. Today there are almost no Indian Buddhists in India, but the world is admiring him more and more."

We had climbed hundreds of steps to reach these revered mountain sites—Hindu and Buddhist caves and monasteries—and were exhausted when we returned. We slept deeply and got up late. The sun remained hidden behind hazy clouds, but the day was bright. We quickly got ready. People go to the temple early in the morning, and it was already nine.

Soumen said, "Let's have a mango for breakfast." Usually, people fast before going to a temple, especially for a worship service in a religious place. But we were young and not too concerned with the rituals. We wanted to see the temple architecture more than earn religious merit. In any case, he looked under the bed but couldn't see the mangos.

"Didn't we put the mangos there?" he asked with a befuddled expression on his face. We quietly searched the room and our belongings, but the mangos were nowhere to be found.

"We will investigate this when we come back," I said. But it bothered me a lot. Had someone entered our room while we were sleeping? They gave us a free room, but they could be in collusion with thieves. Still, we were late, so we left.

As we entered the temple area, many pandas rushed to us and offered their services. Pandas are priest's assistants who help pilgrims and act as guides for visitors. We decided we wouldn't hire a panda. We weren't going to perform a worship service, so why waste money on a panda? We ignored them.

When we reached the gate, however, an old man stopped us. "Who is your panda?" demanded the thin, dark man. He wore a short dhuti, raised almost up to his knees, and no shirt. A white sacred thread hung from his shoulder down to his waist. He had a pair of round, thick glasses set in what looked like tin frames. His dusty feet stuck out of worn-out rubber Hawaiian sandals. And his face looked so old if anyone had told me he was a hundred years old, I'd have believed them.

"We do not have a panda; we are not here to perform a puja," Soumen told him. "We only want to browse in the temple area."

The shriveled man looked at us and said, "You have shoes; you cannot go inside."

Indeed, we knew it was inauspicious bringing the skin of a dead animal inside a holy place. We went back to our room, left the shoes, and returned barefoot.

This time, to avoid the pandas, we went by a huge stone wall that guarded the temple compound. Beautiful sculptures of birds, beasts, creepers, flowers, men and women in different poses, and gods and goddesses in their majestic grandeur lavishly decorated the wall.

As we came near the gate, the same old man caught us. There was a glimmer in his eyes and an expression on his face that said, *No panda yet?*

"We have no shoes now," I implored him with a smile. "Can we get in?"

He looked us up and down, and asked, "What about your belts?"

I was shocked because he was right. We were wearing belts made of leather, forbidden for a Hindu temple. We went back to the Dharamsala and hid our belts under our bedrolls.

"Let's see what he says now, Soumen. We will not give in." I asserted.

When we returned, the surly old man looked at us, somewhat amazed at our impudence. I stood there calmly but smiling inside because I was sure he had no excuse now. He cocked one eyebrow, but acted very cool, and asked, "What about your moneybags?"

Oops, we had leather wallets with us. We couldn't imagine leaving them behind in the Dharamsala, especially after the incident with the mangos;

someone would surely steal them. We were beginning to feel quite put-upon, but we were undaunted. We went back and tucked our 'moneybags' carefully inside our bedrolls, keeping the money with us. What else could the man possibly ask us?

I thought we were now free to enter the temple and we strode toward the gate. The old gatekeeper spotted us, raising his hand like a policeman. The expression on his face seemed to say he had dealt with many boys like us before.

I said confidently, "We have no leather material with us anymore."

In a thunder-like voice he shouted, "What about your umbrella?"

"There is no leather in the umbrella," Soumen boldly asserted.

The gatekeeper snatched the umbrella from Soumen with a force we didn't expect in such an old man. "Have you examined the top of the umbrella?" he demanded. His stooped body suddenly became straight, and his eyes seemed to be burning. "What is this?"

Indeed, there was a small circular patch of leather on top of the umbrella to hold the spokes and the nylon cover together!

We stared at each other in utter disbelief and realized it was hopeless; he would stop us one way or another. We checked our umbrella and hired a panda, a young man, to show us around.

The old man's face brightened when he saw us with the panda. "You will be glad you have a panda," he said as he let us in.

It turned out he was right. We were happy we had the panda to guide us. The panda told us during British times the priests hadn't even let the Viceroy of India in because he was a foreigner, a nonbeliever. Instead, they built a high platform outside the walls so he could get a view of the temples within.

The Lingaraja temple was the largest and most famous, but the complex had several other temples, each rich with local architecture, and the panda gave us an excellent tour. He told us stories about the temples we wouldn't have known otherwise. The Lingaraja temple was a Shiva temple dating back to the 11th century. Although the outside of the temple was ornamental, inside the *Shivalinga*, the emblem of Shiva, had no embellishment to indicate God is simple and does not need all those intricate decorations. The panda showed us the sacred lake, the *Bindu Sagar*, with a tiny island at its center. He told us Shiva had dug this lake to quench the thirst of his wife, Goddess Parvati. Then all the rivers, lakes, and oceans of the world gave drops of water to fill up this lake. That's why it is called Bindu Sagar, which means sea of drops.

We were satisfied with the tour of the temple. But as we walked back, the mystery of the mangos came back to my mind and haunted me.

Majumdar

How could they disappear from our room? Again, we searched the room thoroughly, but we couldn't find the mangos. They had simply vanished. We became suspicious of the Dharamsala workers.

On our way out that evening, we asked the man at the desk, "Do you have another set of keys for our room?"

He admitted they had duplicate keys. "We use them only in emergencies," he said. He smiled, revealing his teeth.

That made us angrier, and I wanted to tell him he must be in collusion with the thieves, but I kept silent. We were certain in our minds that they had stolen our mangos since we had nothing else of value! What kind of a Dharamsala was this? I wished we could catch them red-handed. But we only gave him a suspicious look and went out.

We had walked so much during the trip that sleeping was no problem. But it was sultry; each night we kept the windows open for whatever little breeze we could get.

Three nights passed by quickly. On the last morning, we packed our stuff. I felt a little melancholy. Even though we had lost four mangos, I started to like the city and had become fond of our room, but we had to leave that day. I stared out the windows at the trees in the backyard. The clouds had cleared, revealing a clear, blue sky. The sweet sound of a *koel* bird floated in. Then my gaze shifted to the area below our window. There I saw four large mango seeds on the cornice. I couldn't believe my eyes. I stared at the seeds for a long time, then pulled Soumen over to see them.

We thought perhaps it was an animal known as a Bhaam, a civet—a cat-like mammal, that had taken our mangos. We could never be sure. But we felt stupid and a little repentant. When we left, we donated 10 rupees, or two dollars, to the Dharamsala, an amount much larger than the desk clerk was expecting and more than we had planned to give.

***

When the story ended, Durga gazed at her husband for a few seconds. "Wow! You really were a rebel!" she said, eyes glittering.

He did not reply because he thought there was some truth to her comment; he stared at the horizon where the sky and the water joined and looked tranquil, thinking how that rebel spirit had led him to leave India.

He imagined how his travels had helped him see things from different perspectives, and had helped him develop a questioning mind and a spirit of greater acceptance of the world beyond his father's courtyard. Meanwhile, his father followed the same old rut, a narrow channel of thought he couldn't get out of and didn't want to get out of. Shankar's temple visits had also taught him how deeply India's traditions were ingrained in society. They had been practiced for hundreds, perhaps thousands, of years. There were many like his father who continued to uphold these traditions at great cost to their wives, sons, and daughters, and themselves. Devotion to religion and a feeling of great pride in carrying forward the torch of conservative tradition must have led his father to his course in life.

He signaled to Durga it was time to go home. The sun was lower in the sky when they walked back to their car, both happy they had come to the beach.

When he returned home, Shankar thought again of the shriveled, old panda. How much he had rebelled against that man and his requirement that visitors follow those ancient rules! The old panda was obstinately and unnecessarily protecting useless superstitious ideas. Shankar had been resentful and angry and had wanted to defeat him. He had now forgotten the panda's face, but not his firm demands. It was a challenge, and he didn't succeed, but in the end, he wasn't angry. He was able to let go of his acrimony. He had forgiven the old man. What was there in the panda that occupied his mind now? Did the panda remind him of his father, carrying on similar old Hindu traditions, unfit for modern times? How could he get rid of his resentment and forgive the panda, but not his father?

Chapter Fifty-Six

Struggle at Night

Shankar could not sleep that night. His failure to understand his father and his inability to forgive him haunted him. Now, at night, Parvati was in the center of his thoughts. Though whenever her young face came to his mind, the anger he felt for his long-dead father flared up. She had apologized and asked for forgiveness and he had forgiven her as soon as he read her letter. But was that all he could do for her? Certainly, he could write a letter, saying he was sorry for what had happened, but that seemed so little, kind of futile. His heart ached to do something for her. Had a good doctor seen her? She probably had no one to look after her. With no husband and no children, what happens to a woman in a poor priest's house? Shankar knew the answer and a shiver ran through him. She would not be well taken care of, that was for sure.

He got up from bed and stood near the window. The neighborhood was silent. No wind, nothing moving, a profound stillness pervaded the area. A thin waxing crescent moon was in the sky. He gazed at the moon for some time, transfixed. The shiny sliver of celestial light transcended his anguish and transported him to another world where there was no dissatisfaction, no sadness or sorrow. He felt immersed in the soft light as if he had drunk soma—the invigorating divine drink of the gods. Ancient sages believed the moon to be a vessel for soma. The waxing moon was regenerating the soma, and the vessel will be filled in full moon. Gautama Buddha came to his mind; he was born on a full moon day and achieved

Enlightenment on a full moon night. He drank water from the hands of untouchables, which many would not do even today. He had initiated people of all castes to a caste-free religion. The Buddha was accepted as an Avatar in Hindu religion, but why didn't his father listen to his message? He couldn't envision his father's inner thoughts. Instead, the Buddha's teachings reverberated in his mind—the way to end suffering is through loving kindness, compassion, and awakening one's mind. This clearly came across from all the Jataka stories he had read from the Buddha's past lives; a particular one came to him.

***

Jataka Story

In this story, Buddha was the king of Banaras. He was kind, considerate, generous, and gave alms equally to supplicants and spiritual seekers. Once he let an ascetic stay in the royal garden and instructed his royal gardener to take good care of him. The gardener followed the king's directions sincerely. After a few days, the ascetic went away and returned quietly in the evening; the gardener was unaware of his presence. On the same day, some guests came in the late evening to visit the king and stayed in the royal garden for the night. The gardener received them well, but he had no worthy food to offer to the honored guests. He went to the royal garden to shoot a deer for fresh meat. Hearing a noise and thinking it to be a deer, he shot an arrow, but the ascetic was out, and the arrow pierced him. Hearing a human cry, the gardener quickly ran to the person and attended to his wounds as best as he could. He begged the ascetic to forgive him, but the ascetic was mortally wounded and died. The gardener knew the king could not forgive him for killing the ascetic even though it was an accident. So, he ran away with his family.

After one year, the gardener returned to Banaras and inquired with a friendly minister what the king thought about him. The minister talked with the king about the gardener, but the king acted as if he had not heard him. The minister surmised the king must not be happy with the gardener.

The gardener came back to the city after another year and inquired about the king's feelings toward him. The minister found the same response from the king. On the third year, when the gardener returned, the king told the minister that he would talk with the gardener. The gardener explained to the king what happened and that he had accidentally killed the ascetic. He begged his forgiveness. The king told him not to worry and appointed him to his old post as the royal gardener.

Puzzled, the minister asked the king why only this time did he talk with the gardener and forgive him. He could have done this earlier.

The king said, "For two years I was upset with the gardener, so I was silent. My irritation is appeased now. My goal is to be aware of my feelings and never to act hastily in anger. Only when I was completely calm, could I make a proper judgment." After a short pause, the king murmured, "Compassion does not arise when one is angry."

***

Shankar thought about how long he had been indignant with his father. He felt remorse and sympathy rising in his heart. A sudden calm washed over him, and he went back to bed. Soon, he laid on an infinite ocean of peace. The goddess of sleep embraced him completely.

Chapter Fifty-Seven

Bhai Phonta

With only a few fluffy clouds in the sky, Sunday morning showed all the signs of a beautiful day to come. Shankar sat at the breakfast table and quietly sipped tea. His face was pensive. DeeDee and Raja, dressed in nice clothes, sat with them. Samir was absorbed in reading the paper. Shankar wondered why the children wore fancy clothes and glanced out at the maple tree in the backyard. A few yellow leaves still clung to it, but most were scattered on the lawn, being blown by the wind. Further back in the yard some oak leaves hung on determinedly, waiting for spring. All were quietly engaged except for the sounds of utensils and dishes from the kitchen where Durga and Julie had been busy for a while. The fragrance of cinnamon and something frying drifted through the door.

Finally, Durga, standing in the kitchen doorway, announced, "Today we will observe Bhai Phonta, Brothers-Sisters day. It comes on the second day after Diwali. That was on Thursday, but we'll celebrate it today."

Shankar jerked his head and looked at Durga with an incredulous stare. They had never even discussed Bhai Phonta in the U.S.

Durga seemed to emanate radiance and energy. "This was a wonderful festivity in our family and it still is today," she told Samir and Julie. "A day we enjoyed with our brothers and sisters. With marvelous food, fine sweets, and activities. That's why I have asked DeeDee and Raja to dress up." She entered the breakfast room with a small plate in her hand.

Shankar remembered Bhai Phonta in Dum Dum—the day his sisters put a sandalwood paste dot—phonta—on his forehead while praying for his long life and that God would make him strong.

"You never told me about this, Ma." Samir straightened his shoulders and looked at his mother.

Everyone turned toward Durga expectantly. She smiled at her son and sighed. "I couldn't do this in Ann Arbor because we didn't have a sister for you."

To the grandchildren, she said, "Sisters put a dot of sandalwood paste on the forehead of their brothers to protect them from Yama, the God of Death, and make them strong. They do this with a prayer. Then they eat delicious food and celebrate a wonderful day." Her face beamed as she recounted her family's celebration of Bhai Phonta.

Julie came closer to Durga. "I like it. What do brothers do?"

"Brothers bring gifts for sisters. They also bless and express good wishes for their sisters."

Shankar was amazed and pleased at Durga's passion to bring her family customs to American life. The only Indian festival they had observed in the U.S. was the Diwali celebration. They had followed American customs and celebrations in Ann Arbor, from Memorial Day to Halloween, then Thanksgiving and Christmas, but she had never brought up festivities from India. Bengalis have many festivals throughout the year. They say, 'Thirteen festivals in twelve months.' Speechless, Shankar simply gazed at his wife; she looked so happy.

DeeDee and Raja stood up, delighted to be the center of attention. Julie positioned them on two chairs facing each other. Durga's plate had a small pile of beige sandalwood paste. "Take a bit on the tip of your finger," Durga instructed DeeDee. "Then repeat after me.

I put a phonta on my brother's forehead
To set a thorny barrier on Yama's door
Yamuna gives a phonta to her brother Yama
I give a phonta to my brother
May he become strong as steel.

Now you put a dot on Raja's forehead with the tip of your finger."

"Which finger do I use?" DeeDee's head tilted toward Durga, eyes glowing with curiosity and excitement.

"You use your pinky or the next finger." Durga said, waving the appropriate fingers at DeeDee.

Durga made her repeat the steps three times. Then she instructed Raja to stand up. "You have seen how your mother does pranam to us, touching our feet. You touch DeeDee's feet with your fingers. This way you are asking for her good wishes."

"And DeeDee, you wish good things to come to your brother. You don't say it out loud."

"Do I have to touch her feet?" Raja expressed some resistance but accepted it quickly with a look from his mother.

"This is it—the end of the ceremony. Give a hug to each other." Durga and Julie looked at each other with satisfaction, pleased at how nicely it had gone.

"I prepared a gift for Raja to give to DeeDee," Durga said. "Here it is, Raja. Next year you must get a nice gift for her."

DeeDee opened the gift immediately and shrieked. "A homemade Indian doll! How cute. I love it. Thank you, Grandma."

"Sisters in Bengal do Bhai-Phonta and in a very similar way all over India," Shankar said to DeeDee and Raja.

Durga brought out another box. "DeeDee, give this to Raja. Next year you must get a lovely gift to give to your brother."

Raja tore up the colored papers and opened the package. It was a spaceship Lego set. He was elated. "This is awesome. None of my friends have it. Thank you, Grandma." His face glowed.

"I have cooked special Bengali pulao, lamb curry, fried eggplant, puffed-up Bengali luchi," Durga said, "and Samir has brought sweets from a bakery. Now we will have a feast!" She and Julie started to bring food to the table. The fragrance of the sweet pulao pervaded the room.

"I never thought I would see this here." Shankar's voice choked with emotion as he looked at Durga admiringly. How he had missed this festival! "When I was growing up," he told everyone, "this was a joyous and festive day in our house." Vivid details of the celebration came to him. He sat erect on a mat on the floor as his older sister did the ceremony first, putting a sandalwood phonta on his forehead with the same words in Bengali that Durga taught DeeDee while his mother stood by and watched. Shankar touched his sister's feet for blessings. She put unhusked rice with durva grass on his head with her blessings. Then Parvati followed her. He put rice and durva grass on her head with his blessings and good wishes. His sister's youthful faces came to him; how sincerely they had done the ceremony wishing him long life and good luck.

Then a vision of sick Parvati lying in a cot came to Shankar. His younger sister who had wished him long life each year during Bhai Phonta was dying alone. He remembered her words from the letter: *'I have no one to talk to and no place to go; I prayed for death, but the gods were not kind to me.'* How miserable could her life be to write this to her older brother who had forsaken her. Shankar's eyes misted and became blurred. *'No one from our family ever visited me or wrote to me.'* His eyes teared up and he daubed at them with his handkerchief.

Everyone dove into the marvelous food, but Shankar moved the pulao and pieces of meat with his fork around his plate. He did not lift his hand to put food into his mouth.

As soon as DeeDee finished her sweets, she sprung up. "I'm going to my room to play with my new doll." She ran upstairs without waiting for a response.

Raja also got up, saying, "I want to play with my space set too," and went to the living room.

Shankar couldn't stop the flow of tears. His chest heaved uncontrollably. He rose and faced the window. Durga watched him and was about to get up when Shankar cleared his throat and turned to the table. "I cannot bear this pain anymore," he said. "I have to go to Calcutta immediately," surprising Durga, Samir, and Julie. His eyes glistened with tears.

Durga, Julie and Samir stopped eating and stared at him. After a moment, Shankar spoke, his voice choked with emotion, "I have a lot to tell you." He wiped his eyes with his handkerchief and took Parvati's letter from his pocket. "First, I want you all to read a letter I received Wednesday from my younger sister." He gave it to Durga and sat down.

After reading the letter a second time, Durga's face grew grim; then she read it aloud to her son and daughter-in-law, translating the Bengali words to English. Julie gazed at Shankar with a questioning look. Samir said, "Baba, you'll have to explain everything to us."

Shankar looked at his son, "When you were young, I did not tell you much about our family, deliberately. I'm sorry. You deserve to know everything." Then he described their family's extremely conservative lifestyle in Dum Dum and how his father had thrown him out because he wanted to marry Durga, who belonged to a different caste. His mother had agreed with his father. Shankar thought at least his sister would support him, but she also cast him off. In a rage he rejected his family, and all they represented, and immigrated to the U.S. holding himself to two vows. He would forget his family completely, and never return to India. "I wished to establish a new life in the U.S. without any of the old, conservative constraints from India." He paused. "Those vows were mine and mine alone, not your mother's," he stressed. "I asked your mother only to do one thing: never talk about my family to anyone in the U.S. She has done that out of love for me. Your mother has a wonderful family; you two have met them. I have not asked your mother to abandon her family and told her to keep connection with them in whatever way possible."

The three listened quietly. Shankar looked at Samir and continued, "I've suffered terribly with resentment and anguish. I carried on life as if everything was normal, but I burned inside. I've paid dearly for my actions in many ways, not the least of which is being sorry and sad for depriving you of your family in India."

"You can't blame yourself for all this," Durga spoke up. "You gave up your family because you thought it was the right thing to do—for our love, and to protest the caste constraints of our society. You knew, and my father told you, that you cannot change society easily. So, we came here."

"Do you know any more about auntie's condition?" Samir asked.

Shankar shook his head. "There is no way to call her. I had a feeling from the tone of the letter that if she is alive, she is extremely sick."

"Do you have a plan?" Julie asked.

"The only thing in my mind now is I must not miss a chance to save her."

"I'll go with you," Durga told Shankar.

"My grandparents are already dead," Samir said. "But if there is any hope of helping Auntie, we have to do whatever we can."

"I agree," Durga said.

Julie nodded affirmatively. "Absolutely."

"I blamed everything on my father without ever considering his life," Shankar said. "I should have figured it out a long time ago. My parents could not turn their backs on their way-of-life any more than I could turn my back on my convictions by forsaking Durga. They did what they believed in, right or wrong. This realization has helped me to finally forgive my father. I now feel I am free. It is time to return to India and reconnect with my family. I have missed them for so long."

Tears glistened in Durga's eyes. "You have suffered so much. ... I am so happy ... You have even found compassion for your father."

"I will take Parvati to a hospital and see what can be done. I want her to know she is not alone."

Samir got up and called DeeDee and Raja to come. When they arrived, he announced, "We are all going to India." DeeDee and Raja jumped up. "We're going to India!" DeeDee squealed her surprise and delight.

"I want to go to all the places Grandpa told us about!" Raja said joyfully and turned to Shankar.

"Grandma and I will go immediately," Shankar told them. "You all will come later."

"That'll be great." Julie sat up straight in her chair. "I can squeeze in three weeks in December."

Shankar looked at DeeDee and Raja. Their faces glowed with expectations of a great adventure. He knew DeeDee had started to doubt if his promises to take them to India were real or not. They came over to Shankar. "We'll have a great time, Grandpa!"

"We will, indeed!" Shankar assured them. "And you will meet many cousins in Calcutta."

Durga reached over the table and put her hand on her husband's.

Julie got up. "We need more tea."

After some time, Shankar got up, saying, "I'll send a telegram to let Parvati know we are coming. All of us are coming."

EPILOGUE

Part One

Parvati

No one was at the airport to receive them when Shankar and Durga arrived in the morning. Shankar saw that the Dum Dum Airport, which had been a small building when he left, had been rebuilt, modernized, and renamed Netaji Subhash Chandra Bose International airport, after the Independence fighter hero. The warm air hit them as they came out and took a taxi to Durga's old house in Shalkia. Shankar gazed outside as the taxi drove through the streets of Calcutta. It felt good to see local Bengalis going to markets carrying jute shopping bags for daily fresh vegetables and fish. There were more people on the road than he remembered and many new buildings. He breathed deeply feeling pleasure in seeing old familiar surroundings.

After the exuberance of return, Shankar was eager to visit Parvati and consulted Durga's brother. Durga's brother arranged for their family doctor to accompany Shankar to Bhatpara and advise him. The doctor had a private nursing home and took Shankar in his special car that accommodated a bed for the patient.

Hearing Parvati's situation, the doctor told Shankar that it was most likely she was only suffering from lack of nutrition. "I expect her to be very thin because of loss of fat and muscle mass, perhaps dry hair and dry skin. Don't be surprised to see her with hollow cheeks and sunken eyes. I don't know what to expect but I am telling you this to prepare you for the worst. She might also have difficulty concentrating, even recognizing you, and may be irritable or disoriented."

301

Debu Majumdar

It took them about an hour to reach Bhatpara and some more time to find Parvati's house. The sun has already tilted toward the horizon. They found the Bhattacharya priest family in a dilapidated, poorer section of the town. Shankar entered the shabby one-story house alone. There were several rooms around a large uncemented space, but it was quiet, as if no one lived there. He asked aloud but to no one particular, "Is Mrs. Bhattacharya here?" Not too long later, a thin and bent old woman, wearing a worn-out white cotton sari, came out. She looked at Shankar but there was no life in her eyes.

"I am here to see Parvati," he told her. The woman didn't say anything but pointed her hand to one corner.

Shankar saw that the corner had not been cleaned for some time and rubbish was piled in several places as if no one cared. There was a brown, half-torn curtain hanging on the door. He coughed several times, but no response came. He moved the curtain aside and found someone lying in bed; he could hardly make out if it were a man or a woman. Light came in through a small window; Shankar saw the room was bare. It reminded him of famine-stricken photos he had seen in U.S. magazines. He walked to the bedside and whispered, "Parvati, this is your brother."

The body moved a little, pushed her sari from her face with some effort, and gazed at him. "Who?"

"I got your letter, Parvati. This is Shankar."

"Dada?" She stared at him.

"I got your letter, Parvati. I am here now."

"Are you really here?" She tried to sit up but didn't have the strength and couldn't sit up quickly by herself. She started to cry. "I wished so long … I wished so long to see you."

Shankar held her hand. "Don't cry. I'm here. You are not alone anymore."

"I have lamented all my life. Now you are here before I die!"

Shankar interrupted her. "Stop, Parvati, stop. We will talk later. I want my doctor to see you first." He called the doctor in.

The doctor examined Parvati, especially her eyes, and took her pulse and blood pressure. "Both are low." He gave her a little glucose water to drink, and said, "I am going to put an IV on your arm so I can give you fluid and medicine. Then we will take you to my Nursing Home."

She watched them and let the doctor prick her arm and insert the IV. Shankar and the doctor brought a stretcher from the car. They lifted her and placed her on it. "Parvati, we are taking you to a hospital," Shankar told her. "We may not come back here again. Do you want me to take anything from here?"

She blankly looked around and pointed to one corner.

Shankar found a few of her worn clothes, old letters, and her deities. He collected those and took her out to the courtyard. "Parvati, do you want to say anything to anyone?"

She looked around vacantly. The old woman came out. "Go, Parvati, go. May God give you peace." She then looked at Shankar and said, "I am the wife of her husband's oldest brother. Both of our husbands are dead." She touched her forehead. "Hope we will do better in our next lives." She went inside.

After Parvati was settled properly in the car, the doctor went to the driver's seat. Shankar asked him to wait and went back to the house.

He found the old woman, standing. He gave her a few hundred Rupees, folded his hands, and bent his head. "Thank you for your kindness to my sister."

"May God bless you," she murmured.

Shankar went to see Parvati every day to keep her company and oversee her recovery. After about ten days, Parvati raised her hand a little implying him to hold it. She then struggled to stand up. "I can," she groaned, "the nurses are walking me on the corridor." When she finally succeeded, she dragged herself slowly, clutching onto her brother, to the window and looked at the backyard. There, in front of them, was a medium-height night jasmine tree with the ground covered with silky white fresh flowers. "Shiuli phool." She murmured in Bengali. "It's the season. Remember, we used to play under a shiuli tree?" She turned to her brother.

Shankar nodded and put his arm around her shoulder, pulling her closer.

Parvati leaned on him, whispering, "I've dreamt of this so many days."

Memories swamped Shankar's mind and he stood there mesmerized.

When the doctor said Parvati could have visitors and she felt up for it, Shankar finally brought Durga along. He introduced them, "Parvati, this is Durga, your Boudi," and stepped out of the room. Parvati immediately got up from bed, went to her, bent down, touching Durga's feet and said, "I have missed my Boudi all my life." Her voice choked and she started to cry on Durga's shoulder.

Durga was overwhelmed with Parvati's response, knowing that Parvati's brahmin tradition did not allow her to touch her feet. She hugged her in a warm embrace. "I missed having a sister like you. I am so happy that we could finally meet. Now we will know each other and be together."

Part Two

Liberation

S hankar arranged the funeral ceremony for his parents on the bank of the sacred Ganges River. A clear bright winter sky glowed above, but the temperature was pleasant. The gentle sound of the flowing river added to the gravity of the occasion. The yagna fire for the funeral ceremony rose on the green grass. Shankar sat cross-legged facing the river and fed wood to the fire, which was in front him. The priest lit a five-wick lamp filled with ghee from the fire and set it to one side. There was auspiciousness in the air. Shankar and the priest uttered Sanskrit mantras and offered ghee, flowers, durva grass, unhusked rice, other grains, and *bilva* leaves to the fire. Agni, the sacred fire, rose higher each time ghee was poured on it. Shankar offered small balls of cooked rice and barley mixed with ghee, black sesame seeds, and water to his deceased parents and ancestors to hasten their ultimate peace.

Both the priest and Shankar wore thin shawls over their shoulders. Occasionally when it slipped from his shoulder, Durga could see Shankar's new sacred thread, which the priest had made for him because he had lost his thread long ago. They prayed from the *Rigveda*:

"May all the components of thy body be merged into the five elements. May the power of thy sight be absorbed in the sun and thy breath, the *prana*, be absorbed in the air, the wind. May thy other parts be absorbed in appropriate elements. And in accordance with the meritorious deeds, thou hast performed here, may thy spirit dwell in the appropriate body—to earth or heaven."

Many members of Durga's family came for the event. They sat on mats arranged in a semicircle behind the yagna fire: Durga, Samir, Julie, Parvati, Shankar's older sister Uma and her husband, Durga's brother and two sisters. Some of Shankar's cousins also came. All dressed in light-colored clothes of mourning.

Shankar's older sister, her husband, their two grown children and their families had arrived from Allahabad two days earlier. There was an emotional reunion of the siblings with tears of joy and tears of regret for the many decades of separation. They spent a happy time, talking long into the nights recollecting happy moments of their childhood in Dum Dum.

"Father pushed us away," Uma lamented to Parvati when they had a private moment together, "I am sad I didn't contact you earlier." Parvati saw her older sister's eyes glisten and leaned on her in an embrace.

Shankar's brother-in-law turned out to be a quiet person, a Sanskrit professor at Allahabad university. "You are the one my father wanted me to be!" Shankar told him. "Thank you for making his dream come true."

"Things manifest in ways that we cannot foresee," he said with a glint in his eyes. "That's the amazing part of our lives."

Behind the semi-circle of prayerful adults, the children played during the service in the large unkept field. DeeDee and Raja ran around with their cousins. "It is just like what Grandpa told us," Raja shouted to DeeDee. Julie looked back and put her forefinger on her lips, asking Raja to be quiet. By then he was running toward a bush with the cousins.

When all the prayers were said, Shankar's ancestor's souls received food and water, and mantras were said to make their journey easy, the priest stood up and sprinkled peace water on all present. The adults came forward, passed their hands over the five-wick-lamp burning with ghee and then patted the tops of their own heads, taking in the warmth and blessings of Agni.

Shankar was suddenly filled with long-lost exuberance and freeness, as if he were flying a kite again, high in the sky. The fire that had ushered his parents onto their next life had ushered him into a new life as well. He gazed at the river and wondered if there could ever exist a time and place better than where he was right then.

GLOSSARY OF INDIAN WORDS

Adda	Bengali word for a convivial chat among friends
Ahnik	Prayer and meditation performed by Hindus.
Baba	Common and casual way of saying Father.
Babu-sahib	Honorific term used by common people for a gentleman.
Baithak-khana	Drawing room or sitting room.
Bel tree	Bel (Bilva) tree leaves are considered sacred in Hindu worship services.
Bhagavan	God
Bhagavad Gita	Gospel of Hindu religion. Lord Krishna's words to Arjuna in the Indian epic The Mahabharata.
Bhai	Brother
Bhai Phonta lyric	Sisters utter the following poem or mantra during Bhai Phonta celebration in Bengal:
	"Bhaier kapale dilam phonta,
	Jamer Duare porlo kanta,
	Jamuna Dae Jomke phonta,
	Ami di amar bhaike phonta,
	Bhai jeno hoy lohar vata."
	English translation:
	"On my brother's forehead I put the "phonta,"
	Yamuna applies "phonta" on Yama
	While I give the "phonta" to my brother
	Let my brother be as tough as Iron"
	Yama is the God of Death and Yamuna is his sister)
Bhaja	Fried
Bindi	A decorative bright color dot on the center of a woman's forehead.
Bohurupee	A rural street performer who acts out little vignettes, performs magic, and dances—often in private performances in homes—as a rural art form.
Boudi	This honorific refers to an older brother's wife. It is an affectionate and loving term used by younger siblings to address their older sister-in-law.
Brahma	God, the Creator—along with Vishnu, the preserver and protector, and Shiva, the auspicious one who is also the destroyer.
Brahma muhurta	Brahma's time; traditionally the last period of the night and

	is considered an auspicious time for yoga, meditation, or worship.
Brahmin	A caste of the highest order in Hindu religion.
Bustee	A ghetto where poor people live in small huts or makeshift rooms.
Chira Bhaja	Fried flattened rice.
Chutney	Hot and spicy condiment
Daal	Curried soup made with lentils and spices.
Dharma	Duties, rights, laws, conduct, virtues, and right way of living that makes life good and worthy.
Dharamsala	Place where pilgrims can stay, often without payment.
Dhuti	Plain length of white cloth used by men in place of pants
Didi	Older sister (pronounced the same as DeeDee).
Diwali	Hindu festival of lights to celebrate the victory of good over evil.
Durga	Mother Goddess of the world, wife of Shiva.
Durva grass	A sacred grass whose tender shoots are used in Hindu worship services.
Gamcha	Thin red cotton cloth used as a towel.
Garam masala	Mixture of cardamom, cinnamon, cloves, and sometimes other spices.
Ghar	Room or house.
Ghat	Cemented or brick steps leading down to a body of water, usually a river or a pond.
Ghee	Clarified butter.
Gur	Unrefined sugar.
Ilish Maachh	An extremely popular and coveted fish in the easternpart of India, especially in Bengal. It is Bangladesh's national fish and tastes somewhat like American Shad.
Jhal-muri	Spicy mixture of puffed rice.
Jhal	Hot
Jom	God of death in Bengali (J pronounced like joy), also known as Yama.
Kali	Goddess as a warrior and destroyer; Shiva's wife
Kheer	Rice pudding or plain concentrated and thickened milk.
Khejur	Date

Kul	One kind of berry; it has a distinct flavor and tastes more sour than sweet. Kul trees have thorns.
Kunjo	Clay vessel used to keep water cool.
Lattai	Cylindrical, wooden gadget used to roll the string for kites.
Linga	A linga or lingam, which looks like a phallus, is a Hindu symbol of the great God Shiva.
Lingaraja	The king of Lingam, the iconic phallus symbol of Lord Shiva.
Luchi	Puffed-up, deep-fried, round breads made with fine white flour. A delicacy in Bengal.
Lungi	A sarong-like cloth worn by men in Southeast Asia.
Maach	Bengali word for fish.
Maha	Great
Mahabharata	One of two great Sanskrit epics of India.
Mlechcha	A foreigner, used in a derogatory way.
Meye-Dekha	Literally 'Girl Look.' A visit by a boy's family to consider a girl for marriage.
Mughlai khana	Food cooked in the style of the Mughal emperor's court kitchens.
Muri	Crunchy puffed rice.
Mutton kababs	Ground meat mixed with spices and fried in round balls.
Paisa	Coin used on the Indian subcontinent.
Pajee meye	Cleverly naughty girl.
Panchagavya	A mixture of five elements containing cow dung, cow urine, milk, curd, and ghee.
Panda	Class of people who help pilgrims in temples.
Pandava	Five brothers, the virtuous heroes in the Indian epic Mahabharata.
Pati-shapta	Rice flour crepe with concentrated milk (kheer) and coconut paste inside.
Phool	Flower in North Indian languages.
Pranam	Paying respect, often by touching an elder's feet for his or her blessings.
Prasad	A gracious gift: typically, some food offered to a deity.
Praasaad	Palace
Puja	A Hindu worship service done with reverence for adoration of a deity.
Purano	Old
Payesh	Rice pudding (kheer) made with milk and sugar.

Rooti	Name for chapati in Eastern India—unleavened round, flat, whole wheat bread, cooked on a dry grill.
Sagar	Ocean
Sahib	Originally used to address a white man in India, now used sometimes for any man of higher standing.
Salah	Brother-in-law: it is often used as a derogatory insult.
Sandhya	Ritual of prayer and meditation performed by Hindus.
Sati-daha	Death of a widow on the funeral pyre of her husband.
Shiuli	Night Jasmine Tree flower in Bengal; also known as Shefali or Parijat.
Shiva	One of the three supreme Gods in Hinduism with Brahma and Vishnu.
Shivalinga	A phallus object worshipped as a representation of Lord Shiva.
Sindur	Red vermillion powder—used on the forehead and parting of the hair of married women in India.
Tantric rituals	Ceremonies performed in the Tantric tradition.
Tejya putra	Son discarded by Father.
Tetul	Tamarind, a long, sour fruit.
Tiffin	An Indian-English word for a light meal, a snack between meals or light tea-time snack.
Thakur Ghar	A special room or area in a house designated as a place for worship.
Tiki	Lock of hair, two to three inches long, at the back of a man's head.
Uranta tubri	Fireworks; little fountains that go up in the sky.
Viswakarma	The Hindu god of engineering and craftmanship.
Vishnu	Supreme God in Hinduism, the preserver and protector of the world
Yagnya	Hindu fire ceremony where offerings are made to God through a sacred fire.
Yaksa	Spirits who protect a hoard of treasures. Kuber is the king of the Yaksas.
Yama	God of death.

DISCUSSION QUESTIONS

1. Do you feel children in India have a happy childhood even without fancy toys?
2. Does the title of the novel make sense to you?
3. Do you think all brahmin families still have a strict conservative living style?
4. Do you see any similarities between the Indian caste system and American society?
5. In India, it is unusual to buck family traditions during college time. Societal change is therefore slow. How is this different from the U.S.?
6. Do you see Shankar's son, Samir, as an American or an Indian? Or both?
7. Do you find any similarities with Shankar in your upbringing?
8. Do you understand Shankar better through the stories he described?
9. Which stories made you reflect the most? Are there any you could personally relate to?
10. Can you recollect incidents (as in Shankar's youth) where you wish you had done something but didn't do it?
11. Do you have memories of people whom you ignored because you felt they were beneath you or not worth the effort?
12. Have you rectified, at least repented for, some minor offences from the past? Do they linger with you today as Shankar's did?
13. Do you think Shankar is a weak character? What are his weaknesses?
14. Are there characters like Shankar's father in Western culture?
15. Does Durga fit as a modern liberated woman by Western standards?
16. Does Julie represent a normal American woman? Has her experience in India altered her character?
17. Is there anything in the novel that surprised or perplexed you?
18. Did you feel angry, guilty, or upset with any parts of the book?
19. Was there an event or a story that finally transformed Shankar to act? Or was it a gradual process?
20. Is there a life lesson in this novel?

ACKNOWLEDGEMENTS

Night Jasmine Tree has been in the making for a long time. At first, the stories were written without any thought of a novel, which came during a literary workshop in 2006 in Preston, AZ, where Prof. Melissa Preacher suggested I frame the stories through the character of a grandfather. At the time I did not like the idea, as it called for development of the grandfather's character and a new story. What would the grandfather's life be about? Why did he come to the U.S. and how did his life progress? Thoughts about this brewed for a couple of years. Then two old ideas of mine came together to produce the novel—my total detestation of the Indian caste system and a desire to register my protest through its effect on a protagonist.

I have benefitted from several writers, friends, and writers groups in Idaho and Washington who have provided inspiration, support, and feedback as I worked toward the novel's fruition. My thanks are due to many. I'd be remiss if I didn't acknowledge my thanks to Oren Ashkenazi, Karen Finnigan, Dianne Meyer, Redd Becker, Shannon Hager, Paul Beckel, Sara Andaluz Majumdar, and most of all, immediate feedback from my wife, Catherine. I am indebted to Pat Loughlin for generously painting the beautiful cover picture after reading a draft of the novel. I also thank Kassidy Sikes for the final edits, Jennie Lyne Hiott for her interior design, and Germancreative for designing the cover.

I have a special indebtedness to the Idaho Writers' League for their annual contests where many stories of the novel won prizes thereby encouraging me to keep going. I must acknowledge and thank the following publications where some of the stories of this novel were published: Idaho State University & Caxton Press 1999; Echo, International Publication of IAEA, (Vienna, Austria) 2002 - 04; Sahitya Sankalan (Literary Collection) 2010; Anandalipi 2013, 14, 15, 16, 17; North American Bengali Conference magazine 2018; Whatcom WRITES Anthology 2013 – 19; and Red Wheelbarrow Anthology 2018.

ABOUT THE AUTHOR

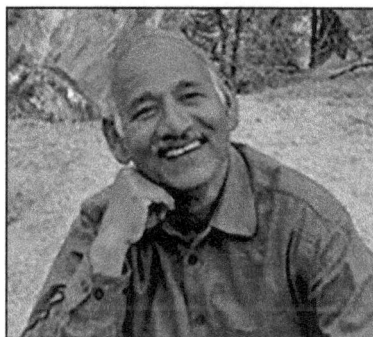

Born in India, Debu Majumdar came to the U.S. in 1964 and received a doctorate degree in physics from SUNY Stony Brook in 1969. He maintained an interest in writing throughout his working life, and after settling in the Rocky Mountain West, he began publishing stories and essays about life as he observed and experienced it.

His first book, From the Ganges to the Snake River, a creative nonfiction, interweaves Indian culture with north-west American reality. His four children's books (Viku and the Elephant series), set in village India, emphasize universal themes of friendship, perseverance, preservation, and bullying. Sacred River: A Himalayan Journey, his first novel, written from a background of India's ancient heritage, describes a daring gold heist from a temple in the Himalayas with romance, history, and a pilgrimage to India for the reader. The spiritual life of India is described and contrasted with Western and Native American beliefs. Night Jasmine Tree, his second novel, is the hidden backstory of an Indian man's immigration to the U.S.—a story of rebellion against conservative caste barriers, romance, sacrifice, loss, and reconciliation that overcomes innate human obstacles. The novel is developed through heartfelt stories told by the protagonist that reveal his turmoil and character.

Dr. Majumdar and his wife now live in Bellingham, WA. For further information, please go to http://www.botreehouse.com/debubooks-example.

www.ingramcontent.com/pod-product-compliance
Lightning Source LLC
Chambersburg PA
CBHW031936090426
42811CB00002B/204